NUCLEAR **NIGHTMARES**

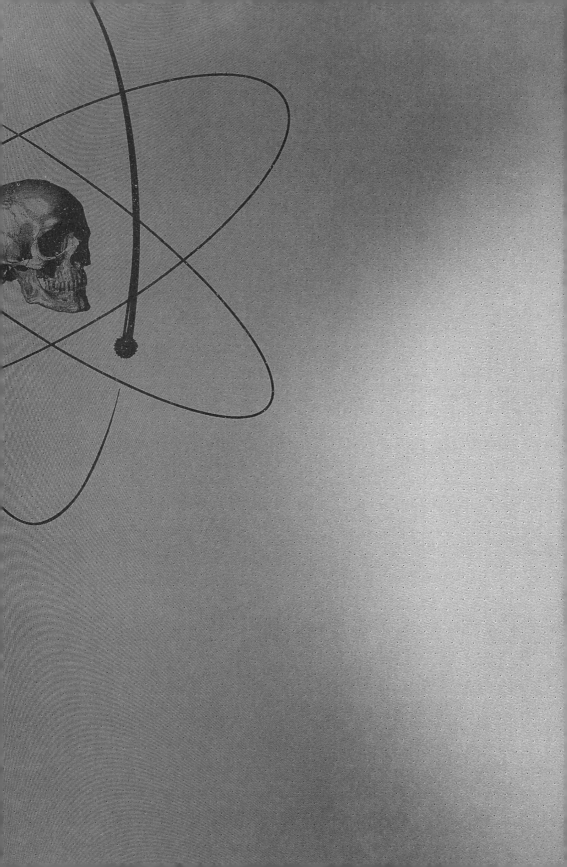

SECURING THE WORLD BEFORE IT IS TOO LATE

JOSEPH CIRINCIONE

COLUMBIA UNIVERSITY PRESS   NEW YORK

COLUMBIA UNIVERSITY PRESS

Publishers Since 1893

New York   Chichester, West Sussex

cup.columbia.edu

Library of Congress Cataloging-in-Publication Data

Cirincione, Joseph.

  Nuclear nightmares : securing the world before it is too late /
Joseph Cirincione.

     pages cm

  Includes bibliographical references and index.

  ISBN 978-0-231-16404-7 (cloth : alk. paper) — ISBN 978-0-231-53576-2 (e-book)

  1. Nuclear nonproliferation.   2. Nuclear terrorism—Prevention.   I. Title.

    JZ5675.C57 2013

    327.1′747—dc23

                         2013026169

JACKET & BOOK DESIGN: VIN DANG

We simply cannot allow the twenty first century to be darkened by the worst weapons of the twentieth century. . . . It took decades—and extraordinary sums of money—to build those arsenals. It's going to take decades—and continued investments—to dismantle them. . . . It's painstaking work. It rarely makes the headlines. But I want each of you to know . . . missile by missile, warhead by warhead, shell by shell, we're putting a bygone era behind us. . . . We're moving closer to the future we seek. A future where these weapons never threaten our children again. A future where we know the security and peace of a world without nuclear weapons.

PRESIDENT BARACK OBAMA, WASHINGTON, D.C. | DECEMBER 3, 2012

CONTENTS

TABLES

NUCLEAR **NIGHTMARES**

INTRODUCTION

Of all the challenges we face, individually, nationally, and globally, only two threaten catastrophe on a planetary scale: global warming and nuclear weapons. Both threats stem from machines that we have made. Both are preventable, even reversible. But to do so, both require new leadership and new ways of thinking.

This is a book about one of those twin threats: the current global arsenal of 17,000 nuclear weapons and the risk of their use, whether by accident or design. Many people have forgotten about these weapons. They believe that the threat ended with the Cold War or that plans are in place that effectively prevent or contain nuclear dangers. They are wrong. These weapons, held by states large and small, stable and unstable, are an ongoing nightmare. As President John F. Kennedy's national security advisor, McGeorge Bundy, said decades ago: "A decision that would bring even one hydrogen bomb on one city of one's own country would be recognized in advance as a catastrophic blunder; ten bombs on ten cities would be a disaster beyond history; and a hundred bombs on a hundred cities are unthinkable."[1]

This book tries to provide a greater understanding of the current threats these weapons represent and the efforts to reduce and eliminate these dangers. In my previous book, *Bomb Scare: The History and Future of Nuclear Weapons*, I provided a primer on the technology and development of nuclear weapons and explained why countries choose to have nuclear weapons or choose not to. In two editions of *Deadly Arsenals: Nuclear, Biological, and Chemical Threats*, my coauthors and I gave detailed descriptions of the nuclear weapon programs in the nations that had them, past and present.

I try not to repeat myself here. My purpose is to provide some understanding of the spread of nuclear weapons (chapter 4), the damage they can do (chapter 5), how much they cost (chapter 6), who has the most weapons and why (chapter 7), which national arsenal poses the greatest danger (chapter 8), the connection between existing arsenals and future arsenals (chapter 9), and, finally, how we can realize feasible solutions to these threats (chapters 10 and 11).

This book, however, is in large part a story about the debate surrounding the nuclear policy of the Obama administration. I actively participate in this debate as an analyst and as the president of Ploughshares Fund, a global security foundation focused on nuclear weapons policy. I try to tell the story honestly as I see it unfolding: the promise, the successes, the failures, and the possibilities of moving toward what President Obama termed "the peace and security of a world free of nuclear weapons."

When President Barack Obama assumed office in 2009, he was determined to reboot America's national security strategy, including modernizing an outdated U.S. nuclear weapons policy. He entered the White House with the most comprehensive, detailed nuclear plan of any president in history, including policies to end the testing of nuclear weapons, end the production of material for weapons, rapidly reduce existing arsenals, and "make the goal of eliminating all nuclear weapons a central element in our nuclear policy."[2] As a member of his campaign's nuclear policy team during 2007 and 2008, I played a small role in developing that plan. It was visionary, practical, and tough.

But the secret of the plan was that it was not really *his* plan. The proposals flowed from a nonpartisan consensus that had developed among the core of America's security elite over the past decade. Many senior strategists—including many former cabinet members and military chiefs who had guided the build-up of the vast nuclear weapons complex—now believed that it was time to reduce that complex. Most believed nuclear weapons represented the greatest threat to our nation and to many other nations. They concluded that the country could be made safer and more secure by moving step-by-step to reduce and ultimately eliminate these arsenals.

The American people feel the same way. Poll after poll reaffirms public support for the elimination of nuclear weapons provided that it is done carefully, mutually with other nations, and verifiably. People are understandably skeptical about the feasibility of actually eliminating all nuclear weapons, but they are overwhelmingly in favor of steps to advance toward that goal. A 2004 poll by the Program on International Policy Attitudes showed that 87 percent of Americans were in favor of a treaty "prohibiting nuclear weapons test explosions worldwide."[3] A November 2010 poll by the Associated Press and GfK Roper Public Affairs & Media showed that 62 percent of Americans thought no countries should have nuclear weapons—including the United States.[4] A mere 16 percent in that poll supported the position that only the United States and its allies should be allowed to have nuclear weapons—even though that came closest to the de facto U.S. position. At the height of a fierce fight in the Senate at the end of 2010 over approval of the New START treaty, 82 percent of the public in a CBS poll favored agreements to limit U.S. and Russian nuclear weapons, even more than the 77 percent who favored the same position when asked by CBS in June of 1979.[5] In a 2012 poll conducted in a joint effort between the Stimson Center and the Center for Public Integrity, when the American public was asked how they would cut Pentagon spending, the number one item that people wanted to cut was nuclear weapons. The general public proposed slashing 27 percent of the nuclear weapons budget, by far the biggest cut they gave to any other part of the military budget.[6]

Previous presidents have wanted to reduce and eliminate nuclear weapons, even during the Cold War. John F. Kennedy warned, "The weapons of war must be abolished before they abolish us."[7] Ronald Reagan said, "My dream is to see the day when nuclear weapons will be banished from the face of the Earth."[8] When confronted with the realities of our nuclear war plans, almost every president at some point turned to his advisors and asked "Why do we have so many of these weapons?"

The end of the Cold War and the increase in the threat of catastrophic terrorism swelled the ranks of those who believed that the liabilities now vastly
outweighed whatever benefits nuclear weapons may have had in the past.
Many of the cabinet officers and ambassadors from previous Republican and
Democratic administrations joined together in articles, op-eds, conferences,
and reports to craft the ideas President Obama carried into the White House.
Major foundations provided millions of dollars in grants to support these efforts, including Ploughshares Fund.

The emerging consensus was epitomized in part by the 2004 and 2008
presidential campaigns. In the September 2004 debate between President
George W. Bush and his challenger, Senator John Kerry, when asked what
was the single greatest threat to the United States, both answered "nuclear
terrorism," although they disagreed on the best strategy for confronting that
threat.[9] By the 2008 campaign, both candidates agreed on the goal of a world
free of nuclear weapons and the need, as Senator John McCain said in May
2008, "to take further measures to reduce dramatically the number of nuclear
weapons in the world's arsenals.... It is my hope to move as rapidly as possible to a significantly smaller force."[10]

The new president was deeply committed to this issue, as was Vice President Joe Biden and several of their senior national security staff. In April
2009, in Prague, the capital of the Czech Republic, President Obama gave his
first foreign policy speech. He chose nuclear policy as his premier issue. The
plan the newly inaugurated president unfolded had integrated three key nuclear security initiatives: reduce, prevent, and secure: reduce the U.S. and Russian arsenals; prevent new states from getting nuclear weapons; and secure
all loose nuclear materials to block terrorists from building a nuclear bomb.

Obama saw these three components working together; one could not be
done without the others. Reductions in existing arsenals would help build the
international cooperation that would encourage nations to secure the materials around the world and prevent others from getting weapons. In turn,
securing materials and preventing new nuclear-armed states would help create the security conditions that would allow further reductions. These steps,
taken together and repeated over time, would decrease risks and increase
security.

In April, the same month Obama delivered his Prague speech, he also met
in London with then-president of Russia Dmitry Medvedev. They pledged
to seek a treaty to immediately reduce the levels of U.S. and Russian strate-

gic offensive forces as a first step toward a follow-on treaty for even deeper reductions. They anticipated that this New START treaty could be reached fairly quickly. After New START, the president and his advisors thought they would consider bringing the 1996 treaty banning all nuclear tests (known as the Comprehensive Test Ban Treaty) up for approval by the Senate.

It did not work out that way. "Everything in war is very simple," Prussian military expert Karl von Clausewitz warned, "but the simplest thing is difficult."[11] His "friction" of war is present in politics as well. Or as President Obama told CBS News in July 2012, "In this office, everything takes a little longer than you'd like."[12]

The Russians used the New START negotiations to air pent-up grievances. Talks dragged on. The Russians seemed to believe the propaganda of the president's opponents that Obama was weak, naïve, and vainglorious. The Russians may have calculated that Obama would be willing to make concessions on missile defense issues in order to secure a new treaty before he traveled to Oslo in December 2009 to accept the Nobel Peace Prize. They were wrong. The president did not yield. The Russians eventually came around and in April 2010 reached agreement on a new treaty that Obama presented to the Senate. Even though the agreement restored the ability of U.S. inspectors to examine Russian weapons (and vice versa) and was supported by the Joint Chiefs of Staff and almost every national security official from previous Republican and Democratic administrations, a major fight erupted over what should have been the rapid approval of a modest treaty making small reductions to the nuclear force.

Three sets of treaty opponents emerged. There were those who had genuine concerns about the treaty, asking honest questions that had to be answered. "What does this word mean? Are we covering this, are we not covering that?" There were also ideological opponents who would never agree to any arms-control treaty, although they were a distinct minority. The majority of the opposition was political. The basic calculation for many Republicans was "Why should we give this Democratic president a victory?" It was 2010, an election year for Congress, and it did not serve the interest of the opposition party to facilitate a major victory for the president.[13] The vote was delayed until after the election when, in December 2010, on the last day of the session, the Senate approved the treaty with 12 Republican votes, 71 to 26.

But by then it was too late to implement the rest of the planned agenda. Consideration of a nuclear test ban treaty would have to wait. Immediate reductions in the arsenal and other changes outlined in the administration's Nuclear Posture Review were put on hold to focus on treaty ratification and then delayed again during the election campaign. Many of the president's team suffered from what some termed "arms control fatigue."[14] And the obstacles just got bigger. As I wrote in *Foreign Affairs* in February 2012 summing up the policy problems of 2011:

> In the past year, Republican opponents and a resistant nuclear bureaucracy have stymied further progress. Contracts raced ahead of policy. Congress pushed through budgets to develop a new generation of nuclear arms before the president and the Pentagon could agree on the specifics of the new course. Unless this is reversed, in the coming decade Washington may actually spend more on the country's nuclear weapons programs than it has in the past.[15]

By 2012, the presidential election was in full swing and policy was at a full stop. Every tough issue was put off until after the elections. This was not just avoiding the risk that political opponents would use a policy initiative as part of the attack on the president's national security acumen (which it would have been). It was also the recognition that international players were hedging their bets. The Russians, the Iranians, and even our allies were waiting for the results of the November election before committing to any new agreements. Thus, the new nuclear guidance developed by the Department of Defense and the Joint Chiefs of Staff—guidance that could reduce the role, numbers, and risks of nuclear weapons—was delayed with other policies until after the elections.

President Obama's reelection in November 2012 reopened the policy window. Brookings Institution president Strobe Talbott wrote in the weeks after the election that Obama had accomplished a great deal in his first time,

> but on two challenges of existential importance, he has come up short: strengthening the global nuclear non-proliferation regime and leading an international effort to slow the process of climate change. Obama had given priority to both goals in his 2008 campaign and first inaugural address but was thwarted on both, largely because of partisan opposition in Washington.[16]

The president would now have the opportunity to complete the policy transformation he envisioned as a senator, campaigned on as a candidate, and began as president. He will need this extra time. Many presidents we now judge as great—Abraham Lincoln, Franklin Roosevelt, Ronald Reagan—would have been considered failures if they had served only one term. It was only in their later terms that they were able to complete what they had started or, in Reagan's case, to turn from a massive military build-up to the most sweeping nuclear arms reductions in history, a goal he previewed in his second inaugural address. "We are not just discussing limits on a further increase of nuclear weapons," he said on January 21, 1985. "We seek, instead to reduce their number. We seek the total elimination one day of nuclear weapons from the face of the Earth."

Can President Obama do the same? Can he, as the *New York Times* implored him to do in February 2013, "follow through with a more sustained commitment" and not "continue to throw money at a bloated nuclear arsenal"?[17] Like all tales of Washington policy, this book can only catch the story in midstream. There is much undecided, much yet to be done. For that reason, we have established a special website, www.nuclearnightmaresbook .com. We will post policy updates so that you can stay as current on these issues as we are.

I hope you find the story as gripping and as important as I do.

PART I

POLICY

ONE
PROMISE

Barack Obama, a most unlikely American president, strode to the podium in Prague, a most unlikely venue, to pledge something that even some of his closest advisors thought impossible. With his speech, the new president would launch a policy initiative that would have to overcome the crises and opponents dominating the political landscape. He was keenly aware of the moment.[1]

A cheering crowd of several thousand people greeted President Obama and First Lady Michelle Obama as they took the stage on this early spring morning, April 5, 2009. At the base of the stage, attendees waved a flurry of small flags. Large Czech, American, and European Union flags hung behind the crowd. Attendees had been gathering since dawn for the late-morning speech. Druhá Tráva, a Czech band, opened the event with a bluegrass set, including a cover of Bob Dylan's "Girl of the North Country"—in Czech. As the audience waited for the president, recorded music from bands like Earth, Wind, and Fire and U2 echoed off the walls of the square.

The presidential podium stood in Prague's Hradcany Square, overlooking the storied, red-roofed city. Above the square towered Prague Castle, a ninth-century fortification that has been the seat of power for kings, the Holy Roman Emperor, and, today, the Czech president. Near the podium stood a statue of Thomas Masaryk, who in 1918 returned to Prague Castle as the first president of the independent Czechoslovak Republic.

In the wings to the left of the president's podium stood his corps of advisors—Press Secretary Robert Gibbs, Senior Advisor David Axelrod, National Security Council Chief of Staff Denis McDonough, and Gary Samore, the National Security Council's coordinator for preventing the proliferation of weapons of mass destruction.

The president and first lady smiled and waved to the enthusiastic crowd. Obama opened his speech by thanking the people of Prague and the Czech Republic. He reminded his audience that fifty years ago, few would have predicted that the United States would elect an African American president who would speak to an audience in Prague, in the heart of a free and united Europe. Obama said, "Those ideas would have been dismissed as dreams. We are here today because enough people ignored the voices who told them that the world could not change." The comments were welcomed with rousing applause, and the president's speech moved through its introduction.

As President Obama thanked Czech president Vaclav Klaus and prime minister Mirek Topolanek, expressing his gratitude for the hospitality of the Czech government, he knew that beneath the formal hospitality, the Czech government was in political turmoil. The Topolanek government had collapsed amid domestic political infighting the week before President Obama's arrival. The global economic crash of 2008 partially undermined the conservative prime minister's economic positions, and public and parliamentary opposition to his agreement with the Bush administration to base antimissile weapons in the country had undercut his principal foreign policy aims. On March 24, 2009, the Czech parliament had delivered a vote of no confidence to his governing center-right coalition. The following day, the prime minister had called President Obama's plan for economic stimulus "the road to hell." The Czech leaders formally welcomed President Obama's visit. Czech domestic politics did not.

Thanks concluded, the president moved to the substance of his speech, with emotional admiration for the dramatic history of the now-democratic Czech Republic. "Few people would have predicted," he said, "that an American president would one day be permitted to speak to an audience like this in Prague." In 1948, a coup d'état had brought a communist government to power in Czechoslovakia and drawn the country into the Soviet orbit. Czechoslovakia would remain behind the "Iron Curtain" until 1989 when a student-inspired, peaceful uprising—the Velvet Revolution—brought down the communist government and lead to a democratic Czech Republic. Obama continued, "Sametová Revoluce—the Velvet Revolution—taught us many things. It showed us that peaceful protest could shake the foundations of an empire, and expose the emptiness of an ideology. It showed us that small countries can play a pivotal role in world events, and that young people can lead the way in overcoming old conflicts. And it proved that moral leadership is more powerful than any weapon."

The cheers in Hradcany Square reflected Czech hopes for a new relationship with the United States. Stiff opposition had grown in the Czech Republic to U.S. plans for the anti-ballistic-missile installation. In July 2008, the Bush administration had secured the permission of governments of Poland and the Czech Republic for the construction of the antimissile weapons systems. The agreements were signed as tensions grew between Russia and Georgia, in the prelude to the Russian invasion later that August.

The Bush administration promoted the weapons as necessary to defend Europe against potential Iranian missiles. But Russia saw the missile defense agreements as a strategic challenge from NATO and the United States. And in the view of some Czech citizens, the proposed radar installation made the Czech Republic a potential Russian military target while giving them little added security. Seventy percent of Czech citizens opposed the deal, and their opinions were vocal. By March 2009, when it became clear the opposition parties could defeat the plan, the Czech prime minister who had endorsed the deal withdrew it from parliament. On the day of Obama's speech, a group of protestors wearing white masks, representing the "invisible" majority of Czechs opposing the new weapons, filled sidewalks around the city. Protestors hung banners from Prague's Charles Bridge that said, "Yes we can—say no to U.S. military base." The Czechs attending were acutely attentive to the president's words on this hot issue.

Obama's speech turned to policy. He had been in office for just over two months. He faced no shortage of pressing international issues, including the wars in Iraq and Afghanistan, a global economic crisis, climate change, and persisting tensions over crises with Iran and North Korea. Obama reminded the crowd, "None of these challenges can be solved quickly or easily. But all of them demand that we listen to one another and work together; that we focus on our common interests, not on occasional differences; and that we reaffirm our shared values, which are stronger than any force that could drive us apart."

President Obama shifted to the core of the speech. "Now, one of those issues that I'll focus on today is fundamental to the security of our nations and to the peace of the world—that's the future of nuclear weapons in the twenty-first century."

Aboard *Air Force One* the night before the address, Robert Gibbs, Obama's press secretary, had talked with reporters about the agenda for the president's stay in Prague. Gen. James Jones, Obama's national security advisor, and Denis McDonough had joined the press gaggle. Press attention had been gathering around the Prague speech in the days before the president's visit. It was billed as a major foreign policy address that would concentrate on nuclear weapons policy. A reporter asked Gibbs for more information on the thrust of the next day's speech. McDonough responded, "Look, the president has been very focused on these issues of proliferation for many years. So tomorrow I think you'll hear the president outline in a very comprehensive way many of the things that he's been talking about and working on for some time."

Barack Obama's concern about nuclear dangers went back to his early years. As an undergraduate at Columbia University in 1983, Obama wrote an article for the college paper titled "Breaking the War Mentality." Obama's article gave attention to student organizations and their efforts as they rallied support for the nuclear-freeze movement—a movement that drew one million supporters to a rally in New York City's Central Park. Later, as a U.S. senator, Obama worked with prominent Republican senators Dick Lugar and Chuck Hagel on programs to stop the spread of nuclear weapons and prevent nuclear terrorism by securing and eliminating the global stockpiles of nuclear bomb materials. Early in his presidential campaign, in October 2007, Senator Obama said: "Here's what I'll say as president: America seeks a world in which there are no nuclear weapons. We will not pursue unilateral disarmament. As long as nuclear weapons exist, we'll retain a strong nuclear deterrent. But we'll keep our commitment under the Nuclear Non-Proliferation Treaty on the long road towards eliminating nuclear weapons." It was a bold move for a young, relatively unknown senator to come out so far on an issue so early in a presidential campaign. Yet he carried his position on nuclear disarmament through the election. When *Time* interviewed President-elect Obama in December 2008, the reporter asked Obama what issues kept him awake at night. Obama listed nuclear proliferation third—just after the ongoing economic collapse and the wars in Iraq and Afghanistan. Obama repeatedly demonstrated his personal commitment to reducing the threat of nuclear weapons to the United States and other nations and working toward their eventual elimination. But politicians say many things while campaigning for office. The question was whether he could turn his nuclear views into policy once in the White House.

Arms-control experts and advocates anxiously anticipated the Prague speech. The question for these nongovernmental organizations was not if but how the president would say it. The broad policy points of the Obama strategy had already been outlined in the campaign. They expected that the president's speech would announce a plan to seek a follow-on agreement to the 1991 Strategic Arms Reduction Treaty and a timeframe for getting the nuclear test ban treaty ratified by the Senate. They knew that the president would have to address the spread of nuclear weapons to North Korea and Iran. What they did not know was how bold the president would be with his speech. Would he offer specific targets for reductions with Russia—perhaps to 1,000 weapons? Could he propose the withdrawal of tactical nuclear weapons from U.S. bases in Europe? Would he redefine the missions of the U.S. nuclear arsenal?

President Obama's moved to a more pressing tone, and he reminded his audiences of the nuclear threats we face:

> Today, the Cold War has disappeared but thousands of those weapons have not. In a strange turn of history, the threat of global nuclear war has gone down, but the risk of a nuclear attack has gone up. More nations have acquired these weapons. Testing has continued. Black-market trade in nuclear secrets and nuclear materials abound. The technology to build a bomb has spread. Terrorists are determined to buy, build, or steal one. Our efforts to contain these dangers are centered on a global nonproliferation regime, but as more people

and nations break the rules, we could reach the point where the center cannot hold.

That very day, the world had been reminded of these threats. At four-thirty a.m. on the morning of Obama's speech, Robert Gibbs woke up the president with word that North Korea had tested a long-range ballistic missile.[2] The North's two-stage missile, theoretically capable of carrying a nuclear weapon, flew over Japan and splashed into the Pacific Ocean after flying 1,300 miles.[3]

Obama continued:

> Some argue that the spread of these weapons cannot be stopped, cannot be checked—that we are destined to live in a world where more nations and more people possess the ultimate tools of destruction. Such fatalism is a deadly adversary, for if we believe that the spread of nuclear weapons is inevitable, then in some way we are admitting to ourselves that the use of nuclear weapons is inevitable.

President Obama then declared:

> So today, I state clearly and with conviction America's commitment to seek the peace and security of a world without nuclear weapons. I'm not naïve. This goal will not be reached quickly—perhaps not in my lifetime. It will take patience and persistence. But now we, too, must ignore the voices who tell us that the world cannot change. We have to insist, "Yes, we can."

Presidents from Harry Truman on had said they wanted to eliminate nuclear weapons. But President Obama was linking that goal to a set of near-term objectives, setting out a practical policy agenda that rejected the existing Cold War paradigms.

As long as these weapons existed, he said, the United States would maintain a "safe, secure, and effective arsenal," but the point of his policy would be to "reduce the role of nuclear weapons in our national security strategy and urge others to do the same." The president pledged to negotiate a new arms reduction treaty with the Russians that year, "setting the stage for further cuts, and we will seek to include all nuclear weapons states in this endeavor." He said he would "immediately and aggressively pursue U.S. ratification for the Comprehensive Test Ban Treaty," to achieve a global ban on nuclear testing and cut off the building blocks needed for a bomb by seeking a new treaty to ban the production of the fissile material (plutonium and highly enriched uranium) for nuclear weapons. He would strengthen the barriers to new nations' getting the bomb with "real and immediate consequences for countries caught breaking the rules." He would "ensure that terrorists never acquire a nuclear weapon" by "a new international effort to secure all vulnerable nuclear material around the world within four years."

There was more. Specifics on the creation of an international fuel bank so nations could not creep up to the nuclear threshold by building national uranium-enrichment facilities. He expressed his desire to negotiate in good faith with Iran and to break up the black markets that trade in nuclear technology. It was a long list, but the crowd listened patiently, even eagerly. They wanted the specifics, not just pretty words. But the president did not disappoint rhetorically. He ended with a stirring cry to action.

> Now, I know that there are some who will question whether we can act on such a broad agenda. There are those who doubt whether true international cooperation is possible, given inevitable differences among nations. And there are those who hear talk of a world without nuclear weapons and doubt whether it's worth setting a goal that seems impossible to achieve.
>
> But make no mistake: We know where that road leads. When nations and peoples allow themselves to be defined by their differences, the gulf between them widens. When we fail to pursue peace, then it stays forever beyond our grasp. . . . That's how wars begin. That's where human progress ends. . . .
>
> I know that a call to arms can stir the souls of men and women more than a call to lay them down. But that is why the voices for peace and progress must be raised together. . . .
>
> Let us bridge our divisions, build upon our hopes, accept our responsibility to leave this world more prosperous and more peaceful than we found it. Together we can do it. Thank you very much. Thank you, Prague.

The crowd roared its approval. The music swelled, the president smiled broadly, and, with the first lady at his side, waved, shook hands, and basked in the waves of applause. The struggle for transformation had begun.

TWO
LEGACY

As Obama knew only too well, presidents don't have the luxury of starting with a blank slate.[1] They inherit the policies and problems of their predecessors. In addition to the country's crashing economy, the new president was now in charge of tens of thousands of troops waging two wars with no clear strategy for victory or resolution. But incoming Obama officials also confronted several critical nuclear problems: one of those wars, in Afghanistan, threatened the stability of neighboring, nuclear-armed Pakistan; Osama bin Laden was hidden in the region, organizing and possibly still seeking a nuclear weapon; Iran was racing ahead with a nuclear program that had barely existed eight years earlier; a nuclear arms race was underway in South Asia; North Korea was now armed with tested nuclear weapons; and relations with the largest nuclear-armed state, Russia, were back to a Cold War chill.

As Bush officials had moved off stage, Secretary of State Condoleezza Rice tried to put the best gloss on their tenure, proclaiming in September of 2008 that the Bush administration would leave the nuclear-proliferation "situation… in far better shape than we found it."[2] But that is not how it looked to the Obama team. To them, it seemed that nearly every nuclear problem President George W. Bush had inherited from his predecessor had grown worse.

The Bush administration has started with great promise and strong resolve in 2001. Officials were determined to clean up the basket of nuclear issues they felt the Clinton administration had dumped in *their* laps. India and Pakistan were expanding their nuclear arsenals after a series of tests in 1998. President Bill Clinton had resolved a crisis with North Korea in 1994 with a negotiated agreement that froze North Korea's production of plutonium, but Bush officials thought the deal did little to end the threat. Iran and Libya were nurturing secret nuclear programs, and, worse, Iraqi dictator Saddam Hussein was flouting UN sanctions and seemed to be secretly continuing chemical, biological, and even nuclear weapons programs. In short, nuclear dangers seemed to be multiplying worldwide in early 2001.

Bush officials were determined to resolve these crises with a radical new approach, a strategy that became popularly known as the Bush Doctrine. This policy would prove tragically flawed. It would lead to war with Iraq, a rapid expansion of the nuclear programs in Iran and North Korea, the collapse of U.S. credibility and prestige around the world, the weakening of the non-proliferation regime, and an unstable, increasingly hostile, nuclear-armed Pakistan. There was nothing inevitable about these developments. Deeply flawed policies created the proliferation crises that would later confront the new Obama administration.

THE BUSH DOCTRINE

Neoconservative institutes had spent years developing alternatives to the consensus security policies in place during the Ronald Reagan and Bill Clinton administrations. Their recommendations heavily influenced the incoming Bush officials. In many cases, experts from these institutes were appointed to key positions. John Bolton, who would serve as Bush's undersecretary of state for arms control and international security and then U.S. ambassador to the United Nations, had summarized his contempt for arms control as a scholar at one of these think tanks, the American Enterprise Institute.

The Clinton administration, Bolton wrote in 1999, suffered from a "fascination with arms control agreements as a substitute for real nonproliferation of weapons of mass destruction."[3] Michael Allen, the special assistant to National Security Adviser Stephen Hadley, later described the incoming teams views: "We're like 'Arms control, what's that?'... I often hear about arms control from the old-timers, but it's so different now.... Most of the times it's 'isolate,' how can we isolate a country even more?"[4]

Gary Schmitt, at the neoconservative Project for the New American Century, explained. "Conservatives don't like arms control agreements for the simple reason that they rarely, if ever, increase U.S. security.... The real issue here, and the underlying question, is whether the decades-long effort to control the proliferation of weapons of mass destruction and the means to deliver them through arms control treaties has in fact worked." He contended that it was no longer "plausible to argue that our overall security was best served by a web of parchment accords, and not our own military capabilities."[5]

Although many neoconservatives assumed high government positions in the Bush administration,[6] it was not until the attacks of September 11, 2001, that they were able to profoundly change the course of U.S. nuclear policy. In the wake of the attacks, their views overwhelmed the pragmatist views of Secretary of State Colin Powell and others who supported existing treaties, favored continuing the negotiated elimination of programs in North Korea and other states, and saw U.S. global leadership in terms of traditional great-power relations. Rather than the realism prescribed by Condoleezza Rice in her 2000 *Foreign Affairs* article outlining the policy Bush purported to follow, the administration ended up closer to the concept of a "benevolent empire" championed by neoconservative thinker Robert Kagan in a 1998 *Foreign Policy* article.[7]

Traditional conservatives and liberals differ in their values and priorities but share a general view that the proper role of the United States is to manage the global order. Neoconservatives believe that the point of U.S. power is to change the world. They viewed the immediate post–Cold War period as a moment where the United States had unrivaled economic and military power. They wanted the United States to be free to exercise this power in pursuit of its national interest while exporting its values abroad. To take advantage of this moment, neoconservatives advocated that the United States use its might to shape the world to its liking—spreading democracy, free markets, and the rule of law. Rather than having the United States be simply a leader promoting change in the world, the United States was to be the dominant power transforming it.

The new order would be built on three interrelated principles, developed by neoconservatives but now known collectively as the Bush Doctrine. First, the United States would favor direct military action over diplomacy and containment. Bush explained why: "Deterrence—the promise of massive retaliation against nations—means nothing against shadowy terrorist networks with no nation or citizens to defend. Containment is not possible when unbalanced dictators with weapons of mass destruction can deliver those weapons on missiles or secretly provide them to terrorist allies."[8] Second, the United States would not wait for a threat to appear before taking military action. As Bush argued, "Some have said we must not act until the threat is imminent. Since when have terrorists and tyrants announced their intentions, politely putting us on notice before they strike? If this threat is permitted to fully and suddenly emerge, all actions, all words, and all recriminations would come too late."[9] Third, the administration pivoted from terrorist groups to nation-states, linking the September 11 attackers directly to regimes that officials believed hostile to U.S. interests. Deputy Secretary of Defense Paul Wolfowitz proclaimed, "It's going to be a broad campaign; it's not going to end quickly. One of those objectives is the [a]l Qaeda network. The second objective is state support for terrorism, and a third is this larger connection between states that support terrorism and states that develop weapons of mass destruction."[10]

The new, action-oriented approach had its roots in positions developed by neoconservatives in the 1990s. Several leaders of this movement, joined by traditional conservatives, summarized their view in a joint letter to President Clinton in 1998, urging war with Iraq. The group included Elliott Abrams, John Bolton, William Kristol, Richard Perle, Donald Rumsfeld, and Paul Wolfowitz. They argued that

> the policy of "containment" of Saddam Hussein has been steadily eroding over the past several months. . . . [W]e can no longer depend on our partners in the Gulf War coalition to continue to uphold the sanctions or to punish Saddam when he blocks or evades UN inspections. . . . The only acceptable strategy is one that eliminates the possibility that Iraq will be able to use or threaten to use weapons of mass destruction. In the near term, this means a willingness to undertake military action as diplomacy is clearly failing. In the long term, it means removing Sadaam Hussein and his regime from power.

Many of the individuals who had developed this policy during the Clinton years were in high positions in the Bush administration by 2002. They formalized their views as the new government policy in two key documents: "The National Security Strategy of the United States of America," released in September 2002, and the "National Strategy to Combat Weapons of Mass Destruction," released in December 2002. The latter called it "a fundamental change from the past."[11] The administration's Nuclear Posture Review, made public in early 2002, reflected these ideas, detailing expanded missions for nuclear weapons, including use against underground bunkers, mobile targets, and many conventional military situations, which would require thousands of nuclear weapons in the U.S. arsenal. "A broader array of capability is needed," said Secretary of Defense Donald Rumsfeld, summarizing the new posture, "to dissuade states from undertaking political, military, or technical courses of action that would threaten U.S. and allied security."[12]

Supporters of the new policy saw nuclear proliferation as part of a larger, global struggle. Bush officials argued that the threats today were different from those of the Cold War—and greater than them. The primary threat came from a small number of outlaw states that had no regard for international norms and were determined to acquire nuclear, biological, and chemical weapons. Previous presidents had viewed the spread of nuclear, biological, and chemical weapons as a paramount concern and sought their elimination through treaties. President Bush, however, asserted that the greatest danger to the United States stemmed from the nexus of outlaw regimes, weapons of mass destruction, and terrorists. The answer was to go after the hostile states, not to pursue new treaties. In essence, Bush had changed the focus from "what" to "who." The new strategy sought the elimination of regimes rather than weapons, believing that the United States could determine which countries were responsible enough to have WMD capabilities and which were not. U.S. power, not multilateral treaties, would enforce this judgment.

David Sanger summarized the strategy in September 2002 for the *New York Times*:

> It sketches out a far more muscular and sometimes aggressive approach to national security than any since the Reagan era. It includes the discounting of most nonproliferation treaties in favor of a doctrine of "counterproliferation," a reference to everything from missile defense to forcibly dismantling weapons or their components. It declares that the strategies of containment and deterrence—staples of American policy since the 1940's—are all but dead. There is

no way in this changed world, the document states, to deter those who "hate
the United States and everything for which it stands."[13]

The strategy seemed to succeed at first. The war in Afghanistan was fast
and cheap. Even though U.S. forces failed to capture bin Laden, the invasion scattered al Qaeda and routed the Taliban from power. Seizing the moment, Bush announced the U.S. withdrawal from the Anti-Ballistic Missile
Treaty in December 2001 with none of the immediate consequences opponents had predicted, as President Vladimir Putin of Russia acquiesced, re-
luctantly, to its abrogation. The administration and the Republican Congress
swiftly increased funding for antimissile programs and the entire defense
budget. Antimissile-program funding increased from $4 billion in fiscal year
2000 to more than $9 billion by fiscal year 2004; overall military spending
spiked from $280 billion to $380 billion over the same period, not including
the price of the wars. (These trends would continue. The defense budget hit
$542.5 billion in fiscal year 2009 and the wars in Iraq and Afghanistan cost an
additional $12 billion per month.)[14]

The administration cowed congressional Democrats into approving military action against Iraq and defied traditional patterns by gaining Republican seats in the 2002 congressional elections, taking control of the Senate
(and increasing their margins in 2004). In 2003, Bush and Vice President
Dick Cheney bulldozed skeptics in their drive for war with Iraq, cheered by
the media and a small army of Washington experts warning of "gathering
storms," "mushroom clouds," and the catastrophic consequences of any delay
to invasion. Inspectors from the International Atomic Energy Agency and
the UN Special Commission on Iraq found no evidence of any weapons or
weapons program in the months preceding the invasion, but administration
officials were skeptical of the analysis and asserted there was "no doubt" the
weapons existed. (Inspectors later estimated that they could have certified
the absence of any weapons with just a few more weeks of investigation.)

The initial phase of the Iraq war appeared to accomplish the mission and
began paying dividends. In April 2003, Iran, which had cooperated in the
overthrow of the Taliban and welcomed the overthrow of Saddam Hussein,
quietly offered to talk with the United States about its nuclear program, its
support for the radical Hamas and Hezbollah movements, and its relationship with Israel. Bush officials rejected the offer and instead began talking of
campaigns to overthrow regimes in Iran, Syria, and even North Korea.[15]

In December, in the most significant nonproliferation success of the Bush administration, Libya agreed to give up its nuclear, chemical, and long-range missile programs. Although the presence of 250,000 U.S. troops in the region undoubtedly played a role, the victory became possible only when the administration departed from its strategy of forcing a change in regimes and sought instead a change in a regime's behavior. The combination of years of sanctions, threats of force, and credible assurances of security won Libya's reversal. Libyan leader Moammar Gaddafi went from being the poster child for rogue-state leaders to a man Bush called a "model" that others should follow. (This brief period of cordial relations ended when the Arab Spring swept the region and swept Gaddafi from power in 2011.) Information Libya provided, along with information from Iranian officials after the disclosure of their secret enrichment program, led to the public exposure of the Abdul Qadeer Khan nuclear black market, another success story, although a partial one.

Finally, in April 2004, Bush officials won passage of UN Security Council Resolution 1540, requiring all nations to take greater legal and diplomatic efforts to block proliferation, a major step forward and one that, again, relied on diplomacy and existing international institutions rather than ad hoc coalitions and forced regime change. Administration officials also short-changed the 2005 nuclear Non-Proliferation Treaty (NPT) Review Conference, sending only low-ranking officials and rebuffing efforts to get a compromise agreement.

The new strategy, however, could not hold. By 2005, the losses started to overwhelm the gains.

FAILURES OF POLICY

The most consequential blunder of the Bush doctrine was the invasion of Iraq. The war was the first implementation of the counterproliferation strategy, justified almost exclusively by the claim that Saddam Hussein had or soon could have nuclear weapons that he would then give to terrorists to attack the United States. Bush told the nation on the eve of war, "The danger is clear: using chemical, biological or, one day, nuclear weapons, obtained with the help of Iraq, the terrorists could fulfill their stated ambitions and kill thousands or hundreds of thousands." Bush dismissed entreaties from U.S. allies to delay the war. "No nation can possibly claim that Iraq has disarmed," he said. "We are now acting because the risks of inactions would be far greater." In passing, at the end of his remarks, the president spoke of his desire to advance democracy, liberty, and peace in the region.[16]

By 2005, government and independent reviews had proven false each of the prewar claims. Iraq did not have nuclear, biological, or chemical weapons, save for a few obsolete chemical-weapon shells; programs for producing such weapons; or plans to restart these programs, which had been shut down in the early 1990s by UN inspectors. None of the key findings in the U.S. National Intelligence Estimate on Iraq was accurate, with the exception of the finding that Hussein was highly unlikely to transfer any weapons to terrorist groups. U.S. and British officials went far beyond the intelligence findings in their public statements.

Tom Ricks summarized the harsh assessment of many national security experts in his 2006 history of the war, *Fiasco*:

> President George W. Bush's decision to invade Iraq in 2003 ultimately may come to be seen as one of the most profligate actions in the history of American foreign policy. The consequences of this choice won't be clear for decades, but it already is abundantly apparent in mid-2006 that the U.S. government went to war in Iraq with scant solid international support and on the basis of incorrect information—about weapons of mass destruction and a supposed nexus between Saddam Hussein and al Qaeda's terrorism—and then occupied the country negligently. Thousands of U.S. troops and an untold number of Iraqis have died. Hundreds of billions of dollars have been spent, many of them squandered.[17]

By the end of the Bush administration, Americans had turned decisively against the war and favored a rapid withdrawal.[18] International opinion of the United States plummeted even faster to historic lows. A 2005 Pew Study found that when the publics of sixteen nations were asked to give favorability ratings of five major leading nations—China, France, Germany, Japan, and the United States—the United States "fared the worst of the group. In just six of the 16 countries surveyed does the United States attract a favorability rating" of 50 percent or higher.[19] Not surprisingly, the United States drew the most negative responses from countries in the Middle East, including U.S. allies Jordan and Turkey.

The failure of the war and of the analysts and officials who championed it has been well documented elsewhere (though few have had their careers harmed by their catastrophic decisions). The damage the Bush Doctrine caused to other areas of U.S. national security has been less well examined. By the end of the Bush administration, there were increased nuclear dangers on almost every front. Here, in brief form, are the major problems that confronted the Obama team as it took office.

The Danger of Nuclear Terrorism Had Increased

The turn from Afghanistan to Iraq allowed al Qaeda and the Taliban to regroup in nuclear-armed Pakistan and counterattack in Afghanistan. U.S. intelligence officials concluded in February 2005 Senate testimony that U.S. policy in the Middle East has fueled anti-U.S. feeling and that the Iraq war has provided jihadists with new recruits who "will leave Iraq experienced in and focused on acts of urban terrorism."[20] After the Iraq invasion, the number of terrorist attacks rose globally, and al Qaeda grew in influence and adherents.[21] Nuclear sites around the world, not just in Pakistan, remain vulnerable to terrorist attack, theft, or diversion. The amount of nuclear material secured in the two years after September 11, 2001, was at best equal to the amount secured in the two years before that date.[22] Brian Finlay of the Henry L. Stimson Center noted, "Top-line nonproliferation funding has remained largely static since 2005, increasing only marginally from $1.25 billion ... to $1.4 billion" during fiscal years 2005–2007.[23] In 2008 a report from former September 11 commission chairs Lee Hamilton and Thomas Kean gave the administration a "C" on its nuclear efforts.[24]

Iran's Nuclear Program Had Accelerated

Iran's early nuclear-research program grew into an industrial-size uranium-enrichment program, going from a few test centrifuges to thousands of operational centrifuges, bringing Iran closer to the capability to produce a nuclear weapon. The United States failed to develop a coherent plan for stopping the program. Most of the construction and development of Iranian nuclear facilities occurred after 2000, including the opening of plants to produce uranium gas, the first successful operation of a centrifuge cascade to enrich uranium, and the construction of a vast facility to house more than 50,000 centrifuges. By late 2008, Iran had installed 8,000 centrifuges at Natanz.

Further, Iran had amassed enough low enriched uranium and enrichment technology that it could produce enough material for the core of a nuclear bomb, given a political decision to so.

The Bush administration stood aside and even thwarted European efforts to negotiate, refusing until the end of the administration even to meet with senior Iranian officials about the program. Regime change was to be the answer, not negotiations. Former undersecretary of state Nicholas Burns now says, "I served as the Bush administration's point person on Iran for three years but was never permitted to meet an Iranian."[25] The United States has also failed to contain Iran's regional ambitions. Senator Chuck Hagel (R-NE) says, "America's refusal to recognize Iran's status as a legitimate power does not decrease Iran's influence, but rather increases it."[26]

North Korea Detonated a Nuclear Bomb and Expanded Its Weapons Program

Pyongyang went from enough material for perhaps two weapons to enough for up to ten. President Clinton's long-term engagement effort—whatever its faults—had made significant progress in transforming North Korea's behavior, getting the North to freeze its plutonium-production facilities and even approach normalizing relations with the United States. Near the end of Clinton's term, talks were underway to end all missile tests and to open up diplomatic-liaison offices in Pyongyang and Washington.

Clinton-administration officials left office confident that incoming secretary of state Powell would continue the dialogue and carry it to a successful conclusion. On March 6, 2001, Powell told reporters, "We do plan to engage with North Korea and pick up where President Clinton and his administration left off." Powell went on to say that "some promising elements were left on the table" and that the United States has "a lot to offer that regime if they will act in ways that we think are constructive."[27]

President Bush, however, overruled his new secretary of state, viewing this strategy as too accommodating and weak on verification.[28] In its first year in office, the administration stepped back from high-level engagement by setting preconditions for the resumption of talks, including "improved implementation of the Agreed Framework," "verifiable constraints" on missile developments, and a less threatening military posture.[29]

The administration followed this curtailment of engagement over the next months by naming North Korea as part of the "Axis of Evil," and including the country in the 2002 Nuclear Posture Review plans as a possible target of U.S. nuclear weapons. With each step, the Bush administration and North Korea moved further from the negotiating table. Almost a decade of improving relations unraveled quickly. In October 2002, the Bush administration confronted Pyongyang with evidence of a North Korean uranium-enrichment program, which the Bush administration said invalidated the 1994 Agreed Framework. Surprisingly, North Korea admitted it had such a program, but dialogue was scuttled. U.S.–North Korean relations went rapidly downhill. Between 2002 and 2006, the U.S. and North Korea would meet in intermittent and unproductive sessions under the umbrella of the Six-Party Talks (which also included China, Russia, Japan, and South Korea), with little progress.

Pyongyang became more aggressive. In December 2002, North Korea threw out IAEA inspectors, removing seals and monitoring equipment with the stated intention of restarting its nuclear facilities at Yongbyong. Soon after, North Korea became the first signatory in history to withdraw from the Nuclear Non-Proliferation Treaty. It ended the freeze on its plutonium program and declared itself to possess enough reprocessed plutonium to produce nuclear weapons. On the Fourth of July 2006, North Korea test-fired seven ballistic missiles, including the failed test of a long-range Taepodong-2. North Korea tested its first nuclear device on October 9, 2006.[30]

The Bush administration never organized a consistent policy toward North Korea, drawing a series of "red lines" that the North Koreans crossed with impunity. The situation deteriorated slowly and painfully as North Korea advanced its nuclear and ballistic-missile capabilities. By September 2008, the "pragmatists" in the Bush administration appeared to have prevailed over the hard-liners opposed to negotiations and resuscitated a process for a verifiable end to the Korean nuclear program, but it was too late to make much progress.

Nuclear Technologies Usable for Weapons Programs Proliferated Around the World

More nations declared their intentions to develop the ability to enrich uranium for nuclear-reactor fuel, the same technologies that can be used to enrich

uranium for nuclear bombs. U.S. proposals to curtail these technologies failed
to win any significant support. In February 2004, President Bush had called
for current nuclear exporters to provide nuclear fuel at reasonable costs for
countries that renounce enrichment and reprocessing. He also urged members of the Nuclear Suppliers Group to cease sales of reprocessing and enrichment equipment to nations without functioning programs.[31] The plan
drew little support, follow-up was ineffective, and efforts to dissuade nations
from pursuing nuclear-enrichment programs have failed. Brazil has continued its enrichment programs,[32] and other nations considering engaging in enrichment activities include Argentina, Australia, Canada, South Africa, South
Korea, and Ukraine. Further, more than a dozen Middle East nations expressed interest in pursuing nuclear energy and research programs, including Algeria, Bahrain, Egypt, Jordan, Kuwait, Libya, Morocco, Oman, Qatar,
Saudi Arabia, Syria, Turkey, and the United Arab Emirates.[33] These civilian
programs could lay the groundwork for weapons capability.

Thousands of Cold War Nuclear Weapons Cut, but Thousands Remained Poised for Attack

The Bush administration made its most dramatic, though largely unheralded,
progress in reducing Cold War nuclear arsenals. When President Bush took
office, Russia and the United States each had deployed some 6,000 strategic
nuclear warheads.[34] President Bush initially made unilateral cuts to a huge
nuclear force that many in the military saw as more of budgetary burden than
an instrument of U.S. power. But bowing to pressure from Congress, he then
pivoted to win Russian agreement to similar reductions in a legally binding
treaty, the Strategic Offensive Reductions Treaty, or SORT, which came into
force in June 2003.

However—consistent with the overall view that the United States should
not be restricted by international treaties—the administration did not include
any verification mechanisms in the treaty and then shut down the negotiation
process supported by every U.S. president since Harry Truman. This meant
that U.S. inspectors would no longer be able to verify Russian reductions after
December 31, 2009, when the START II Treaty would expire.[35] Meanwhile,
the administration's desire to expand NATO by bringing Georgia and Ukraine
into the alliance, coupled with plans to deploy strategic missile interceptors

and radar installations in Poland and the Czech Republic aggravated Russian concerns over U.S. intentions. The Russian-Georgian conflict brought U.S.-Russian relations to their worst point since before the collapse of the Soviet Union.

The strain in U.S.-Russian relations predated the Bush administration and is aggravated in no small part by Russian policies. There was no coherent plan, however, for addressing the danger from the almost 1,300 Russian nuclear warheads poised for attack within fifteen minutes, even as the deterioration of its radar and surveillance satellites introduces grave doubts about the reliability of Russia's early-warning system. The former chairman of the Senate Armed Services Committee Sam Nunn (D-GA) warned, "It's insane for us, 16 years after the Cold War, to think of the Russian president having four or five minutes to make a decision about whether what may be a false warning requires a response before he loses his retaliatory force."[36]

The Currency of Nuclear Weapons Increased in Value

Even as the numbers decreased, new missions for the remaining weapons and proposals to build new types of nuclear weapons seemed to increase their role in U.S. national security strategy. This encouraged the view among other nations that nuclear weapons could substitute for conventional weapons. Stephen Hadley, before becoming President Bush's national security adviser, said "It is often an unstated premise in the current debate that if nuclear weapons are needed at all, they are needed only to deter the nuclear weapons of others. I am not sure this unstated premise is true."[37] Hadley had been a participant in the National Institute for Public Policy's January 2001 report, "Rationale and Requirements for U.S. Nuclear Forces and Arms Control."[38] The group called for a more "flexible" nuclear deterrent against a wide range of targets. These policies were brought into the administration and enshrined in the Nuclear Posture Review delivered to Congress in December 2001, which advocated new nuclear weapons capabilities for use against nonnuclear targets, including chemical and biological weapons stockpiles, underground bunkers, mobile targets, and states without nuclear weapons, such as Iran, Iraq, Libya, and Syria. Congress refused to fund these new weapons, but Russia, France, and Pakistan mirrored U.S. logic in policies justifying the use of nuclear weapons against conventional threats.[39]

The U.S.-India Deal Blew a Hole Through Barriers to the Spread of Nuclear Weapons

Bush's July 2005 decision to reverse U.S. policy toward India and begin sell-ing sensitive nuclear technology and fuel to the country seemed to reward India's nuclear proliferation. By providing India with supplies of uranium, the deal allowed the country to accelerate its production of nuclear weapons, a capability Pakistan would be quick to mirror. The action was a de facto rec-ognition of India as a nuclear state, with all the rights and privileges reserved for those states that have joined the Non-Proliferation Treaty, yet without the same obligations. This raised concerns that states such as Pakistan and Is-rael might follow. Indeed, Pakistan soon demanded a similar deal with the United States,[40] and China reportedly agreed to sell Pakistan two nuclear reactors. The deal made it more difficult to convince other states to accept tougher nonproliferation standards. Representative Ed Markey (D-MA) said, "There are many ways to deepen U.S.-India ties without damaging the nu-clear Non-Proliferation Treaty."[41]

The Nonproliferation Regime Weakened

The 2005 Non-Proliferation Treaty Review Conference (held every five years) ended acrimoniously, failing to act on the consensus of the majority of states for stronger nonproliferation and disarmament efforts or to adopt any of the dozens of useful suggestions proposed by many of the nations present. As other nations concluded that the United States had no intention of fulfill-ing its NPT-related disarmament obligations, including ratifying the Compre-hensive Test Ban Treaty or moving decisively toward nuclear disarmament, they balked at shouldering additional antiproliferation burdens. In 2004, a high-level advisory panel that included Brent Scowcroft, President George H. W. Bush's national security adviser, warned the UN secretary-general, "We are approaching a point at which the erosion of the non-proliferation regime could become irreversible and result in a cascade of proliferation."[42]

Nuclear Smuggling Networks Remained Active

Although the A. Q. Khan nuclear black market in Pakistan was disrupted in 2004, failure to do so earlier allowed Iran, Libya, and possibly North Korea to acquire key components for nuclear weapons production. (This was first detected under the Clinton administration, which failed to shut it down.) The failure to get more cooperation from Pakistan, which used the network for its own nuclear imports, made it difficult to determine if the network had been shut down completely or had simply gone further underground. European intelligence reports indicate that illicit nuclear sales continue to thrive in the region.[43]

Antimissile Programs Failed to Fulfill Their Promise

The Bush administration had hoped to develop a multilayered missile defense system that could protect the United States and its allies. The administration and the Congress swiftly increased annual funding for antimissile programs, from $4 billion in fiscal year 2000 to more than $9 billion by fiscal year 2004, continuing those funding levels through the end of the administration. It also elevated the organization in the Department of Defense responsible for managing these programs to a full-fledged agency, the Missile Defense Agency, increasing its bureaucratic clout.

From 2000 to 2007, the United States spent almost $60 billion on antimissile systems without realizing any substantial increase in military capability. The ground-based interceptors the administration deployed in Alaska and California were widely regarded as ineffective.[44] A rush to deploy similar interceptors in Eastern Europe against a hypothetical long-range Iranian missile threat aggravated relations with Russia. The administration also passed up a Russian offer to field radar bases near Iran that could help counter the existing threat of Iran's short- and medium-range missiles.

REPAIRING THE DAMAGE

By the end of the Bush administration, there was a broad recognition of the failure of the Bush approach, if not yet agreement on all the specifics. Richard Haass, president of the Council on Foreign Relations, summed up the problem with the administration's attraction to regime change as a solution to proliferation: "It is not hard to fathom why: regime change is less distasteful than diplomacy and less dangerous than living with new nuclear states. There is only one problem: it is highly unlikely to have the desired effect soon enough."[45] The former Bush State Department official Nicholas Burns argued, "The next president needs to act more creatively and boldly to defend our interests by revalidating diplomacy as a key weapon in our national arsenal and rebuilding our understaffed and underfunded diplomatic corps." Rather than defaulting to the idea of using U.S. military force against Iran or other nations, Burns said, "dialogue and discussion, talking and listening, are the smarter ways to defend our country, end crises and sometimes even sow the seeds of an ultimate peace."[46]

The nation needed a new course of action. The collapse of the Bush Doctrine was a chance for the Obama administration to fundamentally change U.S. nuclear policy to one that "would take into account the limited present-day need for a nuclear arsenal as well as the military and political dangers associated with maintaining a massive stockpile," as the Manhattan Project veteran Wolfgang Panofsky wrote just before his death. "Given that the risks posed by nuclear weapons far outweigh their benefits in today's world, the United States should lead a worldwide campaign to de-emphasize their role in international relations."[47]

A growing majority of U.S. national security experts across the political spectrum had come to embrace this view. So did both 2008 presidential candidates. Barack Obama said in 2008, "It's time to send a clear message: America seeks a world with no nuclear weapons."[48] Senator John McCain similarly pledged, "The United States should lead a global effort at nuclear disarmament."[49]

The platforms adopted by both parties at their conventions that year concretely demonstrated the consensus that had taken hold among American security elites as to the main dangers and the way to reduce these dangers. The Republican platform said:

> The gravest threat we face, nuclear terrorism, demands a comprehensive strategy for reducing the world's nuclear stockpiles and preventing proliferation. The U.S. should lead that effort by reducing the size of our nuclear arsenal to the lowest number consistent with our security requirements and working with other nuclear powers to do the same. In cooperation with other nations, we should end the production of weapons-grade fissile material, improve our collective ability to interdict the spread of weapons of mass destruction and related materials, and ensure the highest possible security standards for existing nuclear materials wherever they may be located.[50]

Similarly, the Democratic Party platform listed "securing nuclear weapons and materials from terrorists" as the third of Barack Obama's seven national security goals and pledged to "seek deep, verifiable reduction in United States and Russian nuclear weapons and work with other nuclear powers to reduce global stockpiles dramatically" and "create a bipartisan consensus to support ratification of the Comprehensive Nuclear Test Ban Treaty." In language mirroring the Republican analysis, the Democratic platform said:

> America will seek a world with no nuclear weapons and take concrete actions to move in this direction. We face the growing threat of terrorists acquiring nuclear weapons or the materials to make them, as more countries seek nuclear weapons and nuclear materials remain unsecured in too many places. As George Shultz, Bill Perry, Henry Kissinger, and Sam Nunn have warned, current measures are not adequate to address these dangers. We will maintain a strong and reliable deterrent as long as nuclear weapons exist, but America will be safer in a world that is reducing reliance on nuclear weapons and ultimately eliminates all of them. We will make the goal of eliminating nuclear weapons worldwide a central element of U.S. nuclear weapons policy.[51]

Additionally, a number of high-level and grassroots efforts were underway that would encourage and help the new president to implement this vision. The Brookings Institution expert Ivo Daalder and the former assistant secretary of defense Jan Lodal argued in their seminal article, "The Logic of Zero," that "given this remarkable bipartisan consensus, the next president will have an opportunity to make the elimination of all nuclear weapons the organizing principle of U.S. nuclear policy."[52] They and other experts developed concrete plans for practical steps toward elimination that promised to be far more effective than the failed policies of the previous eight years.

Would the new president heed their advice? A struggle would soon begin within the new Obama administration between the "transformationalists," who sought a new vision to transform U.S. nuclear policy, and the "incrementalists," who would focus on gradual steps using the techniques of previous years. The president would have to act quickly, for the policy window that opened in January 2009 would not last long. Delay and indecision could cost him the chance to bring about the visionary change he promised in his campaign and the relief from the nuclear dangers the nation and world so urgently needed.

THREE
PIVOT

When President Barack Obama assumed office in January 2009, confidence in U.S. leadership and global support for the nonproliferation regime were at historically low levels. The Bush policies, as noted in the last chapter, had increased the proliferation threat and weakened most proliferation barriers. After his Prague speech, the president seemed to be sprinting through his efforts to transform U.S. and global nuclear policy.[1] Supported and encouraged by foreign policy heavyweights, President Obama often repeated the pledge first made in Prague, "to seek the peace and security of a world without nuclear weapons."[2] Obama, however, faced stiff resistance from recalcitrant bureaucrats and nuclear hawks and had to contend with Russian officials more interested in using reduction negotiations to relitigate old grievances than in redefining outdated strategies. Still the agenda had broad support within the American national security establishment and from other world leaders. Nuclear policy remained a top priority for the president, Vice President Joe Biden, and their key staff.

Obama's overall goal was to refocus U.S. nuclear policy from the permanent maintenance of an immense nuclear arsenal with multiple missions to the reduction and eventual elimination of all nuclear weapons. This was based on a growing bipartisan consensus of former security and military officials. Former U.S. secretaries of state George Shultz and Henry Kissinger, former secretary of defense William Perry, and former Senate Armed Services chairman Sam Nunn were the leading proponents of this shift, embodied in their January 2007 and 2008 *Wall Street Journal* opinion pieces calling for "a world without nuclear weapons." For their second op-ed, the four garnered the support of almost three-quarters of the still-living former U.S. secretaries of state and defense and national security advisors, including James Baker, Colin Powell, Madeleine Albright, Frank Carlucci, Warren Christopher, and Melvin Laird.

Obama spoke of his strategic vision and program in Cairo, Moscow, the United Nations and other forums. He often said that he was continuing the vision of Presidents John Kennedy and Ronald Reagan, who both championed nuclear disarmament. But he was the first to marry this vision to a series of practical steps when the international conditions were so favorable to change.

By September 2009, the new U.S. orientation was showing modest results. The UN Security Council, with most members represented by their heads of state, unanimously supported UN Resolution 1887, which explicitly linked increased enforcement of nonproliferation rules to a global commitment to a world without nuclear weapons. President Obama, the first U.S. president to chair a session of the Security Council, addressed his fellow heads of state:

> The historic resolution we just adopted enshrines our shared commitment to the goal of a world without nuclear weapons. And it brings Security Council agreement on a broad framework for action to reduce nuclear dangers as we work toward that goal. It reflects the agenda I outlined in Prague, and builds on a consensus that all nations have the right to peaceful nuclear energy; that nations with nuclear weapons have the responsibility to move toward disarmament; and those without them have the responsibility to forsake them.[3]

The next day, President Obama, joined by President Nicolas Sarkozy of France and Prime Minister Gordon Brown of the United Kingdom, exposed the secret uranium-enrichment facility that Iran was building near the city of Qom. The revelation further isolated Iran as supporters walked away in embarrassment of this flagrant breach of Iran's treaty obligations, and the facility's potential use as a covert enrichment site ended.

It was not until April 2010, however, that the framework for the new approach was fully erected. After several delays in external and internal negotiations, the Obama administration ushered in its plans for a strengthened nonproliferation regime with three dramatic developments in eight days: the revamped Nuclear Posture Review on April 6, the New START agreement on April 8, and the Nuclear Security Summit on April 12–13. The Nuclear Posture Review explicitly reduced the role of nuclear weapons in U.S. security policy. The New START treaty, signed by Obama and Russian president Dmitry Medvedev in Prague, was the most important strategic arms reduction treaty in twenty years, restoring critical inspection and verification mechanisms and lowering the level of permitted strategic weapons by one-third. The Nuclear Security Summit in Washington, D.C., gathered fifty world leaders, including thirty-seven heads of state and the heads of the United Nations and the European Union, for the largest, most senior-level conference ever held on nuclear policy. It produced an action plan to secure global stocks of highly enriched uranium and plutonium over the next four years, including immediate steps by many of the participating nations to reduce or eliminate their material stockpiles.

Together, these events impressed global leaders and publics and convinced many domestic skeptics of the viability of the new approach. The *Washington Post* columnist Jim Hoagland, known for his centrist, realist views, wrote: "President Obama has turned the once utopian-sounding idea of global nuclear disarmament into a useful tool for U.S. foreign policy. His well-conceived, confidently executed three-part movement in statecraft this month should banish the notion that Obama's ambitious nuclear goals spring from naiveté or inexperience."[4] In addition, during May, the United States pressed for new UN sanctions on Iran while retaining the possibility of negotiations to resolve the crisis. On May 27, the administration released a new national security strategy with an emphasis on nuclear policy and a clear break from the Bush administration's more unilateralist stance. Finally, on May 28, the Non-Proliferation Treaty Review Conference had a surprising conclusion: the first consensus document in ten years and unanimous agreement on benchmarks for progress in accelerating nuclear disarmament and strengthening the barriers to the spread of these weapons.

Thus, over its first eighteen months, and intensely in April and May 2010, the new U.S. administration invested heavily in the nuclear security agenda. This new agenda reflected and supported the focus on core missions outlined in the May 2010 National Security Strategy: "Defeating al-Qa'ida and its affiliates in Afghanistan, Pakistan and around the globe; and our determination to deter aggression and prevent the proliferation of the world's most dangerous weapons." It also highlighted the return of a traditional pillar of American strength: "We must recognize that no one nation—no matter how powerful—can meet global challenges alone. As we did after World War II, America must prepare for the future, while forging cooperative approaches among nations that can yield results."[5]

Obama seemed to hit the nuclear policy sweet spot: inspiring idealists with his vision and winning pragmatists with his practical programs. Each of the changes introduced by the Obama administration was relatively modest— hence the disappointment among some of his supporters who saw his Prague speech as a call for immediate, dramatic change. Cumulatively, however, the changes marked a significant change of direction and thus spawned criticism from the right. The arc of U.S. policy now bent toward deeper reductions in nuclear arsenals with reduced roles for these weapons in the U.S. national security strategy, a greater emphasis on collective diplomatic action to stop proliferators, and strong cooperative efforts to block nuclear terrorism.

The policy shift tried to strike a deft balance. While continuously asserting the ultimate goal of eliminating nuclear weapons, Obama understood that there was no agreement in the strategic policy community that nations could completely eliminate nuclear weapons or even that they should. There was agreement, however, that many of the practical steps one would take toward elimination—such as reducing arsenals and securing weapon-usable materials—were also steps that reduced the high risks from the 23,000 weapons then held by nine states and the possibility that more nations or groups would get these weapons.

These events seemed to demonstrate the truth of the oft-contested connection between disarmament and nonproliferation. U.S. and Russian commitment to arms reductions helped build the cooperation needed for tougher actions to control the spread of nuclear weapons; actions to control the spread of nuclear weapons increased the security needed for further reductions. It was a nuclear virtuous circle. Obama and his advisors believed that they had charted the correct course for history, reaching internal consensus and forging a smart, effective approach that would pay dividends for American and Western alliance security. It is one that hewed a middle course by understanding that the lines defining the middle had shifted—from a general acceptance of the permanence of nuclear arsenals to a general acceptance on the need to move steadily toward their elimination. Arms control and non-proliferation were quickly becoming the new realism.

Key questions remained, however: did the substance match up to the rhetoric, and did it change the international diplomatic situation for the better?

THE U.S. STRATEGIC POSTURE

The Obama administration's guiding principles for nuclear strategy were set out in the 2010 Nuclear Posture Review (NPR), a Congressionally mandated report asked of each president since the end of the Cold War. While it is essentially an internal document, other nations carefully scrutinize the plan for clues on the future role of nuclear weapons in the U.S. security structure. In a clear break from the Bush era, the Obama administration's posture reduced the role of nuclear weapons in security policy and started a transformation of a nuclear policy to deal with twenty-first-century threats.

Obama's initial challenge in developing the NPR was his assembly of a national security team that contained a number of senior staff who were not as personally committed to the vision of nuclear elimination laid out in Prague. The review process became a struggle within the administration between the "incrementalists" and "transformationalists." It ended in a tie, with an approach that fell short of transformation but delivered significant change. With the personal involvement of President Obama and Secretary of Defense Robert Gates, the document was a delicately crafted posture that diminishes the role of nuclear weapons while maintaining a safe, secure, and robust nuclear deterrent.

The review said that it "altered the hierarchy of our nuclear concerns and strategic objectives" from a force configured for massive retaliation against another nation to a policy that "places the preventions of nuclear terrorism and proliferation at the top of the U.S. policy agenda."[6] The review also ruled out the creation of new weapons, which the previous administration had doggedly pursued, and the need for any new nuclear tests or new nuclear missions. The shifting of priorities and investments reflected a more realistic understanding of the new security environment.

Politically, the most important deliverable from the 2010 posture review may have been the support of Secretary of Defense Robert Gates and the Joint Chiefs of Staff for a permanent end to nuclear testing. As Gates said in his foreword to the review, increased budgets for modernizing the U.S. nuclear weapons complex and the existing stockpile stewardship program "represent a credible modernization plan necessary to sustain the nuclear infrastructure and support our nation's deterrent."[7] Gates thus dropped his hesitation to support Senate approval of the Comprehensive Test Ban Treaty, which he had publicly expressed just eighteen months earlier.[8]

The 2010 review reinforced U.S. security commitments to its allies but also stated that the fundamental purpose of U.S. nuclear weapons was deterrence of nuclear use by others. The general assessment of the Department of Defense was that non-nuclear-weapon states constitute a threat that could be countered by the overwhelmingly superior conventional forces of the U.S. and its allies. Thus, the NPR contained a U.S. pledge to never use or threaten to use a nuclear weapon on a non-nuclear-weapon state that adheres to its nonproliferation obligations.

The NPR also signaled the Obama administration's intention to further promote the reduction of all nuclear weapons across the board. The former secretary of state George Shultz approved of the move, saying, "deterrence is not necessarily strengthened by overreliance on nuclear weapons."[9] In a 2010 briefing, James N. Miller, then the principal deputy undersecretary for policy at the Department of Defense, explained that changes to U.S. nuclear policy were overdue and noted that the Cold War mantra of "mutually assured destruction was a situation, not a strategy."[10] He also noted that every president since the beginning of the nuclear era supported the concept of elimination, save George W. Bush. He rebutted the charges that the president's policy was one of unilateral disarmament, asserting that "the conditions for zero [nuclear weapons] start with the understanding that the U.S. does not 'go it alone.' "[11]

RESPONSES AND IMPLICATIONS

Though many were pleased with the new policies and new mode of thinking, there remained critics on both the right and the left. Those on the right, such as former UN ambassador John Bolton and columnist Charles Krauthammer, objected to any limitation on U.S. use of its arsenal, claiming the United States would not be able to defend itself in the event of a major biological attack.[12] Krauthammer called the new policy "quite insane," "morally bizarre," and "strategically loopy." Reinforcing a theme the right was trying to develop about Obama, Krauthammer said "the naiveté is stunning" and portrayed the new policy as "the theory that our moral example will move other countries to eschew nukes." On the contrary, he said, "The last quarter century—the time of greatest superpower nuclear-arms reduction—is precisely when Iran and North Korea went hellbent into the development of nuclear weapons."[13]

The arguments on the right at first appeared more political but would develop into substantive critiques of the review later on in 2010, during the debate over New START. Some on the left jumped out with strong criticisms of the posture—specifically as it pertained to the budget for the nuclear weapons complex.

In 2010, the administration outlined a massive proposed increase in funding for the maintenance of the U.S. nuclear arsenal and then delivered those numbers in the budget.[14] The administration told Congress that the funding levels for nuclear weapon programs under Obama would total $180 billion over the next decade (later increased to more than $215 billion), a significant increase in funding from the Bush administration (and, as later studies revealed, an underestimate of the true costs).[15] Disarmament advocates argued that calling for nuclear reductions while spending billions to maintain a bloated nuclear arsenal sent out a mixed message at home and abroad. "It's somewhat of a schizophrenic nuclear policy," said Hans Kristensen, director of the nuclear information project at the Federation of American Scientists.[16] Still, nuclear hawks claimed that the budget increases were not enough. Several former U.S. officials disagreed. For example, former National Nuclear Security Administration director Linton Brooks, who served under multiple presidents, including George W. Bush, said that he "would have killed for [the current] budget."[17]

The combination of increased investments and decreased deployments seemed to unite the core government defense constituencies around this new policy path. The NPR was fully supported by the defense agencies and Secretary Gates. The nuclear weapons lab directors Michael Anastasio, George Miller, and Tom Hunter went on record as saying that the U.S. arsenal can be maintained without explosive testing—as would be necessary under the Comprehensive Test Ban Treaty: "We believe that the approach outlined in the NPR, which excludes further nuclear testing and includes the consideration of the full range of life extension options . . . provides the necessary technical flexibility to manage the nuclear stockpile into the future with an acceptable level of risk."[18]

The 2010 NPR revamped the U.S. nuclear posture, but it was more than a national document—the world was watching. It was well received internationally, with U.S. allies praising the new policy as a "concrete" and "important step in the right direction" toward the reduction and eventual elimination of nuclear weapons. Allies also appreciated the NPR's acknowledgement of "the persistence of serious threats to the security of the United States and its allies" and the importance of the United States "maintaining and strengthening reassurance to its allies."[19] Former U.S. ambassador Richard Burt noted the NPR's diplomatic benefits:

> The posture review represents a necessary de-emphasis in the role of nuclear weapons in U.S. defense and foreign policy . . . [that will] strengthen President Obama's hand in re-energizing international support for enhanced nonproliferation measures while raising the costs for any country, such as Iran, that positions itself as a nuclear renegade.[20]

A NEW START

Two days after the release of the NPR, President Obama returned to Prague. There, he and President Medvedev of Russia signed a new strategic arms reduction treaty dubbed "New START." An update from the Strategic Arms Reduction Treaty of 1991 (START I), this new treaty reduced the allowed number of operational strategic nuclear arms to 1,550 warheads on 700 deployed strategic launchers. Once ratified, it would reduce the size of deployed U.S. and Russian strategic arsenals to levels not seen since the Eisenhower presidency. The treaty also established a new, more efficient verification process that authorized the monitoring of nuclear activities in both nations and assured compliance with disarmament pledges. Through this treaty, the U.S. and Russia also worked to reset a relationship that had deteriorated under the previous administration.

Beyond extending and updating the critical verification measures of START I, the Obama administration saw the New START treaty as a key step in gaining the global cooperation needed to prevent nuclear terrorism and nuclear proliferation. By clearly reaffirming U.S. and Russian commitment to disarmament, the United States hoped to convince other states to also take the steps necessary to secure nuclear materials and block nuclear weapons trade and development—steps that are often expensive or cut against the commercial interests of many key nations.

There was broad bipartisan support for the treaty from military leaders and former government officials, including Stephen Hadley and Brent Scowcroft, who served as national security advisors to George W. Bush and George H. W. Bush, respectively, and from former secretary of defense James Schlesinger, who called ratification "obligatory."[21] Senator Jeanne Shaheen (D-NH), for example, asked former secretary of state James Baker during treaty hearings if he thought "the START treaty will be a signal to the international community that the U.S. is serious about carrying out its responsibilities under the nonproliferation treaty." Baker responded, "I think it will, Senator, and I think it was."[22]

Some saw the treaty as critical in influencing partners to crack down on proliferating countries. As former secretary of defense William Perry stated: "To adequately deal with North Korea's and Iran's nuclear aspirations, we need full cooperation of other nations, particularly Russia and China. This treaty will not guarantee that, but this treaty is moving us in that direction of a much better understanding of the relationship with Russia on these vital matters."[23] Countries around the world commended the actions of the world's two largest nuclear states to reduce their arsenals. Britain's foreign secretary David Miliband noted that the treaty "will help pave the way for further reductions worldwide."[24] The diplomatic benefits of New START among non-weapons states such as Indonesia were also clear almost immediately:

> The first steps in the right direction have been taken. The United States and the Russian Federation have signed a new Strategic Arms Reduction Treaty (START). We are also cognizant of some positive aspects of the United States' Nuclear Posture Review. We welcome these developments and what we expect will be the further marginalization of nuclear weapons.[25]

Indonesia's pledge to ratify the Comprehensive Test Ban Treaty, a step it completed in December 2011, was a clear illustration of the connection between disarmament and nonproliferation. As former secretary of defense William Perry noted in his Senate Foreign Relations Committee testimony: "[New START] gives a clear signal to the world that the United States is

serious about carrying out its responsibilities under the Nuclear Nonproliferation Treaty. This will be welcomed as a positive step by all other members
of the NPT."

In fact, the Nuclear Non-Proliferation Treaty was the next item on the
repair list.

GLOBAL STEPS TOWARD NONPROLIFERATION THROUGH NPT

President Obama fielded a senior diplomatic team for the May 2010 Non-Proliferation Treaty (NPT) Review Conference, led by Secretary of State Hillary
Clinton, Undersecretary of State Ellen Tauscher, and NPT Ambassador Susan
Burk. This demonstrated a greater commitment than the U.S. representation
in 2005, which had no one above the rank of assistant secretary. The U.S.
goals this time were modest but critical to the survival of the nonproliferation regime. Despite this, the administration remained divided—some U.S. officials saw the 2010 conference as an event they just had to get through with
minimum damage while others viewed it as an opportunity to gather broad
consensus for reinforcing nonproliferation rules. The latter group proved the
more prescient.

Secretary Clinton trumpeted the New START agreement on the opening
day of the conference and took a small but significant step toward greater
transparency, disclosing the exact size of the U.S. nuclear arsenal: 5,113 warheads in its active stockpile as of September 30, 2009. Drawing attention to
the 84 percent reduction from the peak stockpile in 1967, Secretary Clinton
noted that "for those who doubt that the United States will do its part on
disarmament, this is our record, these are our commitments and they send a
clear, unmistakable message."[26]

Most representatives, save Iran, welcomed the nuclear policy steps taken
by the United States as "encouraging signs of progress," as Minister of Foreign Affairs Marty Natalegawa of Indonesia noted on behalf of the 118 members and 17 observers of the Non-Aligned Movement.[27] To the surprise of
most observers, the conference concluded with a consensus document that,
though watered down from the more far-reaching steps proposed by some
nations at the beginning of the conference, outlined specific steps all nations
should take by the time of the next review conference, slated for 2015. "The
successes achieved at the conference were made possible by the leadership
exhibited from the U.S. team," said U.S. Arms Control Association executive

director Daryl Kimball after the meeting, "and by the shift in U.S. nuclear weapons policy direction under President Obama over the past 15 months."[28]

The specific steps included promises to strengthen IAEA safeguards; deter treaty withdrawals; bring Iran and North Korea back into compliance with the NPT; bring India and Pakistan into the nuclear weapons risk-reduction and elimination process; organize a conference on making the Middle East a zone free of nuclear weapons; accelerate cooperation on securing loose nuclear materials; and advance the nuclear disarmament process by bringing into force the nuclear test ban treaty, negotiating an end to the production of nuclear weapons materials, and reducing the roles and missions of nuclear weapons.

UK ambassador John Duncan summarized the results:

> For the U.S. and UK the principle objective was to re-energize and give renewed focus to a part of the international institutional arena that had been broken and polarized for a decade. At its simplest it was to create a new constituency for action by empowering the center ground against more extreme views. . . . The first task was one of repair. Thus the important outcome lies not in the minutiae of the Final Document, but in the political processes created by last week's agreement. . . . Some commentators complained about a supposed 'lowest common denominator agreement' or that the main success was the absence of failure. This is to rather miss the point. The NPT RevCon is not an end in itself, but like a marketing event in the private sector, the real importance lies in the process of engagement that follows.[29]

NUCLEAR REPRIEVE

Coming out of the NPT Review Conference, there was the sense that the world had brought the nonproliferation regime back from the brink of collapse. This was in large part attributable to the diplomatic space created by U.S. actions on nuclear policy. The analyst Deepti Choubey, attending on behalf of the Carnegie Endowment for International Peace, called the conference a "win for multilateralism." She noted that "states were so eager to get an outcome in part because Obama has created a lot of political capital. The Prague speech created the atmosphere to achieve this outcome."[30]

Obama's new policy declarations and his concrete actions had made a difference. The diplomatic situation by the end of 2010 was quite different than it had been two years previously. That did not mean the road ahead would be easy. Thus far, it was only a course correction, and it was not yet clear how budgets, deployments, and diplomacy would shift or whether the new policy would thwart national nuclear ambitions more effectively than the policies of Obama's predecessor.

President Obama seemed to understand this and made it clear that the U.S. cannot succeed without the help of the international community: "We are clear-eyed about the shortfalls of our international system. But America has not succeeded by stepping out of the currents of cooperation—we have succeeded by steering those currents in the direction of liberty and justice, so nations thrive by meeting their responsibilities and face consequences when they don't."[31] The new U.S. nuclear agenda had engaged the nations of the world in a more cooperative and determined process to reduce nuclear dangers and to at least talk about working toward the reduction and eventual elimination of nuclear weapons. But how far would this cooperative enterprise advance? It had proven more effective than any recent alternative approaches, but could it last?

PART II
NIGHTMARES

FOUR
ARSENALS AND ACCIDENTS

A reader who has gotten this far into the book may be wondering if all this policy talk really matters.[1] Treaties, agreements, dialogues, debates—who cares? Didn't the collapse of the Soviet Union and the end of the Cold War mark the end of the nuclear threat? Nothing could be further from the truth. There are multiple nuclear nightmares still out there. On any given day, we could wake up to a crisis that threatens our country, our region, our planet. If we ignore these nuclear nightmares, we do so at our peril.

The American poet Robert Frost famously mused on whether the world will end in fire or in ice. Nuclear weapons can deliver both. The fire is obvious: modern hydrogen bombs duplicate the enormous thermonuclear energies of the sun on the surface of the earth—with catastrophic consequences. But it might be nuclear cold that kills the planet. A nuclear war with a few hundred weapons exploded in urban cores could blanket the Earth in smoke and particulates, ushering in a years-long nuclear winter, with global droughts, massive crop failures, and mega-famines.

The nuclear age is now in its seventh decade. For most of these years, citizens and officials lived with the constant fear that long-range bombers and ballistic missiles would bring instant, total destruction to the United States, the Soviet Union, many other nations, and, perhaps, the entire planet. In 1957, Nevil Shute's best-selling novel, *On the Beach*, portrayed the terror of survivors as they awaited the radioactive clouds drifting toward Australia from a Northern Hemisphere nuclear war. There were then some 7,000 nuclear weapons in the world, with the U.S. stockpile outnumbering the Soviet Union's ten to one.

By the 1980s, the nuclear danger had grown to grotesque proportions. When Jonathan Schell's chilling book, *The Fate of the Earth*, was published in 1982, there were then almost 60,000 nuclear weapons stockpiled with a destructive force equal to roughly 20,000 megatons (20 billion tons) of TNT, or over 1 million times the power of the Hiroshima bomb. President Ronald Reagan's "Star Wars" antimissile system was originally intended to defeat a first-wave attack of some 5,000 Soviet SS-18 and SS-19 missile warheads streaking over the North Pole. "These bombs," Schell wrote, "were built as 'weapons' for 'war,' but their significance greatly transcends war and all its causes and outcomes. They grew out of history, yet they threaten to end history. They were made by men, yet they threaten to annihilate man."[2]

The threat of a global thermonuclear war today is low. The treaties negotiated in the 1980s, particularly the START agreements, which began the reductions in U.S. and Soviet strategic arsenals, and the Intermediate-Range Nuclear Forces Treaty of 1987, which eliminated an entire class of nuclear-tipped missiles, began a process that accelerated with the end of the Cold War. Between 1992 and 2012, the nuclear weapons carried by long-range U.S. and Russian missiles and bombers decreased by 74 percent.[3] And the number of all the nuclear weapons in the world (short- and long-range, deployed and nondeployed) has been cut by almost three-quarters, from a Cold War high of more than 65,056 in 1986 to about 17,200 as of March 2013. What has not changed is the concentration of these weapons. The United States and Russia at the beginning of 2013 had over 95 percent of all these weapons, or about 16,200, with seven other countries holding the remaining 1,000 or so.[4]

The U.S. and Russian stockpiles are on track to decline for at least the rest of this decade. As their numbers come down, so does the risk of nuclear war.

But the risk is not zero. Even a small chance of nuclear war each year, for whatever reason, multiplied over a number of years sums up to an unacceptable chance for catastrophe.

These are not mere statistical musings. We came much closer to Armageddon after the Cold War ended than many realize. In January 1995, a global nuclear war almost started by mistake. Russian military officials mistook a Norwegian weather rocket for a U.S. submarine-launched ballistic missile. Boris Yeltsin became the first Russian president to ever have the "nuclear suitcase" open in front of him. He had just a few minutes to decide if he should push the button that would launch a barrage of nuclear missiles. We believe his senior military officials advised him that he had to launch. Thankfully, he concluded that his radars were in error. The suitcase was closed.

Such a scenario could repeat today. The presidents of Russia and the United States are still followed everywhere they go by an aide carrying a suitcase (or the "football" as the White House calls it) with the codes and communications that could launch Armageddon. The Cold War is over, but the Cold War weapons remain. And so do the Cold War postures that keep thousands of these weapons on hair-trigger alert, ready to launch in under fifteen minutes. As of January 2013, the active U.S. stockpile contains nearly 4,650 nuclear warheads. About 1,950 of them are deployed atop Minuteman III intercontinental ballistic missiles based in Montana, Wyoming, and North Dakota; the rest are deployed in a fleet of fourteen nuclear-powered Trident submarines that patrol the Pacific, Atlantic, and Artic oceans and at air force bases housing the long-range B-2 bombers in Missouri and the B-52s in North Dakota and Louisiana (see table 4.1). The United States also has approximately 3,000 intact warheads in storage awaiting dismantlement, for a total inventory of some 7,700 warheads.

Russia has more than 4,500 warheads in its active stockpile, with 2,484 atop its SS-18, SS-19, SS-25, and SS-27 missiles deployed in silos in six missile fields arrayed between Moscow and Siberia (Kozelsk, Tatishchevo, Uzhur, Dombarovskiy, Kartalay, and Aleysk); on eleven nuclear-powered Delta submarines that conduct limited patrols with the Northern and Pacific fleets from three naval bases (Nerpich'ya, Yagel'Naya and Rybachiy); and on Bear and Blackjack bombers stationed at Ukrainka and Engels air bases (see table 4.2). Russia also retains an estimated 4,000 intact warheads in storage awaiting dismantlement, for a total stockpile of some 8,500 weapons.[5]

Though the Soviet Union collapsed in 1991 and Russian and American presidents now call each other friends, Washington and Moscow continue to maintain and modernize these huge nuclear arsenals. In July 2007, just before President Vladimir Putin of Russia vacationed with President George W. Bush at the Bush home in Kennebunkport, Maine, Russia successfully tested a new submarine-based missile. In operation, the missile would carry six nuclear warheads and could travel more than 6,000 miles; that is, it is designed to strike targets in the United States, including, almost certainly, targets in the very state of Maine that Putin visited. For his part, President Bush's administration adopted a nuclear posture that included plans to produce new types of weapons; begin development of a new generation of nuclear missiles, submarines, and bombers; and expand the U.S. nuclear weapons complex so that it could produce thousands of new warheads on demand. President Barack Obama, as noted in previous chapters, has updated this strategy, but it still retains many of the nuclear-war-fighting aspects that could lead, by intention, miscalculation, or accident, to a thermonuclear exchange.

In October 2012, many organizations and experts marked the fiftieth anniversary of the Cuban Missile Crisis, when the United States and the Soviet Union almost started a global thermonuclear war. But this crisis was not the only time we almost used or exploded nuclear weapons; it is only the most well known. Jeffrey Lewis, director of the East Asia Nonproliferation Program at the James Martin Center for Nonproliferation Studies, compiled a list that month for *Foreign Policy* magazine of twelve other near misses—or one for each month of the year—in his article "Nightmare on Nuke Street." It was not hard to do. The Department of Defense, Lewis noted, has a report documenting thirty-two nuclear weapon accidents between 1950 and 1980. These include incidents where a total of six nuclear weapons were lost and never recovered. The department also tallied up 1,152 "moderately serious" nuclear false alarms between 1977 and 1984—or roughly three per week. "I kind of get the feeling that if NORAD went more than a week without a serious false alarm," Lewis quipped, "they would start to wonder if the computers were ok."[6]

Examples of crises provided by Lewis, who also edits the popular blog *ArmsControlWonk.org* include:

⊙ A November 1979 incident when someone at North American Aerospace Defense Command (NORAD) "played a training tape showing a massive Soviet attack ... NORAD issued warnings that went out to the entire intercontinental ballistic missile (ICBM) force and put the president's airborne command post in the air."

⦿ Several accidents involving B-52s armed with nuclear weapons that crashed in 1962 (Goldsboro, North Carolina), 1966 (Palomares, Spain), and 1968 (Thule, Greenland). "After the third crash, the Air Force finally figured out that it's a terrible idea to keep nuclear armed bombers in the air at all times."

⦿ A 1958 incident where a B-47 crew accidentally dropped a hydrogen bomb that landed near Myrtle Beach, South Carolina—and exploded. "Fortunately, only the high explosives detonated. But the impact crater can still be seen today."

⦿ Three different false alarms from June 3 to June 6, 1980, caused by new software and a faulty forty-six-cent computer chip that failed in NORAD headquarters that "showed different Soviet attacks from one moment to the next," alarming "many officials in the Carter administration."

⦿ A 1956 bomber crash at Lakenheath Air Base in Britain where a B-47 plowed into nuclear weapons storage "igloos," killing the crew and scattering Mark Six nuclear warheads. General Curtis LeMay, head of the Strategic Air Command, cabled back home: "Preliminary exam by bomb disposal officer says a miracle that one Mark Six with exposed detonators didn't go off."

⦿ A 2007 incident where "a weapons crew at Minot Air Force Base in North Dakota mistakenly loaded six nuclear-armed cruise missiles onto a B-52 bomber, which then flew the nuclear weapons across the country to Barksdale Air Force Base in Louisiana. The nuclear weapons were unsecured for 36 hours." Crew in Barksdale eventually noticed that the missiles hanging from the bomber's wings were nuclear, not conventional, weapons. Officials at Minot did not know the weapons were missing until the alarmed officers in Louisiana notified them.

As the 1995 and 2007 incident demonstrates, the dangers from the accidents, miscalculations, and misunderstandings involving the existing nuclear arsenals are not confined to the Cold War past. For example, although much was made at the time of the 1994 joint decision by Presidents Bill Clinton and Boris Yeltsin to no longer target each other's countries with their weapons, this announcement had few practical consequences. Target coordinates can be uploaded into a warhead's guidance systems within minutes. The warheads remain on missiles on a high-alert status similar to what was maintained during the tensest moments of the Cold War. This greatly increases the risk of an unauthorized or accidental launch. Because there is no time buffer built into each state's decision-making process, this extreme level of readiness enhances the possibility that either side's president could prematurely order a nuclear strike based on flawed intelligence.

Bruce Blair, a former Minuteman launch officer who is now a leader of the Global Zero movement, says, "If both sides sent the launch order right now, without any warning or preparation, thousands of nuclear weapons— the equivalent in explosive firepower of about 70,000 Hiroshima bombs— could be unleashed within a few minutes."[7]

Blair describes the scenario in dry but chilling detail:

> If early warning satellites or ground radar detected missiles in flight, both sides would attempt to assess whether a real nuclear attack was under way within a strict and short deadline. Under Cold War procedures that are still in practice today, early warning crews manning their consoles 24/7 have only three minutes to reach a preliminary conclusion. Such occurrences happen on daily basis, sometimes more than once per day. If an apparent nuclear missile threat is perceived, then an emergency teleconference would be convened between the American/Russian President and his top nuclear advisers. On the U.S side, the top officer on duty at Strategic Command in Omaha, Neb., would brief the president on his nuclear options and their consequences. That officer is allowed all of 30 seconds to deliver the briefing.
>
> Then the U.S or Russian president would have to decide whether to retaliate, and since the command systems on both sides have long been geared for launch-on-warning, the presidents would have little spare time if they desired to get retaliatory nuclear missiles off the ground before they—and possibly the presidents themselves—were vaporized. On the U.S side, the time allowed to decide would range between zero and 12 minutes, depending on the scenario. Russia operates under even tighter deadlines because of the short flight time of U.S. Trident submarine missiles on forward patrol in the North Atlantic.[8]

Russia's early-warning systems remain in a serious state of erosion and disrepair, making it all the more likely that a Russian president could panic and reach a different conclusion than Yeltsin did in 1995.[9] As Russian capabilities continue to deteriorate, the chance of an accident only increases. Limited spending on the conventional Russian military has led to greater reliance on an aging nuclear arsenal whose survivability would make any deterrence theorist nervous. (See more on this in chapter 5.) Yet the missiles remain on the same launch status that began in the worst days of the Cold War.

As Blair concludes, "Such rapid implementation of war plans leaves no room for real deliberation, rational thought, or national leadership."[10] Former chairman of the Senate Armed Services Committee Sam Nunn agrees: "We are running the irrational risk of an Armageddon of our own making.... The more time the United States and Russia build into our process for ordering a nuclear strike the more time is available to gather data, to exchange information, to gain perspective, to discover an error, to avoid an accidental or unauthorized launch."[11]

U.S. NUCLEAR FORCES

As of early 2013, the active U.S. stockpile contained approximately 4,650 nuclear warheads. This included about 2,150 deployed warheads: 1,950 strategic warheads and 300 nonstrategic warheads, including cruise missiles and bombs. Approximately 2,650 additional warheads were held in the reserve or inactive/responsive stockpiles or awaiting dismantlement.

Table 4.1 ► U.S. Nuclear Forces, 2013

NAME/TYPE	LAUNCHERS	WARHEADS
ICBMs	450	500
SLBMs	288	1,152
Bombers	113	300
Total Strategic Weapons	851	~1,950
Tomahawk cruise missile	0	0
B-61-3, -4 bombs	N/A	200
Total Nonstrategic Weapons	N/A	200
Total deployed weapons	1,702	~2,150
Total non-deployed weapons		~2,500
Total retired awaiting dismantlement		~3,000
Total Nuclear Weapons		~7,700

Source: Hans M. Kristensen, "US Nuclear Forces," in SIPRI Yearbook (Stockholm: Stockholm International Peace Research Institute, 2013), 286.

RUSSIAN NUCLEAR FORCES

As of March 2013, Russia had approximately 4,500 operational nuclear war-heads in its active arsenal. This included about 2,484 operational strategic warheads and approximately 2,000 nonstrategic warheads, including artil-lery, short-range rockets, and landmines. An additional 4,000 warheads were believed to be in reserve or awaiting dismantlement, for a total Russian stock-pile of approximately 8,500 nuclear warheads.[12]

GLOBAL ARSENALS

The arsenals of the other nuclear-weapons states under the NPT are min-iscule compared to the U.S. and Russian arsenals. France has the next larg-est arsenal, totaling approximately 300 weapons, deployed on bombers and

Table 4.2 ▸ Russian Nuclear Forces, 2013

NAME/TYPE	LAUNCHERS	WARHEADS
CBMs	326	1,050
SLBMs	160	624
Bombers	72	810
Total Strategic Weapons	558	2,484
Total Nonstrategic Weapons		~2,000
Total Active Weapons		~4,500
Total Retired Weapons		~4,000
Total Nuclear Weapons		~8,500

Note: Russia has approximately 2,484 strategic warheads assigned to 558 launchers. However, because several nuclear-powered ballistic-missile sub-marines are in overhaul and do not carry their allocated missiles and war-heads, and bombers under normal conditions are not loaded with nuclear weapons, approximately 1,490 of Russia's strategic warheads are deployed on 434 operational missiles. Russia's nonstrategic weapons are said to be in central storage. The number of ICBN launchers is up slightly from the 322 in 2012 because some assumed SS-25 retirements did not occur. The number of SLBM launchers is higher than the 144 from 2012 because the Borei SSBN entered service.

Source: Robert S. Norris and Hans M. Kristensen, "NRDC Nuclear Notebook, Russian Nuclear Forces, 2013," *Bulletin of the Atomic Scientists*, forthcoming.

a small SSBN (submarine) force.[13] China's arsenal is not as transparent, but independent experts estimate its force at no more than 240 warheads total, approximately 138 on land-based missiles and 20 on bombers. Although the Chinese have built two submarines, neither is operational. An additional 62 Chinese warheads were either built for the submarines or are slated for dismantlement.[14] The British have the smallest nuclear deterrent of the original five nuclear-weapons states with 225 total warheads; 160 are deployed on four SSBNs with an additional 25 in reserve.[15]

Four countries have nuclear weapons programs but are not members of the Non-Proliferation Treaty: India, Pakistan, Israel, and North Korea (which joined then left the NPT). Israel has a nondeclaratory policy, meaning it does not officially acknowledge or deny its nuclear weapons; however, it is widely estimated that the country possesses 80 to 100 nuclear weapons deployed on land-based missiles and aircraft.[16] There is also a high probability that their fleet of three submarines is armed with nuclear-capable cruise missiles.[17]

India and Pakistan both have rapidly growing arsenals. Based on the amount of plutonium it has produced, Kristensen and Norris estimate India has 80–100 warheads. India can deploy nuclear weapons on missiles and bombers and is expected to have an operational nuclear-armed submarine within a decade.[18] Similarly, Pakistan is also estimated to have between 90–110 warheads on a range of missiles and bombers. Both arsenals are examined in more detail in chapter 8.

Finally, North Korea has tested three nuclear devices; however, there are no signs of operational delivery vehicles, despite the regime's claims to have intercontinental ballistic missiles that could bring "a sea of fire" down on the United States, and no publicly available information that the nation has operationalized its nuclear devices.[19] The tests in late 2012 indicated that North Korea has made progress in both its missile and weapon capabilities. The nation may have enough material for between three and ten nuclear weapons. Iran is often mentioned as having nuclear weapons, but it does not. The best available intelligence is that Iran is constructing facilities that could allow it to build nuclear weapons, but it has not yet made a decision to do so. It would likely take Iran two to three years to produce an operational nuclear warhead that could fit on a missile. The programs in Iran and North Korea are explored further in chapter 10.

No other nation has nuclear weapons or is suspected of programs that could build nuclear weapons. Indeed, the vast majority of the world is

Table 4.3 ► Global Nuclear Stockpiles, 2013

United States	7,700
Russia	8,500
France	300
China	240
United Kingdom	225
Pakistan	90–110
India	80–100
Israel	80[a]
TOTAL	~17,200

Note: Figures include estimates of total warheads, including strategic and nonstrategic, deployed and non-deployed weapons, as well as those awaiting dismantlement. All figures except Israel are from Hans M. Kristensen and Robert S. Norris's "Nuclear Notebook" series in the Bulletin of Atomic Scientists, at http://bos.sagepub.com/cgi/collection/nuclearnotebook; and Federation of American Scientists, "Status of World Nuclear Forces," December 18, 2012, http://www.fas.org/programs/ssp/nukes/nuclearweapons/nukestatus.html.

[a] Estimate from Shannon N. Kile, Phillip Schell, and Hans Kristensen, "Israeli Nuclear Forces," in SIPRI Yearbook (Stockholm: Stockholm International Peace Research Institute, 2012), http://www.sipri.org/research/armaments/nbc/nuclear.

nonnuclear. One hundred and eighty-four nations have signed the NPT as non-nuclear-weapons states and have pledged never to develop or possess nuclear weapons. With the possible exception of Iran, all seem to mean it. Many of these nations do not have the economic or technical ability to build nuclear weapons. But many do. Several dozen nations, such as Japan, Germany, and Brazil, could build nuclear weapons if they wanted to—some quite quickly. They have decided not to.

Whether these countries and others will continue to decide not to proliferate depends a great deal on what happens with the existing nuclear arsenals in the world. The Stanford University professor Scott Sagan warns in his 2012 "A Call for Global Nuclear Disarmament" that fifty years after the Cuban Missile Crisis, "we live in a nuclear world that has not just two superpowers but nine nuclear-weapon states, with new ones looming on the horizon. The governments of these emergent nuclear states may not make the same mistakes that Russia and the United States made during the cold war, but they will make others."[20] Sagan, like many other experts, favors a step-by-step approach to disarmament that lowers the levels of existing arsenals, starting with the United States and Russia and then folding in the other nuclear nations. His plan would also curtail national uranium-enrichment and plutonium-reprocessing facilities that have civilian uses but can be used to make bomb-grade materials and turn countries into "latent nuclear-weapons states." He acknowledges the skepticism about reaching full abolition of nuclear weapons:

> The strategic challenges we face are daunting and we may end up with small nuclear arsenals rather than attain the global-zero landmark. But even that would be a much safer world than the one we live in now. If we fail to work together to achieve nuclear disarmament, the world we are heading towards—bristling with nuclear-weapons states, with more nuclear weapons, and the ever-present threat of nuclear terrorism—is even more fraught with danger.[21]

Whether we can move steadily toward that world depends, in part, on how seriously nations calculate the threat from the existing arsenals. That is the subject of the next chapter.

FIVE
CALCULATING ARMAGEDDON

There are major uncertainties in estimating the consequences of nuclear war.[1] Much depends on the time of year of the attacks, the weather, the size of the weapons, the altitude of the detonations, the behavior of the populations attacked, and so on. But one thing is clear: the number of casualties, even in a small, accidental nuclear attack, would be overwhelming. If the commander of just one Russian Delta IV ballistic-missile submarine were to launch twelve of its sixteen missiles at the United States, 7 million Americans could die.[2]

Experts use various models to calculate nuclear war casualties. The most accurate experts estimate the damage done from all three of a nuclear bomb's sources of destruction: blast, fire, and radiation. Fifty percent of the energy of the weapon is released through the blast, 35 percent as thermal radiation, and 15 percent through radiation.

Like a conventional weapon, a nuclear weapon produces a destructive blast, or shock wave. A nuclear explosion, however, can be thousands and even millions of times more powerful than a conventional one. The blast creates a sudden change in air pressure that can crush buildings and other objects within seconds of the detonation. All but the strongest buildings within 3 kilometers (1.9 miles) of a 1-megaton hydrogen bomb would be leveled. The blast also produces super-hurricane winds that can destroy people and objects like trees and utility poles. Houses up to 7.5 kilometers (4.7 miles) away that have not been completely destroyed would still be heavily damaged.

A nuclear explosion also releases thermal energy (heat) at very high temperatures, which can ignite fires at considerable distances from the detonation point, leading to further destruction, and can cause severe skin burns even a few miles from the explosion. The Stanford University historian Lynn Eden calculates that if a 300-kiloton nuclear weapon were dropped on the U.S. Department of Defense, "within tens of minutes, the entire area, approximately 40 to 65 square miles—everything within 3.5 or 6.4 miles of the Pentagon—would be engulfed in a mass fire" that would "extinguish all life and destroy almost everything else." The creation of a "hurricane of fire," Eden argues, is a predictable effect of a high-yield nuclear weapon, but war planners do not take this into account in their targeting calculations.[3]

Unlike conventional weapons, a nuclear explosion also produces lethal radiation. Direct ionizing radiation can cause immediate death, but the more significant effects are long term. Radioactive fallout can inflict damage over periods ranging from hours to years. If no significant decontamination takes place (such as rain washing away radioactive particles or their leaching into the soil), it will take eight to ten years for the inner circle near the explosion to return to safe levels of radiation. In the next circles, such decay will require three to six years. Longer term, some of the radioactive particles will enter the food chain.[4] For example, a 1-megaton hydrogen bomb exploded at ground level would have a lethal radiation inner circle radius of about 50 kilometers (30 miles) where death would be instant. At 145 kilometers radius (90 miles), death would occur within two weeks of exposure. The outermost circle would be at 400 kilometers (250 miles) radius where radiation would still be harmful but the effects not immediate.

In the accidental Delta IV submarine strike noted above, most of the immediate deaths would come from the blast and "superfires" ignited by the bomb. Each of the 100-kiloton warheads carried by the submarine's missiles

Table 5.1 ► Immediate Deaths from Blast and Firestorms in Eight U.S. Cities, Submarine Attack

CITY	NO. OF WARHEADS	NO. OF DEATHS
Atlanta	8	428,000
Boston	4	609,000
Chicago	4	425,000
New York	8	3,193,000
Pittsburgh	4	375,000
San Franciso	8	739,000
Seattle	4	341,000
Washington, D.C.	8	728,000
TOTAL	48	6,838,000

Source: Bruce G. Blaire, et al., "Accidental Nuclear War—a Post-Cold War Assessment," The New England Journal of Medicine 338, no. 18 (April 1998): 1326-32.

would create a circle of death 8.6 kilometers (5.3 miles) in diameter. Nearly 100 percent of the people within this circle would die instantly. Firestorms would kill millions more (see table 5.1). The explosion would produce a cloud of radioactive dust that would drift downwind from the bomb's detonation point. If the bomb exploded at a low altitude, a swath of deadly radiation 10 60 kilometers (6–37 miles) long and 3–5 kilometers (2–3 miles) wide would kill all exposed and unprotected people within six hours of exposure.[5] As the radiation continued and spread over thousands of square kilometers, it is possible that secondary deaths in dense urban populations would match or even exceed the immediate deaths caused by fire and blast, doubling the total fatalities in table 5.1. The cancer deaths and genetic damage from radiation could extend for several generations.

CALCULATING GLOBAL WAR

Naturally, the number of casualties in a global nuclear war would be much higher. U.S. military commanders, for example, might not know that the commander of the Delta IV submarine had launched by accident or without authorization. They could very well order a U.S. response. One such response could be a precise "counter-force" attack on all Russian nuclear forces. An American attack directed solely against Russian nuclear missiles, submarines, and bomber bases would require some 1,300 warheads in a coordinated barrage lasting approximately thirty minutes according to a sophisticated analysis of U.S. war plans by experts at the Natural Resources Defense Council in Washington, D.C.[6] It would destroy most of Russia's nuclear weapons and development facilities. Communications across the country would be severely degraded. Within hours after the attack, the radioactive fallout would descend and accumulate, creating lethal conditions over an area exceeding 775,000 square kilometers (300,000 square miles)—larger than France and the United Kingdom combined. The attack would result in approximately 11–17 million civilian casualties, 8–12 million of which would be fatalities, primarily from the fallout generated by numerous ground bursts.

American war planners could also launch another set of plans designed and modeled over the nuclear age: a "limited" attack against Russian cities, using only 150–200 warheads. This is often called a "counter-value" attack, and, though using fewer weapons, it would kill or wound approximately one-third of Russia's citizenry. An attack using the warheads aboard just a single U.S. Trident submarine to attack Russian cities will result in 30–45 million casualties. An attack using 150 U.S. Minuteman III ICBMs on Russian cities would produce 40–60 million casualties.[7]

If, in either of these limited attacks, the Russian military command followed their planned operational procedures and launched their weapons before they could be destroyed, the results would be an all-out nuclear war involving most of the weapons in both the U.S. and Russian arsenals. The effects would be devastating. Government studies estimate that between 35 to 77 percent of the U.S. population would be killed (105 to 230 million people, based on current population figures) and 20 to 40 percent of the Russian population (28 to 56 million people).[8]

A 1979 report to Congress by the U.S. Office of Technology Assessment, *The Effects of Nuclear War,* noted the disastrous results of a nuclear war would go far beyond the immediate casualties:

> In addition to the tens of millions of deaths during the days and weeks after the attack, there would probably be further millions (perhaps further tens of millions) of deaths in the ensuing months or years. In addition to the enormous economic destruction caused by the actual nuclear explosions, there would be some years during which the residual economy would decline fur-

ther, as stocks were consumed and machines wore out faster than recovered production could replace them. . . .

For a period of time, people could live off supplies (and, in a sense, off habits) left over from before the war. But shortages and uncertainties would get worse. The survivors would find themselves in a race to achieve viability . . . before stocks ran out completely. A failure to achieve viability, or even a slow recovery, would result in many additional deaths, and much additional economic, political, and social deterioration. This postwar damage could be as devastating as the damage from the actual nuclear explosions.[9]

According to the report's comprehensive analysis, if production rose to the rate of consumption before stocks were exhausted, then viability would be achieved and economic recovery would begin. If not, then "each postwar year would see a lower level of economic activity than the year before, and the future of civilization itself in the nations attacked would be in doubt."[10] It is doubtful that either the United States or Russia would ever recover as viable nation-states.

CALCULATING REGIONAL WAR

There are grave dangers inherent not only in the thousands of nuclear weapons maintained by countries such as the United States and Russia but also in hundreds of weapons held by China, France, the United Kingdom, Israel, Pakistan, India, and North Korea. While these states regard their own nuclear weapons as safe, secure, and essential to security, each views the others' arsenals with suspicion.

Existing regional nuclear tensions already pose serious risks. The decades-long conflict between India and Pakistan has made South Asia the region most likely to witness the first use of nuclear weapons since World War II. An active missile race is under way between the two nations even as India and China continue their rivalry. And though some progress toward détente has been made, with each side agreeing to notify the other before ballistic missile tests, for example, quick escalation in a crisis could put the entire subcontinent back on the edge of destruction. Each country has an estimated 60 to 110 nuclear weapons, deliverable via fighter-bomber aircraft or possibly by the growing arsenal of short and medium-range missiles each nation is building. Their use could be devastating.

Table 5.2 ▸ Casualties and Fatalities in a South Asian Nuclear War

TARGETS	WEAPON USED	CASUALTIES (MILLIONS)	FATALITIES (MILLIONS)
Main cities (13 in India, 12 in Pakistan)	50 KT	31	12.1
Main cities (13 in India, 12 in Pakistan)	1 MT	98	59.2
All strategic military targets in both countries	Various	6.8–13.4	2–4
All transportation and power targets in both countries	Various	7.5–13.7	2.55–4.74
All targets in both countries (city centers, strategic military targets, power, and transportation)	Various	40–111	15.5–63.7

Source: Robert T. Batcher, "The Consequences of an Indo-Pakistani Nuclear War," International Studies Review 6, no. 4 (December 2004): 143–50.

South Asian urban populations are so dense that a 50-kiloton weapon would produce the same casualties that would require megaton-range weapons on North American or European cities. Robert Batcher with the U.S. State Department Office of Technology Assessment, notes:

> Compared to North America, India and Pakistan have higher population densities with a higher proportion of their populations living in rural locations. The housing provides less protection against fallout, especially compared to housing in the U.S. Northeast, because it is light, often single-story and without basements. In the United States, basements can provide significant protection against fallout. During the Cold War, the United States anticipated 20 minutes or more of warning time for missiles flown from the Soviet Union. For India and Pakistan, little or no warning can be anticipated, especially for civilians. Fire fighting is limited in the region, which can lead to greater damage as a result of thermal effects. Moreover, medical facilities are also limited, and thus, there will be greater burn fatalities. These two countries have limited economic assets, which will hinder economic recovery.[11]

In addition to immediate casualties, a limited nuclear exchange would have devastating long-term consequences.

CALCULATING NUCLEAR WINTER

In the early 1980s, scientists used models to estimate the climatic effect of a nuclear war. They calculated the effects of the dust raised in high-yield nuclear surface bursts and of the smoke from city and forest fires ignited by airbursts of all yields. They found that "a global nuclear war could have a major impact on climate—manifested by significant surface darkening over many weeks, subfreezing land temperatures persisting for up to several months, large perturbations in global circulation patterns and dramatic changes in local weather and precipitation rates."[12] Those phenomena are known as "nuclear winter."

Since this theory was introduced, it has been repeatedly examined and reaffirmed. By the early 1990s, as tools to assess and quantify the effects of the production and injection of soot by large-scale fires, scientists were able to refine their conclusions. The prediction for the average land cooling beneath the smoke clouds was adjusted down a little bit, from the 10–25 degrees Celsius (50–77 degrees Fahrenheit) estimated in the 1980s to 10–20 degrees (50–68 degrees Fahrenheit). However, it was also found that interior land temperatures could decrease by up to 40 degrees Celsius (104 degrees Fahrenheit), more than the 30–35 degrees (86–95 degrees Fahrenheit) estimated in the 1980s, "with subzero temperatures possible even in the summer."[13]

In a *Science* article in 1990, the authors summarized: "Should substantial urban areas or fuel stocks be exposed to nuclear ignition, severe environmental anomalies—possibly leading to more human casualties globally than the direct effects of nuclear war—would be not just a remote possibility, but a likely outcome."[14] Carl Sagan and Richard Turco, two of the original scientists to develop the nuclear-winter analysis, concluded in 1993: "Especially through the destruction of global agriculture, nuclear winter might be considerably worse than the short-term blast, radiation, fire, and fallout of nuclear war. It would carry nuclear war to many nations that no one intended to attack, including the poorest and most vulnerable."[15]

In 2007, members of the original group of nuclear winter scientists collectively performed a new comprehensive quantitative assessment using the latest computer and climate models.[16] They concluded that even a small-scale, regional nuclear war could kill as many people as died in all of World War II and seriously disrupt the global climate for a decade or more, harming nearly everyone on Earth. The scientists considered a nuclear exchange involving 100 bombs of the same size as that dropped on Hiroshima (15 kilotons) used on cities in the subtropics, and found that

> smoke emissions of 100 low-yield urban explosions in a regional nuclear conflict would generate substantial global-scale climate anomalies, although not as large as the previous 'nuclear winter' scenarios for a full-scale war. However, indirect effect on surface land temperatures, precipitation rates and growing season lengths would be likely to degrade agricultural productivity to an extent that historically has led to famines in Africa, India and Japan after the 1784 Laki eruption or in the northeastern United States and Europe after the Tambora eruption of 1815. Climatic anomalies could persist for a decade or more because of smoke stabilization, far longer than in previous nuclear winter calculations or after volcanic eruptions.[17]

The scientists concluded that the nuclear explosions and firestorms in modern cities would inject black carbon particles higher into the atmosphere than previously thought and higher than normal volcanic activity. Blocking the sun's thermal energy, the smoke clouds would lower temperatures regionally and globally for several years, open up new holes in the ozone layer protecting the Earth from harmful radiation, reduce global precipitation by about 10 percent, and trigger massive crop failures. Overall, the global cooling from a regional nuclear war would be about twice as large as the global warming of the past century "and would lead to temperatures cooler than the pre-industrial Little Ice Age."[18] A 2012 study by Dr. Ira Helfand of Physicians for Social Responsibility found that these conditions could lead to widespread famines that could kill a billion people.[19]

NUCLEAR BALANCE

Despite the horrific consequences of their use, many national leaders continue to covet nuclear weapons. Some see them as a stabilizing force, even in regional conflicts. There is some evidence to support this view. Relations between India and Pakistan, for example, have improved overall since their 1998 nuclear tests. Even the conflict in the Kargil region between the two nations that came to a boil in 1999 and again in 2002 (with more than one million troops mobilized on both sides of the border) ended in negotiations, not full-scale war. The Columbia University scholar Kenneth Waltz argues, "Kargil showed once again that deterrence does not firmly protect disputed areas but does limit the extent of the violence. Indian rear admiral Raja Menon put the larger point simply: 'The Kargil crisis demonstrated that the subcontinental nuclear threshold probably lies territorially in the heartland of both countries, and not on the Kashmir cease-fire line.'"[20] It would be reaching too far to say that Kargil was South Asia's Cuban Missile Crisis, but since the near-war, both nations have established hotlines and other confidence-building measures (such as notification of each side's impending missile tests), exchanged cordial visits of state leaders, and opened transportation and communications links. War seems less likely now than at any point in the past.

This calm is deceiving. Just as in the Cold War standoff between the Soviet Union and the United States, the South Asian détente is fragile. A sudden crisis, such as a terrorist attack on the Indian parliament or the assassination of President Asif Ali Zardari of Pakistan, could plunge the two countries into confrontation. As noted above, it would not be thousands that would die, but millions. Michael Krepon of the Stimson Center, one of the leading American experts on the region and its nuclear dynamics, notes:

> Despite or perhaps because of the inconclusive resolution of crises, some in Pakistan and India continue to believe that gains can be secured below the nuclear threshold. How might advantage be gained when the presence of nuclear weapons militates against decisive end games? . . . If the means chosen to pursue advantage in the next Indo-Pakistan crisis show signs of success, they are likely to prompt escalation, and escalation might not be easily controlled. If the primary alternative to an ambiguous outcome in the next crisis is a loss of face or a loss of territory, the prospective loser will seek to change the outcome.[21]

Many share Krepon's views both in and out of South Asia. The Indian scholar P. R. Chari, for example, further observes:

> Since the effectiveness of these weapons depends ultimately on the willingness to use them in some situations, there is an issue of coherence of thought that has to be addressed here. Implicitly or explicitly an eventuality of actual use has to be a part of the possible alternative scenarios that must be contemplated, if some benefit is to be obtained from the possession and deployment of nuclear weapons. To hold the belief that nuclear weapons are useful but must never be used lacks cogency.[22]

A new and quickly escalating crisis over Taiwan or disputed territories in the South China Sea is another possible scenario in which nuclear weapons could be used, not accidentally as with any potential U.S.-Russian exchange, but as a result of miscalculation. Neither the United States nor China is eager to engage in a military confrontation over Taiwan's status or ownership of remote islands. Both sides believe they could effectively manage such a crisis. But crises work in mysterious ways—political leaders are not always able to manipulate events as they think they can, and events can escalate quickly. A Sino-U.S. nuclear exchange may not happen even in the case of such confrontations, but the possibility should not be ignored.

The likelihood of use depends greatly on the perceived utility of nuclear weapons. This, in turn, is greatly influenced by the policies and attitudes of the existing nuclear-weapon states. Advocacy by some in the United States of new battlefield uses for nuclear weapons (for example, in preemptive strikes on Iran's nuclear facilities) and for programs for new nuclear weapon designs could lead to fresh nuclear tests and possibly lower the nuclear threshold, i.e., the willingness of leaders to use nuclear weapons. The five nuclear-weapon states recognized by the Non-Proliferation Treaty have not tested since the signing of the Comprehensive Test Ban Treaty in 1996, and until North Korea's October 2006 test, no state had tested since India and Pakistan did so in May 1998. Despite North Korea's tests, no other nation has broken this informal global test moratorium.

If the United States again tested nuclear weapons, political, military, and bureaucratic forces in several other countries would undoubtedly pressure their governments to follow suit. Indian scientists, for example, are known to be unhappy with the inconclusive results of their 1998 tests. Indian governments now resist their insistent demands for new tests for fear of the damage they would do to India's international image. It is a compelling example of the power of international norms. New U.S. tests, however, would collapse that norm and trigger tests by India then perhaps China and other nations. The nuclear test ban treaty, an agreement widely regarded as a pillar of the nonproliferation regime, would crumble, possibly bringing down the entire regime.

All of these scenarios highlight the need for nuclear-weapons countries to decrease their reliance on nuclear arms. While the United States has reduced its arsenal to the lowest levels since the 1950s, it has received little credit for these cuts because the reductions were conducted in isolation from a real commitment to disarmament. To demonstrate a serious intent to commit to disarmament, the United States, Russia, and all nuclear-weapons states need to return to the original purpose of the NPT bargain—the elimination of nuclear weapons. The failure of nuclear-weapons states to accept their end of the bargain under Article VI of the NPT has undermined every other aspect of the nonproliferation agenda.

Universal Compliance, a 2005 study concluded by the Carnegie Endowment for International Peace, reaffirmed this premise:

> The nuclear-weapon states must show that tougher nonproliferation rules not only benefit the powerful but constrain them as well. Nonproliferation is a set of bargains whose fairness must be self-evident if the majority of countries is to support their enforcement. . . . The only way to achieve this is to enforce compliance universally, not selectively, including the obligations the nuclear states have taken on themselves. . . . The core bargain of the NPT, and of global nonproliferation politics, can neither be ignored nor wished away. It underpins the international security system and shapes the expectations of citizens and leaders around the world.[23]

While nuclear weapons are more highly valued by national officials than chemical or biological weapons ever were, that does not mean they are a permanent part of national identity. Steps to reduce the nuclear dangers and move towards the eventual elimination of these weapons are explored in the final chapter. But before that, we need to put together a few more pieces of the nuclear puzzle.

SIX
EXPLODING
BUDGETS

Fiscal constraints and the end of the wars in Iraq and Afghanistan are forcing reductions in America's military budgets.[1] As
of now, it is unclear how much we can expect these budgets to
be reduced. But, barring another national emergency or war, it
is almost certain that as the troops come home, the budgets
will come down. The Department of Defense began its budget
submission to Congress in January 2012 with this historical
context:

> After every major conflict, the U.S. military has experienced significant
> budget draw downs. The new budget level for the Defense Department
> will rise from FY 2013 to FY 2017; however, total U.S. defense spend-
> ing, including both base funding and war costs, will drop by about 22%
> from its peak in 2010, after accounting for inflation. By comparison,
> the 7 years following the Vietnam and Cold War peak budgets saw a
> similar magnitude of decline on the order of 20 to 25 percent.[2]

This estimate of the reductions (which includes substantial savings from ending the wars) may be too low. Even with American troops still suffering casualties in the Afghanistan war, polls show little public support for keeping the large Pentagon budgets of the past ten years. A July 2012 survey, "Consulting the American People on National Defense Spending," conducted by the Program for Public Consultation, the Stimson Center, and the Center for Public Integrity, showed that three-quarters of the American people favor lowering the level of spending on the base budget (excluding spending for the wars), including two-thirds of Republicans and nine in ten Democrats. On average, those surveyed favored lowering the base budget by 23 percent—far more than either the Congress or the administration is considering. The majority favored lowering the budget at least 11 percent.[3]

Those taking the survey were allowed to choose where they would make cuts in the military programs. Nuclear budgets took the hardest hit. Two-thirds of respondents decreased the budget for nuclear weapons, including eight in ten Democrats and two-thirds of Republicans, with the public as a whole cutting the budget an average of 27 percent—the largest percentage cut for any program in the survey.[4]

The participants in this survey were presented with arguments for and against nuclear weapons before they were asked their opinion on budget levels. In a fascinating side note to the results—which may tell us something profound about the nature of the overall debate on nuclear weapons—the respondents found the arguments for and against equally compelling. But they still cut the budgets. The pollsters vetted the arguments with advocates for each side to ensure they were consistent with the way the advocates themselves would present them.

The case for nuclear weapons emphasized, as advocates do in real debates, the vital strategic importance of the weapons and their low cost:

America's nuclear arsenal is our country's ultimate insurance policy against aggression. It helps protect our influence in a world with many threats and at a relatively modest cost. It provides assurance to our allies, decreasing incentives to develop their own nuclear weapons, and communicates our resolve to be a global power. It also deters threatening actions by our enemies. Developing newer models of nuclear warheads, as well as more modern bombers, more accurate missiles, and submarines to carry them, ensures that the deterrent remains reliable, useable and therefore credible.[5]

About two-thirds of the respondents found this convincing, with 22 percent finding it very convincing. There was some difference according to political party: about 60 percent of Democrats and independents agreed; 74 percent of Republicans agreed.

The argument against the nuclear weapons budget focused on the huge size of the nuclear arsenal and its irrelevance to today's threats:

> America's nuclear arsenal consists of thousands of weapons, most far more destructive than the one that obliterated Hiroshima. The idea that we need thousands of weapons to deter an adversary is absurd: We can effectively destroy a country with a small number of weapons. Their use is also highly unlikely against today's foes—some of whom use crude road bombs. Advanced conventional arms can accomplish virtually every mission that nuclear arms can, without killing thousands of civilians and producing long-lasting nuclear fallout.[6]

A similar 67 percent of the respondents found this convincing, with 26 percent finding it very convincing. There was little difference according to political leanings with 72 percent of Democrats, 66 percent of Republicans, and 62 percent of independents agreeing with the argument.

Yet, in the end, all cut the nuclear weapons budgets—and cut them far more than the budgets for ground forces, naval forces, or air forces. Republicans cut it by 18 percent, independents by 26 percent, and Democrats by 35 percent. It seems that whether one agrees or disagrees with the arguments on nuclear policy, most agree we can do what we need to do for far less money.

Shrinking budgets will soon force military leaders to prioritize among competing weapons programs. U.S. leaders, like the public, may well choose to preserve conventional military capabilities over nuclear forces that many now see as irrelevant to current threats. This will set up a major budget crunch for the nuclear weapon programs, many of which set ambitious expansion goals in the years when defense budgets were increasing. It will be impossible to accommodate all these new programs with budgets that are flattening or contracting.

Another factor that will add to the nuclear budget pressure is the miserable management track record of the chief agency in charge of programs for developing, producing, and modernizing nuclear warheads and materials, the Nuclear National Security Administration. Almost all NNSA programs are over-budget, behind schedule, and underperforming. In 2012, it was revealed that several major projects originally estimated to cost several hundred million dollars had each ballooned to several billion dollars. NNSA was forced to delay a plant for producing dozens of new plutonium bomb cores—likely killing the project—when the budget skyrocketed from $800 million to over $6 billion without a clear rationale for the extra capacity.[7] *The Albuquerque Journal*, the leading paper in New Mexico, home to two nuclear laboratories, Sandia National Laboratories and Los Alamos National Laboratory, editorialized in November 2012 that NNSA "has turned the nuclear weapons complex into a bureaucratic quagmire that defies attempts at efficiency. Its inability to move forward with essential projects is a threat to our nuclear security."[8]

The ability of security officials and policy makers to make smart budget decisions is complicated by the failure of the government to track total spending on nuclear weapons programs. There is no comprehensive accounting for these systems. In 2012, Ploughshares Fund commissioned several studies of the nuclear budget. One of these, *Resolving Ambiguity: Costing Nuclear Weapons*, produced by the Stimson Center in Washington, D.C., estimated that the United States spends about $31 billion each year on the missiles, bombers, submarines, and warheads that compose America's offensive strategic force.[9]

In addition, the government spends about $10 billion a year on antiballistic-missile weapons designed to intercept enemy missiles; about $9 billion a year on environmental cleanup and health costs related to the manufacture and maintenance of nuclear weapons; about $6 billion a year on programs working to secure nuclear weapons and materials in other nations and prevent their spread; and just under $1 billion a year on nuclear incident management programs to deal with the consequences should a bomb explode in the United States. This spending is about to increase with plans to start new nuclear weapons programs. A Ploughshares Fund study in September 2012 found that the United States is on track to spend approximately $640 billion from 2013 through 2022 on nuclear weapons and related programs.[10]

Some of this budget would remain even if nuclear weapons were eliminated tomorrow. A large portion would be necessary even with reduced arsenals. A good deal of this spending, however, is unnecessary. As detailed in previous chapters, the U.S. nuclear arsenal is still configured to counter the Cold War threat of a massive Russian nuclear attack—even though military and intelligence officials agree that the greatest threats to the nation come from nuclear terrorism and the spread of nuclear weapons to other states. Reconfiguring the nuclear force to address the actual twenty-first-century threat environment could reduce force numbers dramatically over the next decade without sacrificing vital military missions. Negotiating with other nations to verifiably eliminate nuclear weapons over the next two decades would allow the government to shift funds from the oversized nuclear budget to other pressing defense and domestic needs and avoid most of the planned expenditure of several hundred billion additional dollars for the development and production of a new generation of long-range nuclear weapon delivery systems that would keep thousands of nuclear weapons on airstrips, in silos, and prowling the oceans into the 2070s.

THE CURRENT FISCAL CRISIS

In 2012, the federal government ran an annual budget deficit of over one trillion dollars. The total national debt has ballooned from $5.6 trillion in 2000 to over $16 trillion in 2012. In 2011 alone, the United States paid $454 billion in interest to finance this debt. Of that, $36 billion went to China—in effect, the amount required to fund more than one-quarter of China's estimated annual defense budget.[11]

As Roger Altman and Richard Haass noted in 2010:

> The U.S. government is incurring debt at a historically unprecedented and ultimately unsustainable rate. . . . As the world's biggest borrower and the issuer of the world's reserve currency, the United States will not be allowed to spend ten years leveraging itself to these unprecedented levels. If U.S. leaders do not act to curb this debt addiction, then the global capital markets will do so for them, forcing a sharp and punitive adjustment in fiscal policy.[12]

Their view is now the common wisdom, as are the grave consequences for the national defense. Former secretary of defense Robert Gates warned in 2011, "This country's dire fiscal situation—and the threat it poses to American influence and credibility around the world—will only get worse unless the U.S. Government gets its finances in order. And as the biggest part of the discretionary federal budget the Pentagon cannot presume to exempt itself from the scrutiny and pressure faced by the rest of our government."[13] Cuts in Pentagon spending need not sacrifice security, though the two are often conflated. Baker Spring, a Heritage Foundation research fellow, said the Obama administration's proposed defense budget for fiscal year 2013 was "simply too small." He wrote:

> The Obama Administration's budget policies are reducing America's military capacity so drastically that upholding these commitments will become impossible over time. A conservative Congress, which as the name implies should focus on preserving essential American values, institutions and commitments, would necessarily reject the Obama Administration's defense budget proposal.[14]

However, national defense spending has grown out of proportion to the military threats confronting the nation. National defense spending doubled after the attacks of September 11, rising from $334 billion in fiscal year 2001 to a peak of $717 billion in fiscal year 2011 (this includes the budget for the wars in Iraq and Afghanistan).[15] The 2011 budget spent more on military programs than in any year since the end of World War II—more than during the Korean War, the Vietnam War, or any year of the Cold War. From 2002 to 2012, Congress appropriated close to $7 trillion for national defense, including $1.3 trillion for the wars in Iraq and Afghanistan. The United States spends as much on defense as the next fourteen countries in the world combined (many of whom are U.S. allies) and spends five times more than China, which ranks second in defense spending at roughly $143 billion a year.[16]

In January 2011, Secretary Gates proposed scaling back the growth of the defense budget for the next five years to realize $78 billion in savings from previous plans. The 2012 and 2013 budget requests reflected this priority: the 2012 budget request totaled $671 billion ($118 billion of that was war costs) and the 2013 budget request was $614 billion (with $88 billion in war costs).[17] This likely marked only the beginning of the necessary reductions.

There is fierce political debate over the proper size of the Pentagon budget. At first, in the immediate aftermath of the 2008 fiscal crisis, members of Congress on both sides of the aisle agreed that any serious effort to reduce government spending must include cuts in military programs. Shortly after becoming Republican majority leader, Representative Eric Cantor (R-VA) explicitly included cuts in defense budgets as one option for congressional action on reduced government spending. "Every dollar should be on the table," Cantor said, "No one can defend the expenditure of every dollar and cent over at the Pentagon."[18] In early February 2011, House Budget Committee chair-

Table 6.1 ▸ Largest Military Budgets, 2011

COUNTRY	DOLLARS (IN BILLIONS) FOR FY2011
1. United States	711.0
2. China	143.0
3. Russia	71.9
4. UK	62.7
5. France	62.5
6. Japan	59.3
7 India	48.9
8. Saudi Arabia	48.5
9. Germany	46.7
10. Brazil	35.4
11. Italy	34.5
12. South Korea	30.8
13. Australia	26.7
14. Canada	24.7
15. Turkey	17.9
TOTAL	**713.5**

Source: Stockholm International Peace Research Institute (SIPRI), "The Fifteen Countries with the Highest Military Expenditure in 2011 (Table)," September 2011, http://www.sipri.org /research/armaments/milex/resultoutput/milex_15/the-15 -countries-with-the-highest-military-expenditure-in-2011- table/view.

man Paul Ryan (R-WI) proposed a 2 percent cut from the DOD budget request.[19] A number of senators and representatives propelled into Congress by the Tea Party movement broke from the traditional conservative opposition to cuts in military spending. Newly elected senator Rand Paul (R-KY) said in 2011, "As our country's economic crisis continues, many progressives and conservatives alike are deeply concerned about skyrocketing deficits. Sharing this concern myself, I urge Congress to cut defense spending. I believe that large cuts in defense spending are indispensable if we hope to return to balanced budgets any time in the foreseeable future."[20]

The bipartisan National Commission on Fiscal Responsibility and Reform (known as the Simpson-Bowles Commission after its two cochairs, Senators Alan Simpson and Erskine Bowles) proposed nearly $4 trillion in deficit reductions through 2020, which would include capping discretionary spending, or nonmandatory spending, at 2011 levels. The Department of Defense accounts for 54 percent of all discretionary spending.[21] The commission also recommended holding spending growth at half the rate of inflation after 2013, requiring substantial budget cuts through 2020. The commission argues these cuts would save $1 trillion in costs from security-related programs alone.[22]

Some business leaders also weighed in. Republican financier Peter G. Peterson noted that military spending makes up 23 percent of all government spending and recommended "eliminating costly weapons systems, reducing troop deployments overseas, lowering the number of nuclear weapons, and reforming military pay and benefits."[23] Specifically, Peterson argued:

> The U.S. nuclear weapons program provided a powerful deterrent when the Soviet Union posed a significant threat during the Cold War. Many defense analysts argue that now that the Soviet Union has disintegrated, the U.S. needs far fewer warheads to maintain our security and deter potential enemies, and that we should reduce the size of the arsenal and limit funding for nuclear research.[24]

In an effort to reconcile sharply divergent budget priorities, Congress passed the Budget Control Act (BCA) in August 2011, capping security and nonsecurity spending. The BCA included $487 billion in defense cuts over the next ten years and provided a mechanism for finding more savings: the so-called Super Committee, a bipartisan group of twelve members of Congress. But the Super Committee failed to agree on a package for more savings, triggering across-the-board spending cuts that would automatically go into effect in 2013, returning the Department of Defense budget to its FY 2007 level and yielding ten-year reductions of about $960 billion (relative to the FY 2012 plan).[25]

When planning for fiscal year 2013, policy makers largely ignored the Budget Control Act; both Congress and the president broke the BCA spending caps by several billion dollars in their marks for the fiscal year 2013 budget.[26] As the 2012 political campaigns heated up, many political figures distanced themselves from cuts to the Pentagon budget. GOP presidential nomi-·

nee Mitt Romney promised to increase military spending by at least 4 percent of GDP. A major part of the Republican campaign against the Democrats was the claim that President Obama wanted to slash defense budgets. Republican leaders in Congress championed increased military spending and struggled to put back in the budget programs that the administration had eliminated, including nuclear weapons programs.

Conservatives remain deeply divided between the defense hawks and the deficit hawks, however. The columnist David Brooks summarized the divide on the PBS *Newshour* in August 2012:

> You have got the defense hawks, who really think cuts in defense spending in general would devastate our national security. And they're led by John Mc-Cain and Lindsey Graham.
>
> On the other hand, you have the more Tea Party–oriented people, who are not against defense spending, necessarily, but it's not a priority for them. Lowering taxes and domestic economy are a priority for them, and they are quite happy to see the defense budget really decrease, not all of them . . . but certainly a lot of them.
>
> So are you seeing this rift opening up between the defense hawks versus the tax cut hawks. I would say, if you look at the balance of the Republican Party, they are in the tax cut hawk [camp]. So support for high defense spending is probably decreasing in the Republican Party.[27]

Grover Norquist, a prominent Republican lobbyist, is a leading tax-cut hawk. He argued for cutting wasteful military spending in August 2012, trying to convince Republicans in Congress to "cut the defense budget to avoid a major federal tax hike." Many wasteful projects could be cut without harming national security, Norquist argued: "You need to decide what your real defense needs are. That doesn't mean chairmen of certain committees get to build bases in their states. That's not a defense need . . . [but] a political desire."[28]

There is a potential alliance between these Republicans and prominent Democratic defense leaders in Congress who are looking at nuclear weapons programs as one area where budgets can be cut without harm. When a CSPAN reporter asked Representative Adam Smith (D-WA), the ranking member on the House Armed Services Committee, in July 2012 where, specifically, he would cut the budget, he responded by citing savings from ending the wars in Iraq and Afghanistan and stating that "our nuclear policy is based on a premise of deterrence and mutually assured destruction with the then–Soviet Union. I think there is clearly savings to be found in that area as well."[29] After listening approvingly to the president's State of the Union address in January 2012, Smith added, "We can reduce the size of our nuclear arsenal, potentially saving billions of dollars and strengthening national security."[30]

Similarly, Senator Carl Levin (D-MI), chairman of the Senate Armed Service Committee, said in June 2012, the administration "should consider going far lower" that the 1,550 strategic nuclear weapons allowed under the New START treaty.[31] Saying that spending on the nuclear arsenal is "ripe for cuts," Levin added, "I can't see any reason for having as large an inventory as we are allowed to have under New Start, in terms of real threat, potential threat."[32]

Whether these lawmakers will find the political will necessary to rein in defense spending in future years remains to be seen. But their critique is correct: the U.S. nuclear posture is still configured much as it was during the conflict with the Soviet Union. The Cold War has been over for twenty years, but thousands of weapons remain deployed, on hair-trigger alert and intended to strike hundreds of targets in Russia (see chapter 4). Decisions over the next few years will either maintain the status quo, or set the nation on a path to increased security with lower force levels and greater savings. The former vice chairman of the Joint Staff General James Cartwright stresses the gravity of this decision point: "We are at a 50-year inflection point in the department. We are about to recapitalize most of our capital assets, which will have generally somewhere between 30 and 50 years of life. So the decisions we make about our submarines, the decisions we make about our ICBMs, the decisions we make about our bombers, are 50-year decisions."[33]

PAYING FOR THE SWORD OF DAMOCLES

President John F. Kennedy famously warned in 1963: "Each of us lives under a nuclear sword of Damocles, hanging by the slenderest of threads, capable of being cut at any moment by accident, miscalculation or by madness."[34] When Kennedy spoke, the United States was nearing the end of a huge nuclear build-up—surging from 300 warheads in 1950 to more than 28,000 in 1963.[35] The United States has steadily reduced its nuclear stockpile over the past twenty-five years through negotiated agreements with Russia, but nuclear weapons budgets have remained at Cold War levels or higher.

As already noted, the United States spends about $56 billion per year on nuclear-weapons-related programs.[36] If the scope is narrowed to offensive strategic nuclear weapons—those that are counted by most arms-control treaties—the costs are still staggering. For fiscal year 2011, this included $22.71 billion for the Department of Defense and $8.25 billion for the National Nuclear Security Administration's weapons budget, for a total of $30.96 billion.[37] These are just the annual costs. The ten-year estimate developed by Stimson Center analysts for nuclear spending on offensive strategic weapons (warheads, missiles, bombers, and submarines) is $352–$392 billion.[38] Unless the president and the Congress chart a new path soon, the budgets for nuclear weapons will soon explode.

A 2012 Ploughshares Fund study expanded the Stimson ten-year estimate, adding in other nuclear-weapons-related programs.[39] These included:

- Missile defenses: $95.9–$97.4 billion: Most policy makers and analysts intimately link antimissile programs to nuclear policy. The study projected spending of $95.58 and $97.44 billion on these programs over the next ten years. This estimate used the Department of Defense projection for missile defense spending from FY13–FY17. Costs were assumed to grow with inflation through FY22.[40]

- Environmental and health costs: $100.7 billion: The study estimated that the U.S. would spend $100.7 billion managing and cleaning up radioactive and toxic waste resulting from nuclear weapons production and testing activities, as well as compensating victims of such contamination.[41]

- Nuclear threat reduction: $62.7 billion: This includes funding for nonproliferation, securing and disposing of fissile materials, the Mixed Oxide Fuel facility, converting HEU-fueled reactors, and other programs.

- Nuclear incident management: $8.5 billion: This estimate included programs to prepare for emergency responses for a nuclear or radiological attack against the United States. It did not include relevant expenditures by the National Guard and federal and local agencies that would be involved in nuclear incident response.

The full ten-year estimate of between $620 and $662 billion is conservative. It did not include relevant costs that are difficult to calculate—including intelligence programs, some missile defense funds, and aerial refueling costs. The study did not account for programs that did not yet have official budget estimates—such as a new ICBM. The estimate also did not account for cost growth—an unfortunate reality for acquisition programs. Contractors often low-ball initial estimates, hoping that moving quickly to production will create jobs that lock in political support even as programs double or triple in costs. Finally, the study provided a range of possible future budgets. The low estimate assumed that defense budgets grow at less than the rate of inflation in keeping with the president's budget plans. The high estimate simply assumes defense programs grow with inflation. The average of the two estimates is $640 billion.

Even if some of these programs are scaled back, the government will still have to spend billions each year. There is no quick exit to the cost of nuclear weapons. The question is, where are we going? Are we steadily reducing the costs, as well as the numbers and role of nuclear weapons? Or are we locking in spending at current levels for the next two generations of Americans?

When President Obama committed to reducing and eventually eliminating nuclear weapons, he also committed to maintain a "safe, secure and effective arsenal to deter any adversary and guarantee that defense to our allies."[42] Some have interpreted this goal to mean the indefinite preservation of the current nuclear force posture and nuclear weapons complex. Senator Jim DeMint (R-SC) said, "While the goal of reducing global levels of nuclear weapons is noble, it cannot take priority over our duty to protect Americans."[43] Senator Jon Kyl (R-AZ) echoed this view in a 2010 *Wall Street Journal* op-ed, arguing that nuclear budgets were too low for our security needs:

> Despite pledging over $100 billion to maintain and modernize nuclear delivery systems, the [New START] plan makes a commitment only to a next-generation submarine—not to a next-generation bomber, ballistic missile or air-launched cruise missile. The administration has also made no decision about whether or how it will replace the B-52 bomber, which first flew in 1952, and under current plans will continue to fly until possibly 2037. Nor does the White House intend to decide what the new U.S. nuclear force structure will look like.[44]

Senator Kyl was correct that the budget plans did not yet include these future program costs. But the opposite is also true: President Obama's desire to negotiate reductions in global nuclear arsenals had not yet impacted the long-term plans of the Departments of Defense or Energy as of late 2012. Procurement was racing ahead of policy. Contracts were being let for nuclear weapons mandates by guidance dating from decades past, and policy decisions to change that guidance languished. Commenting on the growing budgets for these programs, *Time* magazine said: "Something profound is happening in the proposed 2012... defense budget... but few are paying attention. You may want to, because it sets the nation on a path that, if history is any guide, will last for a half-century, and cost hundreds of billions of dollars."[45]

ARE NEW NUCLEAR WEAPONS AFFORDABLE?

In addition to the substantial monetary costs associated with these programs, there are also substantial opportunity costs. The U.S. Navy plans to replace its current fleet of fourteen ballistic-missile submarines, which collectively deploy half of the U.S. strategic arsenal, with twelve new submarines at the rate of one boat per year between 2031 and 2044. The Congressional Budget Office (CBO) estimated that the navy's preliminary plans will consume at least 25 percent of its entire shipbuilding budget, crowding out new ships for conventional missions.

Cost estimates for the new fleet doubled in just three years. In 2010, the navy issued plans for the new class of submarine—the SSBN(X)—estimating that the first boat off the line would cost $7 billion.[46] By 2012, the navy's estimate grew to $11.7 billion for the first submarine, with a goal of reducing average costs per submarine to $6–$7 billion. But the CBO estimated that the first submarine would actually cost $13.3 billion, with an average cost of $7.2 billion per boat. In total, the entire program was estimated to cost from $100–$110 billion.[47] The navy is increasingly concerned about the effects of the SSBN(X) costs on the shipbuilding program, as noted in the FY 2013 Shipbuilding Plan: "Spending $5–$6B per year for a single ship over a 10 to 12-year period will strain the Department of the Navy's yearly shipbuilding accounts."[48]

If the SSBN(X) project is completed as planned, in 2040 U.S. Navy submarines will likely deploy 800 nuclear warheads.[49] It is not at all clear why. A rationale for this military capability has not been presented to Congress. Nor did President Obama explain how this force fits with the April 2010 Nuclear Posture Review plan to take concrete steps towards a world without nuclear weapons "by reducing the number of nuclear weapons and their role in U.S. national security strategy."[50]

As for the other legs of the nuclear triad, plans for a new class of land-based intercontinental ballistic missiles and a new strategic nuclear bomber are only beginning to form. The Minuteman III missile—of which the United States has 450—is about to complete a $7 billion upgrade to extend its service life to 2030.[51] The development of a replacement heavy bomber will cost $292 million in the FY2013 budget and an additional $5 billion projected for FY2014–FY2017.[52] Early estimates are that the new bomber will cost upward of $55 billion to develop and procure.[53] The air force also plans to develop a new air-launched, nuclear-armed cruise missile for the bomber fleet. A 2009 study by the Air Force Association estimated the replacement triad would cost $216 billion through 2050,[54] but there are no truly reliable cost estimates yet for these new weapons systems. It will likely cost two to three times that amount to fully replace the current generation of intercontinental ballistic missiles, bombers, and submarines, as is now planned, well in excess of half a trillion dollars over the next few decades.

TOWARD SMALLER ARSENALS AND REASONABLE BUDGETS

How many nuclear weapons do we need? Often the discussion of this question is conducted at a high level of abstraction and decisions on force levels are often based more on political calculations than strategic ones. As Jeffrey Lewis of the Monterey Institute for International Studies notes about justifications for hundreds or thousands of nuclear weapons, "Much of this is just crazy talk."[55] In 1953, President Dwight D. Eisenhower famously tried to put the power of nuclear weapons in perspective with his "Atoms for Peace" address to the United Nations:

> Atomic bombs are more than twenty-five times as powerful as the weapons with which the atomic age dawned, while hydrogen weapons are in the ranges of millions of tons of TNT equivalent. Today, the United States stockpile of atomic weapons, which, of course, increases daily, exceeds by many times the total equivalent of the total of all bombs and all shells that came from every plane and every gun in every theatre of war in all the years of the Second World War. A single air group whether afloat or land based, can now deliver to any reachable target a destructive cargo exceeding in power all the bombs that fell on Britain in all the Second World War.[56]

President John F. Kennedy added in his address to the United Nations in 1961:

> The mere existence of modern weapons—ten million times more powerful than any that the world has ever seen, and only minutes away from any target on

earth—is a source of horror, and discord and distrust. . . . And men may no longer pretend that the quest for disarmament is a sign of weakness—for in a spiraling arms race, a nation's security may well be shrinking even as its arms increase.[57]

In 2008, Ivo Daalder, ambassador to NATO from 2009 to 2013, and a former senior defense department official, Jan Lodal, wrote a cogent *Foreign Affairs* analysis on the decreasing utility of nuclear weapons in the twenty-first century. "The Logic of Zero" begins from the assessment that whatever security benefits nuclear weapons may have held during the Cold War, they are now outweighed by the security threats they pose: "Only one real purpose remains for U.S. nuclear weapons: to prevent the use of nuclear weapons by others. That reality has yet to sink in. U.S. nuclear policies remain stuck in the Cold War, even as the threats the United States faces have changed dramatically." Not only do massive arsenals do nothing to deal with the real threats the United States confronts today—nuclear terrorism and the spread of nuclear weapons to other states—but they actually make these problems worse. "The more nuclear weapons there are in the world, the more likely it is that terrorists will get their hands on one," say Daalder and Lodal. "How can Washington expect to persuade other countries to forgo the very capabilities that the U.S. government itself trumpets as 'critical' to national security?"[58] As long as these weapons exist, there is a risk of their use. The only way to prevent nuclear terrorism and nuclear proliferation is to eliminate all nuclear weapons. "The logic of zero is driven by this threat," write Daalder and Lodal.

Many experts and advocates agree. The former CIA operations officer Valerie Plame Wilson and Queen Noor of Jordan, a leader of the international movement Global Zero, discussed their nuclear nightmares in November 2012 on a *Today Show* interview. Plame argued that the elimination of nuclear weapons "has to be the goal . . . nuclear technology is so widely available . . . far beyond where we were at the height of the Cold War where it was just the United States and Russia. And now we have to drain the swamp, there is no other way ahead."[59] U.S. leadership is essential, they argued, to rally other nations in a joint effort to both stop the spread of these weapons and reduce global stockpiles.

Daalder and Lodal recognize the economic benefits of zero. In addition to potentially preventing trillions of dollars in economic losses resulting from the use of just one nuclear weapon on a major city, they argue that the direct economic costs of maintaining a robust regime to verify nuclear disarmament "are likely to be low in comparison to the economic savings resulting from the elimination of nuclear weapons."[60]

Reducing the size of the U.S. nuclear arsenal may not yield proportional cuts to the U.S. nuclear weapons budget at first. Some areas of the U.S. nuclear budget—including maintaining a nuclear weapons production complex—are largely sunk costs and cannot be quickly reduced. Indeed, some targeted investments in facilities will be necessary to retain sufficient capacity at the complex for years to come. However, by requiring fewer warheads and fewer delivery vehicles, the United States can still shave billions of dollars off annual budgets over the next few decades.

REAPING THE SAVINGS

How much money would reducing the weapons arsenal save? In 2006, Steven Kosiak of the Center for Strategic and Budgetary Assessments proposed a number of options for scaling back the U.S. nuclear arsenal to achieve greater budgetary savings. In one option, he argued the United States could retool its strategic arsenal to deploy 1,000 warheads for an average cost of $13.5 billion a year through 2035, or one-third of the current annual expenditures.[61]

This option is predicated on reducing the size of the nuclear force and on buying smaller replacement systems. It calls for the development and deployment of 150 smaller, single-warhead ICBMs. The strategic nuclear bomber force would be reduced to 32 bombers—including a smaller replacement for the B-52H to be procured in 2030—with 288 deployed nuclear bombs. Finally, it calls for the development and deployment of eight new, smaller ballistic-missile submarines. Six would be deployed at any time, with twelve missiles apiece and eight warheads per missile, for a total of 576 submarine-based nuclear warheads. Kosiak, now in charge of defense programs at the Office of Management and Budget, argued that this scaled-back force structure would yield substantial savings in operations and support for the nuclear forces, while requiring fewer replacement weapons systems at relatively lower costs. Further reductions would yield further savings. Though the savings do not track one-to-one with reductions (there are costs associated with maintaining a bomber base, for example, regardless of how many bombers are stationed there), rationalizing the force further down to a few hundred weapons would save tens of billions more.

Benjamin Friedman and Christopher Preble of the Cato Institute proposed a series of substantial budget cuts to military spending, totaling more than $1.2 trillion over ten years.[62] Their proposal illustrates the dramatic scale of the budget cuts being brought to the table. They recommended cutting $87 billion over ten years from the nuclear weapons budget. A later Cato report in May 2012 found several billion dollars in nuclear budget savings in fiscal year 2013 alone.[63]

Daryl Kimball of the Arms Control Association also has suggested "right-sizing" the nuclear submarine fleet to find significant savings. Procurement of the Ohio-class replacement was pushed back from 2029 to 2031, a move that will save $6 to $7 billion over the next decade according to Pentagon projections. Kimball suggests that adjusting the size of the fleet could save billions more. He writes, "By reducing the Trident nuclear-armed sub fleet from 14 to eight or fewer boats and building no more than eight new nuclear-armed subs, the United States could save roughly $27 billion over 10 years, and $120 billion over the 50-year lifespan of the program."[64]

Additional savings could be found by delaying a new bomber replacement, as today's B-2s and B-52s are being refurbished to last until the 2040s. Kimball estimates that this would save $18 billion in ten years. Finally, he suggests cutting one squadron of ICBMs at each of the three air force bases, bringing their total number down to 300. This would "save approximately $360 million in operations and maintenance costs in fiscal 2013 alone and far more in future years," Kimball writes.[65]

Looking forward, going down to zero weapons over the next two decades could save most of the $31 billion spent each year on strategic offensive forces. This would be enough to finance the annual budgets of five of America's largest cities: Atlanta, Chicago, Los Angeles, San Francisco, and Seattle.[66]

HOW LOW CAN WE GO?

Under the New START treaty, the United States and Russia will reduce both sides' long-range strategic nuclear forces to no more that 1,550 warheads on no more than 700 delivery vehicles. However, the treaty does not deal with shorter-range nuclear weapons (also known as tactical weapons) or the weapons each side holds in reserve. Both of these categories are likely to be the subject of the next round of negotiations between the two nations.

Some want to block any further reductions in nuclear forces. In a November 2012 Heritage Foundation report, Baker Spring and Rebeccah Heinrichs argued for a dramatic increase in the number of U.S. nuclear weapons, arguing that the "failure to maintain a dynamic and effective nuclear force because of a misunderstanding of deterrence or an ideological pursuit of ridding the world of nuclear weapons could empower America's foes and increase the likelihood of a holocaust."[67]

Their report calls for a stockpile of between 2,700 and 3,000 nuclear weapons, including "a minimum of 800 short-range nuclear weapons that are modernized for rapid delivery in order to meet counterforce targeting requirements relative to the Russian short-range nuclear weapons."[68] As a reference point, the U.S. currently has an estimated 1,950 operationally deployed warheads.[69] The U.S. arsenal had 2,702 deployed nuclear warheads in when President George W. Bush left office in 2009. To meet Heritage's proposed numbers, the United States would have to reverse reductions taken by President George W. Bush and build up above the SORT and New START treaty ceilings.[70]

The majority of experts, in and out of the military, believe that U.S. national security objectives can be met at far lower numbers. Ambassador Steven Pifer and the scholar Michael O'Hanlon of the Brookings Institution outlined several possible scenarios in their 2012 book, *The Opportunity: Next Steps in Reducing Nuclear Arms*. They argued that the aim of the next round of negotiations between the United States and Russia could and should be to reduce "deployed strategic nuclear inventories to 1,000 warheads and their inventories of non-deployed strategic and nonstrategic nuclear warheads to another 1,000–1,500, [where] they would retain a clear numerical dominance over the medium nuclear powers."[71] This would "aspire to a time line in which negotiations on a treaty would begin within ten years, with the global elimination of nuclear weapons ideally to occur by 2030 or 2035."[72]

Many respected nuclear policy experts have recommended seeking deeper near-term reductions as stepping-stones toward zero. A 2012 report from the Global Zero Nuclear Policy Commission, whose authors include former vice chairman of the Joint Chiefs of Staff General James Cartwright (ret.), former NATO commander general Jack Sheehan (ret.), Secretary of Defense Chuck Hagel, and Ambassadors Richard Burt and Thomas Pickering, as well as the nuclear expert Bruce Blair, concludes that the United States needs no more than 900 total nuclear weapons to provide a reliable deterrent. As one illustration of how the force might look at these levels, 720 strategic warheads could be assigned to 10 Trident submarines, and 180 gravity bombs, to 18 B-2 bombers. The ICBM force could be eliminated. Additionally, the report suggests that the new nuclear force would be on a de-alerted operational status, meaning they would take twenty-four to seventy-two hours to prep for an offensive strike.[73]

The authors argue that while some may still see nuclear arsenals as playing a role in deterring a nuclear-armed state like North Korea, outsized arsenals are not needed for this purpose:

> We surely do not need thousands of modern nuclear weapons to play this role vis-à-vis a country with a handful of primitive nuclear devices. In fact, strong conventional forces and missile defense may offer a far superior option for deterring and defeating a regional aggressor. Non-nuclear forces are also far more credible instruments for providing 21st century reassurances to allies whose comfort zone in the 20th century resided under the U.S. nuclear umbrella. Precision-guided conventional munitions hold at risk nearly the entire spectrum of potential targets, and they are usable.[74]

The nuclear scientist Sidney Drell and Ambassador James Goodby of the Hoover Institution at Stanford University suggested going down to 500 deployed strategic warheads with another 500 as a responsive force. They propose, for example, keeping four or five submarines (three at sea) with ninety-six warheads each, one hundred ICBMs in silos, and twenty to twenty-five bombers. The nondeployed "responsive force" would consist of fifty to one hundred ICBMs taken off high-alert status, with warheads removed, and twenty to twenty-five bombers on hand for maintenance or training.[75]

Going deeper, the International Commission on Nuclear Non-Proliferation and Disarmament suggested in 2010 that the United States and Russia seek reductions down to a total of 500 warheads by 2025.[76] The nuclear experts Hans Kristensen, Robert Norris, and Ivan Oelrich have also supported reducing to 500 warheads as part of a strategy of fielding a "minimal deterrent" nuclear force. They recommend removing the submarine leg of the nuclear triad and deploying only 200 single-warhead ICBMs and 250 gravity bombs for strategic bombers, holding perhaps 50 warheads in reserve.[77] Friedman and Preble, mentioned earlier in this chapter, offer a force structure at this level, which they estimate could cut $97 billion from the Departments of Defense and Energy between 2011 and 2020. They propose reducing the force to a dyad—dropping the bomber leg—with eight submarines (six on patrol) holding up to 192 warheads and 150 ICBMs.[78]

In a 2010 article in *Strategic Studies Quarterly*, an air force journal, Col. B. Chance Saltzman, chief of Strategic Plans and Policy Division at Air Force Headquarters, and his coauthors, James Forsyth Jr. and Gary Schaub Jr., asked a simple question: "What size force is needed for deterrence?" They gave a surprising answer: "The United States could address military utility concerns with only 311 nuclear weapons in its nuclear force structure while maintaining a stable deterrence."[79] This proposition would include 192 single-warhead, submarine-launched ballistic missiles on 12 Ohio-class submarines, 100 single-warhead ICBMs, and air-launched cruise missiles loaded on 19 stealth B-2 bombers. The authors argue that this relatively small, survivable force is sufficient for keeping the United States secure under a strategy of minimum nuclear deterrence. It would also allow the United States to relieve itself of the tremendous costs and catastrophic risks associated with the current arsenal of thousands of warheads.

Some conservatives thinkers believe efforts to eliminate nuclear weapons undermine U.S. security and argue for maintaining or increasing the number of nuclear weapons. Former Bush administration deputy assistant secretary of defense Keith Payne holds that the elimination of nuclear weapons is "divorced from reality" and "recommendations for deep reductions within 10 years rest on a set of assertions contrary to obvious facts and no small amount of unwarranted idealism regarding international relations."[80] Payne does not believe deterrence is reliable with a smaller arsenal, basing his case on uncertainty and our own inability to predict the future:

> Confident and near-universal claims that we should expect deterrence to function predictably at relatively low numbers of US nuclear forces—whether 300, 500 or 1,000—seemingly know how opponents will perceive US deterrence threats, value the stakes at risk, calculate costs and benefits and make the implement decisions.[81]

Senator Kelly Ayotte (R-NH) and several other Republican senators wrote to President Obama in April 2012 arguing that the president's "budget proposal currently underfunds nuclear modernization, endangering our nation's nuclear deterrent and the security of all Americans." They argued:

> A reliable and modern nuclear deterrent is central to American national security. A credible nuclear arsenal deters potential enemies from launching a nuclear attack against our country or our allies. A strong and dependable U.S. nuclear deterrent also helps prevent nuclear proliferation by assuring friendly nations that a nuclear program is unnecessary. When the U.S. fails to maintain a reliable and modern nuclear deterrent we undermine these objectives, which are central to the security of our country.[82]

Former U.S. ambassador to the United Nations John Bolton says simply and strongly, "We should also announce our withdrawal from the New START arms-control treaty, and our utter disinterest in negotiations to prevent an 'arms race' in space. Let Moscow and Beijing think about all that for a while."[83] And Senator Jim DeMint (R-SC) summarized a common theme among some conservative analysts that holds the United States cannot further reduce its strategic offensive nuclear arms until Russia cuts it nonstrategic (or tactical) weapons. "New Start is another Obama giveaway at the expense of U.S. citizens," he says. "The treaty mandates strategic nuclear weapons parity with the progeny of an old Cold War foe, yet allows the Russians to maintain a 10-to-1 tactical nuclear-weapons advantage."[84]

These conservatives fight hard and persistently for their positions but appear to be waging a losing battle. Force levels have been going down for almost thirty years, and there is every indication that they will continue to do so. It is a question of speed, not direction. All the reduction proposals call for maintaining a capability to deter a nuclear attack on the United States for as long as other nations retain nuclear weapons. At these lower levels, however, the United States would create the conditions for serious negotiations with other nuclear-armed nations for step-by-step reductions down to tens of nuclear weapons held in each national arsenal and eventually to zero nuclear weapons.

The United States would likely continue to maintain the science and technology base that could support renewed nuclear weapon production even under a disarmament treaty, if simply as a hedge against the treaty failing in practice. However, the sprawling complex that developed, manufactured, and maintained nuclear weapons since World War II could be shuttered. The extraordinarily expensive bombers, missiles, and submarines could be retired or converted for conventional military use. An emergency nuclear production capability could likely be sustained at a few billion dollars per year, until such time as this insurance policy is no longer needed.

CONCLUSION

In 2010, President Obama began to reorient U.S. nuclear policy to reflect the "logic of zero." The April 2010 Nuclear Posture Review concluded:

> The massive nuclear arsenal we inherited from the Cold War era of bipolar military confrontation is poorly suited to address the challenges posed by suicidal terrorists and unfriendly regimes seeking nuclear weapons. Therefore, it is essential that we better align our nuclear policies and posture to our most urgent priorities—preventing nuclear terrorism and nuclear proliferation.[85]

However, as of early 2013, this promised realignment had yet to occur. The budgets and force plans guiding U.S. nuclear weapon development had not yet moved from a Cold War focus on Russia and China to the new standard of how these forces prevent—or exacerbate—nuclear terrorism and nuclear proliferation. Indeed, senior defense officials still seemed gripped by Cold War thinking. On March 1, 2013, Deputy Secretary of Defense Ash Carter announced that he would protect two areas of military spending from the effects of the sequester: operations in Afghanistan and nuclear budgets. While the department intended to ground air forces and tie up ships in port, it would keep nuclear weapon programs at full throttle. "The very notion that nuclear deterrence should be exempt from sequestration," wrote Jeffrey Lewis in *Foreign Policy*, "helps illustrate the incredibly convoluted and confused thinking that underpins the U.S. approach to nuclear weapons."[86]

New guidance from the president on nuclear weapons is needed to break this obsolete thinking and reshape budgets. It will become increasingly important as the United States moves into the process established by the Nuclear Posture Review of multilateral negotiations for nuclear disarmament. According to a 2010 study, *Elements of a Nuclear Disarmament Treaty*,

> As the United States and Russia reduce their deployed weapons through New START, the United States will pursue negotiations for deeper reductions and greater transparency in partnership with Russia. Over time, we will also engage with other nuclear weapon states, including China, on ways to expand the nuclear reduction process in the future.[87]

In the foreword to that study, former secretaries of defense Frank Carlucci and William Perry note that "precedents exist in past or existing international agreements, and in state practices for most of the measures that would have to be put in place to govern, verify and enforce a disarmament agreement." They conclude: "The overriding obstacles are not technical; they are political."[88] If these political obstacles can be overcome, the elimination of nuclear weapons will provide considerable economic benefits to all nations.

The administration needs to bring fiscal responsibility to the nuclear weapons bureaucracy. It should commission studies on the cost savings and strategic benefits of rationalizing the nuclear force to levels of 1,000 and to 500 nuclear weapons over the next ten years and to zero nuclear weapons in twenty or thirty years. The administration should integrate the president's nuclear-reduction goals into all budget and planning processes. The navy, the air force, U.S. Strategic Command, and the National Nuclear Security Agency should be tasked to develop deployment plans and budgets for sharply reduced nuclear forces over the next twenty or thirty years. These can be presented to the president and Congress along with plans to maintain the current nuclear force indefinitely. Not providing these alternatives condemns policy makers to the tyranny of the status quo.

The fiscal logic of zero reinforces the strategic appeal of preventing nuclear catastrophe by eliminating nuclear weapons. The realization that policy makers can reduce both strategic and financial threats to the United States may broaden the support for moving towards the peace, security, and economic benefits of a world without nuclear weapons.

SEVEN
THE 95 PERCENT

The United States and Russia possess 95 percent of the world's nuclear weapons.[1] How these two nuclear superpowers configure and view their nuclear forces has a profound impact on how the other nuclear-armed states perceive the value of their weapons and how seriously other nations consider acquiring or not acquiring their own nuclear arsenals. This chapter briefly summarizes how the U.S. and Russia view their nuclear weapons and offers practical policy recommendations for how both nations can achieve their stated goal of reducing the role of nuclear weapons in national security strategies.

The New START treaty limits the United States and Russia to no more than 1,550 deployed strategic nuclear warheads each, carried by no more than 700 operational delivery vehicles each. This means that each nation can maintain 1,550 thermonuclear bombs on missiles and airplanes that can reach the territory of the other.[2] In addition, both countries have hundreds of nonstrategic (or "tactical") nuclear weapons assigned for battlefield use, plus hundreds of weapons held in reserve that could become operational on fairly short notice (that is, uploaded onto existing missiles and planes), plus thousands of weapons that have been decommissioned but not yet dismantled. Each country keeps about a thousand of its warheads on missiles on heightened alert status (or "hair-trigger alert"), ready to launch in fifteen minutes or less. (See chapter 4 for details on each nation's arsenal.)

EVOLVING PERSPECTIVES, DIMINISHED UTILITY

The force structure and use doctrines of both Russia and the United States remain rooted in Cold War strategy. That means that despite the various desires and claims of the leaders of the United States and Russia over the past twenty years, both still configure their forces to deter the other by holding targets of strategic value at risk of nuclear destruction. These targets include nuclear forces, conventional forces, industrial and economic assets, and political leadership.

Moreover, the guidance that the president of the United States provides to the military (and presumably that the president of the Russian Federation provides to his military) still requires very high confidence of an "assured kill" of the target. Target destruction is determined by blast damage. The calculations largely ignore radiation and fire damage, even though both will contribute to massive destruction in the targeted areas.[3] It means, for all practical purposes, that many targets have to be in or near the crater dug by the nuclear explosion—with two warheads usually allocated for hard-to-kill targets like ICBM silos. This results in both states creating requirements for a very large number of warheads.

For example, before the end of the Cold War, while I was working in Congress on the professional staff of the House Armed Services Committee, I was briefed on the Single Integrated Operational Plan (SIOP) that coordinated the war-time use of U.S. nuclear weapons. In an unclassified illustration of the methodology, we walked through the possible targets in one Soviet city and the warheads required to destroy each of them, even though the bomb blasts, fire, and radiation would overlap. The exercise resulted in sixty high-yield hydrogen bombs targeted for delivery on Odessa, Ukraine—a port city of about one million people. This vivid demonstration of "overkill" makes no military sense, except from the narrow point of view of the target officers, who are just following their instructions.

The guidance has barely changed over the years. Today's U.S. targeting plans yield similar results for Moscow, St. Petersburg, and dozens of other cities, even though, technically, the cities are not targeted, just plants, buildings, and bases within or near the cities. Similar plans exist for other nations, including China. Less is known about Russian plans but it would be logical to assume that New York, Washington, and other U.S. cities are similarly redundantly targeted.

A 2012 report from the Government Accountability Office confirmed the failure of nuclear policy to adapt to the post–Cold War world. R. Jeffry Smith of the Center for Public Integrity reported:

> Little has changed in U.S. objectives or in the targeting process over the past two decades—a period in which the political map of Eastern Europe was redrawn, NATO was expanded and wars erupted in the Balkans, the Persian Gulf and the Middle East. "The fundamental objectives of U.S. nuclear deterrence policy have remained largely consistent since 1991, even as the threat environment and the size of the nuclear weapons stockpile has changed," the GAO report states.

White House officials said President Obama had been reviewing new recommendations for precise targeting of U.S. nuclear forces. But defense officials told the GAO that the presidential guidance governing those forces was still that written by President George W. Bush in 2002.[4]

EVOLUTION OF VIEWS AND DOCTRINES

These plans and strategies, as extensive as they are, have been scaled down considerably from the height of the Cold War; at its peak in the mid-1980s, the United States and Russia fielded more than 65,000 nuclear weapons on thousands of long-range missiles and bombers. Arms-control agreements negotiated during the Cold War and continuing today have reduced those arsenals by almost 75 percent.

Current U.S. and Russian views imperfectly mirror each other:

- Both nations view nuclear weapons as an important part of their strategic identity, with the weapons playing a more pronounced role in Russia than in the United States.

⊙ Both nations' militaries still see value in nuclear weapons. This view is decidedly decreasing in the U.S. military but still strong in the Russian military, particularly to offset perceived conventional military shortfalls.

⊙ Both nations devote a sizable portion of their defense budgets to nuclear weapons. The United States spends about $56 billion each year on nuclear weapons and weapons-related programs.

⊙ Both have significant modernization plans underway for new nuclear-armed missiles, submarines, and bombers.

⊙ The force posture of each nation is still largely determined by the force posture of the other. Both nations are reluctant to fall below the force numbers of the other or to negotiate asymmetrical limits.

⊙ The number and deployments of nuclear weapons by both nations are also major factors in other nations' strategic calculations, particularly NATO members and China.

⊙ The presidential leadership of each nation has embraced the goal of a world free of nuclear weapons and has taken concrete steps toward that goal. The presidents face significant opposition from their nuclear bureaucracies and from political and ideological opponents.

⊙ There is a significant, open debate in both nations on the role of nuclear weapons and the desirability and feasibility of eliminating nuclear weapons, though this debate is more transparent and more developed in the United States.

The current shift in U.S. and Russian strategic thinking began with President Ronald Reagan and President Mikhail Gorbachev. During Reagan's first term, the seemingly belligerent policies of the U.S. military build-up and aggressive Soviet actions under General Secretary Leonid Brezhnev convinced millions of Americans and Europeans that the two would start a global thermonuclear war. A mass movement to reduce and eliminate nuclear weapons arose to counter this danger. Its impact rippled through the U.S. Congress and European parliaments and stimulated new strategic thinking that continues to this day.

Reagan saw the build-up as part of a strategy to force negotiations to end the arms race. He wanted to convince the Soviets that they could not win an arms race and thus would have to end it. As one biographer observed, "Ronald Reagan harbored an intense dislike of nuclear weapons and the concept of mutually assured destruction. That antinuclearism was based on his deeply rooted personal beliefs and religious views. Reagan was convinced that it was his personal mission to avert nuclear war."[5] Reagan spoke often of his desire to make nuclear weapons "impotent and obsolete" and to move steadily to a world without any nuclear weapons. He found a partner in Gorbachev, who wrote,

> The road to this goal began in November 1985 when Ronald Reagan and I met in Geneva. We declared that "a nuclear war cannot be won and must never be fought." This was said at a time when many people in the military and among the political establishment regarded a war involving weapons of mass destruction as conceivable and even acceptable, and were developing various scenarios of nuclear escalation.[6]

Reagan and Gorbachev tried but failed to conclude an agreement at their summit in Reykjavik, Iceland, in 1986 to eliminate all nuclear weapons within ten years. But their talks later helped them negotiate two treaties, the Intermediate Nuclear Forces Treaty and the START I treaty (concluded by George H. W. Bush) that eliminated thousands of long-range weapons. President Bush negotiated START II, which would make additional nuclear cuts, with Gorbachev's successor, Boris Yeltsin. These policies enjoyed broad bipartisan support, as demonstrated by the role played by President Bill Clinton in winning Senate approval of START II in 1996 and continuing to reduce the role and numbers of nuclear weapons.

Arms control has not always come through formal treaties. In 1991, President George H. W. Bush and Soviet leader Mikhail Gorbachev coordinated deep reductions in their countries' nuclear forces. President Bush announced plans to eliminate all ground-launch short-range nuclear weapons, remove all nuclear weapons from surface ships and attack submarines, take U.S. strategic nuclear bombers off strip alert, stand-down from alert all ICBMs scheduled for deactivation under START, and forgo a series of nuclear modernization programs.[7] In kind, Gorbachev announced plans to eliminate nuclear artillery munitions, mines, and warheads for tactical missiles and to remove nonstrategic nuclear weapons from surface ships and submarines. Russian president Boris Yeltsin reaffirmed and clarified Gorbachev's pledges, including committing to halve Russian stocks of air-defense missiles and air-launched nonstrategic munitions and to eliminate one-third of sea-based nonstrategic weapons.

President Bush's cuts were applauded by most officials and experts even though he took them unilaterally, without a formal agreement of any kind.

"The President wanted to take the initiative in arms control," explained Brent Scowcroft, then national security adviser. "He saw intuitively that there was a new world forming, and didn't want to be behind the power curve and be driven either by the Congress and the budget, or by the Pentagon's resistance."[8] Under these initiatives, the United States and Russia reduced their deployed nonstrategic stockpiles by an estimated 5,000 and 13,000 warheads, respectively.[9] Lacking a treaty, these numbers cannot be publicly verified. Nor is it certain whether the United States and Russia kept all their commitments, but it appears that most were implemented.

EVOLUTION INTERRUPTED

This doctrinal shift was interrupted by the administration of George W. Bush, who continued reductions of nuclear forces but also sought to expand their missions. Although the president did not appear to harbor any ideological attachment to nuclear weapons—and made unilateral cuts of his own— many officials in his administration came into office in 2001 with a disdain for what they considered the naïve practice of arms control (as discussed in chapter 2). These officials sought to remove any constraints on U.S. defense and foreign policy. They convinced President Bush to renounce previous arms-control commitments, withdraw from the 1972 Anti-Ballistic Missile Treaty, and reject any new negotiated nuclear reductions with Russia until compelled by Congress to do so. The 2002 Strategic Offensive Reductions Treaty (SORT) that his officials worked out with the Russians codified unilateral nuclear reductions plans already underway in the United States and Russia but abandoned the verification mechanisms of the 1991 START treaty, developed by the previous Republican administrations. A high-ranking U.S. official quipped that the SORT treaty was simply "two force postures stapled together and called a treaty."[10]

The Bush administration formalized its views in the congressionally mandated Nuclear Posture Review, submitted to Congress on December 31, 2001. The NPR greatly expanded the role and missions of nuclear weapons in U.S. national security strategy. Although classified, most of the document was leaked in early 2002. While this is essentially an internal document, other nations carefully scrutinize the plan for clues on the future role of nuclear weapons in U.S. security structure.

The NPR identified a wide range of potential uses for nuclear weapons, including responding to a biological or chemical weapon attack, striking hardened conventional targets, striking mobile targets, and responding to a surprise or unusual conventional attack. It specified China as a target for U.S. nuclear weapons as well as "rogue" states that did not have nuclear weapons, including Libya, Iran, Iraq, North Korea, and Syria. It called for the development of several new types of nuclear weapons, including low-yield weapons and earth-penetrating "bunker busters." It also called for research, development, and production of a new generation of nuclear-armed missiles, submarines, and bombers—plans that the Obama administration is now implementing.

STRATEGIC PIVOT

President Barack Obama, in a clear break from the Bush years, released an unclassified Nuclear Posture Review in April 2010 that reasserted the basic policies of Ronald Reagan, George H. W. Bush, and Bill Clinton. The 2010 NPR reduced the role of nuclear weapons in security policy and started a fundamental reorientation of U.S. nuclear policy. The review "altered the hierarchy of our nuclear concerns and strategic objectives," shifting emphasis from a force configured for massive retaliation against another nation toward a policy that places "the prevention of nuclear terrorism and proliferation at the top of the U.S. policy agenda."[11]

The 2010 NPR reinforced U.S. security commitments to its allies but moved decidedly away from suggestions that it would use nuclear weapons to deter or respond to attacks involving biological, chemical, or conventional weapons. It declared that the fundamental purpose of U.S. nuclear weapons is deterrence of nuclear use by others. The NPR contained a clear U.S. pledge to never use or threaten to use a nuclear weapon on a non-nuclear-weapon state that adheres to its nonproliferation obligations.

The NPR also signaled the Obama administration's intention to further promote the reduction and elimination of all nuclear weapons, suggesting that missile defenses and precision-guided conventional weapons could be substituted for missions that previously required a nuclear weapon. Former secretary of state George Shultz applauded the move, stating, "Deterrence is not necessarily strengthened by overreliance on nuclear weapons."[12] With the

NPR, President Obama tried to implement his pledge from Prague in April 2009: "To put an end to Cold War thinking, we will reduce the role of nuclear weapons in our national security strategy and urge others to do the same."

In part, this reflects a growing bipartisan consensus in the U.S. security establishment that whatever benefits nuclear weapons may have had during the Cold War are now outweighed by the threat they present. As George Shultz, Henry Kissinger, William Perry, and Sam Nunn argued, "We face a very real possibility that the deadliest weapons ever invented could fall into dangerous hands." The only way to prevent this, they said, was to move to eliminate all nuclear weapons. These four statesmen worked out their views with the close advice of the former Reagan nuclear negotiator Max Kampelman and the physicist Sid Drell. As Philip Taubman wrote:

> It was one thing if Max Kampelman favored the abolition of nuclear weapons, quite another if George Shultz, Henry Kissinger, Bill Perry, and Sam Nunn endorsed the idea. This was the heart of the foreign policy establishment talking, two mainstream Republicans and two benchmark Democrats breaking with their clans to embrace a quixotic cause that had inspired plenty of soaring presidential rhetoric over the years but little serious consideration.[13]

Thus, a view that thirty years ago was identified primarily with left political movements became solidly part of the American security elite. The center shifted; arms control became the new realism. It is seen as an essential element in efforts to prevent nuclear terrorism and the spread of nuclear weapons. Secretary of State Hillary Clinton concisely summarized this logic: "Clinging to nuclear weapons in excess of our security needs does not make the United States safer.... It gives other countries the motivation or the excuse to pursue their own nuclear options."[14] More formally, the 2010 NPR states: "By demonstrating that we take seriously our NPT [Nuclear Non-Proliferation Treaty] obligation to pursue nuclear disarmament, we strengthen our ability to mobilize broad international support for the measures needed to reinforce the non-proliferation regime and secure nuclear materials worldwide."[15]

This strategy has harsh critics. Senator John Cornyn (R-TX) said on the Senate floor during the December 2010 New START debate, "I fear that the New START treaty will serve as another data point in the narrative of weakness, pursuing diplomacy for its own sake—or indulging in utopian dreams of a world without nuclear weapons—divorced from hard reality."[16] Senator Jon

Kyl (R-AZ) is another who believes it foolish to eliminate nuclear weapons: "Is 'zero' really desirable? If nuclear deterrence has kept the peace between superpowers since the end of World War II, which itself cost over 60 million lives by some estimates, are nuclear weapons really a risk to peace or a contributor to peace?"[17]

This debate never ends. Critics in the House of Representatives, wanting to refight the New START debate they lost in 2010, attached legislation to the Defense Authorization Bill for Fiscal Year 2012, denying the president funds to implement the New START agreement or dismantle any U.S. nuclear weapons, even those long slated for destruction. The Heritage Foundation, which campaigned against the New START treaty, works diligently to block any new agreements. A 2011 Fact Sheet from the group, for example, described any new reductions as "dangerous," "weak" "concessions to the Russians" that place "the U.S. irreversibly on the path to nuclear disarmament."[18]

Despite its critics and, more significantly, the partial and sluggish policy implementation by the executive bureaucracy, the president's strategy has made progress. The April 2010 Nuclear Security Summit brought fifty world leaders to Washington and won their support for a four-year action plan to secure and eliminate stocks of highly enriched uranium and plutonium—the core ingredients for nuclear weapons. The leaders gathered again in Seoul, South Korea, in 2012 to assess their progress and push for new actions. The 2010 Non-Proliferation Treaty Review Conference reversed the failure of the 2005 conference, securing the consensus of the 189 member states for a joint program to strengthen the barriers to the spread of nuclear weapons, though the steps have yet to be implemented.

Meanwhile, U.S.-Russian relations—though often strained—improved considerably from the low point of 2008, following the Russia-Georgia conflict. The United States and Russia increased collaboration in securing vulnerable nuclear materials worldwide. Russia allowed overland transportation of coalition supplies into Afghanistan and joined the U.S.-led international efforts to contain the nuclear programs in Iran and North Korea.

When the U.S. Senate approved the New START Treaty in December 2010 and the Russian Duma did so in January 2011, they restored inspections in both countries and paved the way for another round of negotiations for deeper cuts in strategic weapons and, for the first time, in tactical nuclear weapons and nondeployed weapons. These negotiations, when they start, are expected to take several years. Meanwhile, NATO is slowly undergoing its own strategic review. Several member states have urged the withdrawal of U.S. tactical nuclear weapons from Europe, and all members support new negotiations with Russia for mutual reductions. The NATO "Deterrence and Defense Posture Review" released at the May 2012 summit in Chicago, was a disappointing document, however. As several analysts noted, "NATO leaders missed an important opportunity to change the Alliance's outdated nuclear policy and open the way to improving European security by the removal of the remaining 180 U.S. nuclear bombs in Europe, which serve no practical military value for the defense of the Alliance."[19] But the review did conclude:

> NATO is prepared to consider further reducing its requirement for non-strategic nuclear weapons assigned to the Alliance in the context of reciprocal steps by Russia, taking into account the greater Russian stockpiles of non-strategic nuclear weapons stationed in the Euro-Atlantic area.
>
> Allies look forward to continuing to develop and exchange transparency and confidence-building ideas with the Russian Federation in the NATO-Russia Council, with the goal of developing detailed proposals on and increasing mutual understanding of NATO's and Russia's non-strategic nuclear force postures in Europe.[20]

RUSSIAN VIEWS

Russia reacted predictably to the policies of President George W. Bush. Following his withdrawal from the ABM Treaty, the Russian Duma voted 326 to 3, on January 16, 2002, to adopt a nonbinding resolution that described the U.S. withdrawal as "mistaken and destabilizing since it effectively ruins the existing, highly efficient system of ensuring strategic stability and paves ground for a new round of the arms race."[21] Russia later declared the START II treaty dead and began plans to test a multi-warhead version of one of its missiles, something the treaty had prohibited, and to develop a new, multi-warhead missile to replace the huge SS-19 scheduled for retirement.

But Russian views weren't simply reactive. President Vladimir Putin had already begun to implement a more assertive strategic policy. His January 2000 National Security Concept said that Russia would use "all available means and forces, including nuclear weapons, in case of the need to repel an armed aggression when all other means of settling the crisis situation have been exhausted or proved ineffective"[22] The Russian expert Yury Fedorov noted in 2007, "While the role of nuclear weapons in Western security thinking is more modest than it was during the Cold War, Russian strategic thinking is evolving in a different direction. Russian military, political, and bureaucratic elites consider nuclear weapons to be the main foundation of Russian security and see them as an instrument that ensures Russia's national interests." Fedorov concludes, "As the second largest nuclear power in the world, Russia hopes to strengthen its international influence by relying on its nuclear assets."[23]

The Russia-Georgia war of 2008 plunged U.S.-Russian relations to their worst levels since the end of the Cold War. Russian views of nuclear weapons correspondingly shifted further. Nikolai Patrushev, head of Russia's Security Council, said in October 2009 that Russia would not rule out the use of a pre-emptive nuclear strike and suggested an enlarged role for nuclear weapons to apply "not only to full-scale wars, but also to regional and even to local wars."[24]

Patrushev's views, however, appear to be a lagging indicator of Russian opinion. As the Stanford University scholar Pavel Podvig notes in a 2011 assessment, the determined effort by the Obama administration to "reset" U.S.-Russian relations created a process that shifted Russian views back toward a narrowing of the role and missions of Russian nuclear weapons. In particular, the U.S. decision to renew arms-control negotiations and cancel the deployment of antimissile interceptors in Eastern Europe "changed the dynamics of the domestic security debate in Russia, shifting its focus toward negotiations and cooperation with the United States."[25]

This process appears to have contributed to the change reflected in the 2010 Russian Military Doctrine. The new doctrine narrowed the role of nuclear weapons and the circumstances in which they would be used. While still considered essential as a deterrent and to be used in response to aggression, the new doctrine, like the U.S. 2010 NPR, says that the use of nuclear weapons would only occur in the most extreme cases:

> The Russian Federation reserves the right to utilize nuclear weapons in response to the utilization of nuclear and other types of weapons of mass destruction against it and/or its allies, and also in the event of aggression against the Russian Federation involving the use of conventional weapons *when the very existence of the state is under threat*.[26]

The prominent Russian security analyst Alexei Arbotov notes, "on the whole, it is obvious that the new Military Doctrine expresses a more restrained attitude toward the role and missions of nuclear weapons than the previous 2000 Doctrine and certain statements by Moscow politicians and strategists."[27]

Conversations I have had with Russian officials, experts, and retired military officers over the past three years indicate a strong belief among the security establishment that nuclear weapons, particularly tactical nuclear weapons, remain an essential part of Russia's national security strategy. Some discuss in great detail the need for hundreds of tactical weapons in the event of attacks on Russia from some of its neighbors, however illogical these scenarios appear to non-Russians. Many are reluctant to engage in new negotiations with the United States until they see how the New START treaty will be implemented and if the new direction in U.S. policy is permanent. Mirroring some corresponding American opinions, there are strong Russian ideological currents that still consider the United States an enemy, out to trick Russia and ultimately destroy it.

These attitudes may reflect long-standing Russian insecurities but also indicate deep concern that budget pressures will reduce the size of the Russian nuclear arsenal well below the limits set by New START. Arbotov calculates that under current plans the Russian strategic nuclear force will shrink to 1,000–1,100 strategic warheads by 2020, well under the New START limits of 1,550 that will be in effect by that time. "For the first time in the history of strategic treaties," he says, the Russian strategic forces "will make a unique 'dive' beneath treaty ceilings" and will require new programs and new funding to build back up.[28] To counter this decline, it first appeared that Russia would extend the operational lives of the SS-18 and SS-19 missiles. There are now plans for a new heavy ICBM that can carry up to ten warheads, to be deployed in 2018.[29]

At the same time, President Dmitri Medvedev's views, at least in his public statements, seemed more in line with President Obama's: "As leaders of the two largest nuclear weapons states, we agreed to work together to fulfill our obligations under Article VI of the Treaty on Non-Proliferation of Nuclear Weapons (NPT) and demonstrate leadership in reducing the number of nuclear weapons in the world," he said at his meeting with Obama in July 2009. Medvedev praised the New START treaty at its signing in April 2010, saying it "enhances strategic stability and, at the same time, enables us to rise to a higher level for cooperation between Russia and the United States." It is unclear where Putin stood on this issue, but it is unlikely that Medvedev would have proceeded without his backing.

The main opposition to reductions seemed to come from the entrenched nuclear weapons bureaucracy, still wed to the jobs, contracts, and prestige the programs offer, and from political and ideological opponents. Vladimir Zhirinovsky, leader of the Liberal Democratic Party, said about the United States and arms control, "They play the fox, using these agreements to learn the locations of our factories, where we build our rockets, but they don't grant us such access.... They say that they want to destroy us, that they don't need Russia."[30]

THE IMPACT OF U.S. AND RUSSIAN DISARMAMENT ON NONPROLIFERATION

One of the most hotly debated issues in nuclear policy is what impact, if any, U.S. and Russian strategic views and postures have on the decisions taken by other nuclear-armed states or potential nuclear-armed states. For example, former secretary of defense Harold Brown and former CIA director John Deutch argued in a 2007 *Wall Street Journal* op-ed,

> A nation that wishes to acquire nuclear weapons believes these weapons will improve its security. The declaration by the U.S. that it will move to eliminate nuclear weapons in a distant future will have no direct effect on changing this calculus. Indeed, nothing that the U.S. does to its nuclear posture will directly influence such a nation's (let alone a terrorist group's) calculus.[31]

Scott Sagan of Stanford University and Jane Vaynman of Harvard University argue the opposite in a comprehensive 2010 survey of national attitudes on nuclear weapons. They say that Brown, Deutch, and others set up "straw men" to knock down. They also cite former the Bush administration official Christopher Ford, who argues against the idea "that a hearty re-endorsement of nuclear 'zero' as the ultimate goal would do the trick: moving faster on disarmament was the key to getting nonproliferation under control." Ford says, "My point is not to complain that the Obama Administration hasn't 'solved' all of today's proliferation problems. (After all, the Bush Administration didn't solve all of them either, and it had eight years.) Instead, my point is that they seem spectacularly unaffected by Washington's Prague-era disarmament posturing." "We know of no serious policy maker or analyst," Sagan and

Vaynmen say, "who thinks that the simple proclamation that the U.S. government seeks global nuclear disarmament would lead Iran or North Korea to give up their nuclear ambitions." But they argue that their case studies do show that foreign governments look very carefully at "both pronouncements of U.S. intent and U.S. actions," make judgments on how these actions and policies change the overall security environment, and adjust their own nuclear policies only when "they judge such changes to be in their broader interests."[32]

Sagan and Vaynman believe their work provides "valuable new evidence that many, but by no means all, foreign governments have indeed been strongly influenced by Washington's post-Prague disarmament policy and nuclear posture developments." Specifically, they find that the new U.S. posture and actions have "opened the door for states to make changes in their own policies and produce compromises in negotiated settlements."[33] They have encouraged some governments to reduce the role of nuclear weapons in their doctrines (UK and Russia); have helped reinforce the nuclear nonproliferation regime (specifically at the NPT Review Conference and the Nuclear Security Summit), and have encouraged new domestic discussion in some states (Japan and South Korea) on the proper role of conventional forces versus nuclear weapons in extended deterrence guarantees in East Asia. But not all nations have "walked through the door." U.S. policies and actions have had "minimal direct influence" on France, China, India, and Pakistan.[34] Many states are hedging their bets, waiting to see if President Obama can get the Senate to approve his other arms-control treaties, particularly the nuclear test ban treaty, before they commit to further steps in either disarmament or nonproliferation. The impact of nuclear postures on other nations' nuclear policies is explored in more detail in chapter 9.

U.S.-RUSSIAN COOPERATION STRENGTHENS POSITIONS TOWARD IRAN

The United States and Russia have a shared interest in keeping Iran from acquiring nuclear weapons but have different views of Iran. The United States sees Iran's nuclear program as a pressing threat that must be confronted and has led an international coalition to pressure Iran back to the negotiating table. Russia sees Iran's nuclear program as a problem that must be managed along with its geopolitical and economic interests with Tehran. Russia's approach to Iran has thus differed from the U.S. approach—sometimes frustratingly so. However, as U.S.-Russian relations have improved, Russia has been more willing to back the United States.

When U.S.-Russian relations have been cool, as during the last few years of the George W. Bush administration, Russia tacked against the U.S. position. Beginning in 2006, Russia stalled or heavily diluted Security Council sanctions against Iran being sought by the Bush administration. Even so, Russia did cooperate in other ways. WikiLeaks cables recently revealed that in 2006 President Vladimir Putin delayed the construction of the Bushehr reactor and held up supplying fuel for the facility.

As U.S.-Russian relations improved under the Obama administration, so did Russian cooperation on Iran. Obama's policy of engagement with Iran also helped reduce Russian fears of another U.S. war in the region. Russia became a key partner with the United States in arranging a nuclear fuel swap with Iran in 2009, though the deal ultimately fell through. When the Obama administration sought tough Security Council sanctions against Iran in 2010, Russia voted in support of Security Council Resolution 1929. In what Vice President Biden called "an unambiguous sign of international resolve" toward Iran's nuclear program, Russia canceled, and lost money on, a deal to sell Iran its sophisticated S-300 air defense system.[35] It has continued to support efforts to sanction Iran and to help broker a deal that could resolve the nuclear crisis with Iran, although favoring diplomacy over threats of the use of force.

The U.S. and Russia will always have different strategic interests, particularly regarding the border regions of Russia, but U.S.-Russian cooperation on Iran has been a significant diplomatic success. Keeping Russia on board will be a practical test of how improved U.S.-Russian relations can benefit global nonproliferation efforts.

SEVEN EASY STEPS TO ENHANCE U.S. AND RUSSIAN SECURITY

It is possible that the United States and Russia could proceed to reduce their nuclear arsenals in the manner favored by officials in the George W. Bush administration, that is, joint consultations but no formal treaties and no verification measures. This would give each side maximum flexibility in reductions and allow for rapid increase if future events warranted. Most military leaders prefer the certainty that verified treaties provide for force planning. It is almost certainly true that the reductions in Russian tactical nuclear weapons that the U.S. Senate ordered the president to undertake as part of its advice and consent to the New START treaty cannot be achieved without detailed negotiations and rigorous new verification methods. However, there are steps that the president can take without the Russians and without the Senate that would modernize the U.S. nuclear posture and develop a military defense in line with twenty-first-century requirements.

Step one would be to recognize that deterrence does not require numerical parity. Given that Russia is no longer an enemy and the chance of a premeditated nuclear exchange is close to zero, a fresh approach could do more than the past exercises, which have merely trimmed U.S. nuclear target sets by reducing or eliminating particular categories of targets. The Joint Chiefs could be directed to develop an entirely new set of target options based on what is sufficient to deter the leadership of Russia. This "zero-based targeting" would significantly reduce the number of required targets and, consequently, facilitate reductions in U.S. weapons and delivery systems.

Step two would be for the president to tell the military that he or she no longer requires them to maintain a capability for launch on warning or launch under attack to ensure the credibility of the deterrent. The military could then choose if it wanted to retain that capability, but it would no longer be under a presidential directive to do so. It could weigh the costs and resources devoted to these cumbersome Cold War practices with other military needs.

Both of these steps are similar to actions taken by previous presidents (George H. W. Bush, for example, reduced the target set and took nuclear bombers off high alert.) Both would rationalize the nuclear force without any loss of deterrent capability. Both would save money. And both would send a signal to other nations, including Russia, that the United States is serious about reducing the roles and missions of nuclear weapons in national security strategy.

But such action would not be sufficient. As noted above, other nations will evaluate U.S. and Russian views on nuclear weapons based on both declarations and actions. While policies have clearly shifted in both nations, procurements have not. Both have ambitious nuclear modernization plans. The Obama administration is continuing the research and development of a new generation of nuclear delivery vehicles called for in President Bush's nuclear posture review. If implemented, the United States will spend roughly $640 billion on nuclear weapons and weapons-related programs over the next ten years. Other nations will have to decide which reflects a nation's views more accurately: policy or procurement?

Under plans in effect as of March 2013, the United States will deploy in 2020 approximately 1,550 nuclear warheads as follows:

- 420 warheads on 420 Minuteman III ICBMs
- 1,090 warheads on 240 Trident SLBMs on 14 Trident submarines
- 40-60 B-2 and B-52 bombers[36]

Russia will deploy a smaller force of, at most, 1,258 warheads:

- 542 warheads on 192 Topol, Topol-M, RS-24, and SS-18 ICBMs
- 640 warheads on 128 Bulava SLBMs on 3-4 submarines
- 76 Tu-160 and Tu-95 bombers[37]

These forces are considerably larger than either country requires for military missions other than attacks on each other. The United States and Russia could implement additional steps over the next few years that would continue to reduce the saliency of nuclear weapons in their national security strategies and enhance efforts to prevent nuclear terrorism and the spread of nuclear weapons, without any decrease in the national security of either state. These steps would build on and accelerate agreements already agreed to by the two nations and should enjoy the support of the military leadership of both.

Step three would be to accelerate the reductions in strategic weapons agreed to in New START. The treaty provides that reductions will be implemented within seven years of the entry into force (February 5, 2018). The United States and Russia could implement the reductions more quickly, preferably announcing that the new, lower levels would be achieved by the 2015 Non-Proliferation Treaty Review Conference. Military officials might also see this as an effective cost-saving measure: early removal of weapons already slated for retirement could free up resources for other military needs. This step would not require a new treaty.

Step four would be to increase the transparency of both nations' nuclear arsenals. The United States and Russia should exchange information on nuclear weapons types and numbers beyond that required by the New START treaty—including nonstrategic weapons, nondeployed warheads, and retired warheads awaiting dismantlement. This would reduce uncertainties in strategic planning, facilitate the reductions and negotiations urged in steps five and six, and increase incentives for other nuclear-armed states to disclose more details about their nuclear arsenals.

Step five would be to initiate additional reciprocal nuclear reductions, similar to those implemented in 1991 by Presidents Bush and Gorbachev. As indicated above, Russian forces are likely to decline to 1,000–1,100 strategic warheads accountable under New START by 2020. Moscow and Washington should announce in parallel statements that each side would reduce its holdings to 1,000 strategic warheads and consider coordinating further reciprocal reductions if conditions allow. The New START limits are a ceiling, not a floor, and should not artificially promote levels that neither side needs for any conceivable military purpose. These reductions should include accelerating the dismantlement of thousands of weapons decommissioned but still stored in warehouses. These reductions could and should also include nonstrategic weapons and extend transparency measures to their inventory and storage.

Step six would be to begin negotiations for a new round of reductions, as envisioned by the U.S. Nuclear Posture Review and the statements of both President Obama and President Dmitri Medvedev of Russia. The treaty, as preliminary consultations between the two nations have explored, should reduce strategic, tactical, and nondeployed nuclear weapons. The talks should aim at a new treaty that is approved by the Congress and the Duma before the 2015 Non-Proliferation Treaty Review Conference for maximum effect on the ability of that conference to strengthen nonproliferation barriers.

Step seven, finally, should be to steadily take portions of both nations' strategic forces off heightened alert status. This would reduce the risks of accidental launch, save funding and resources for other military needs, and allow hundreds of highly trained officers to undertake more meaningful assignments. As importantly, it would be another step toward demonstrating the reduced relevance of nuclear weapons in both nations' security strategies.

There is growing expert support for accelerating nuclear reductions. In November 2012, the International Security Advisory Board chaired by former secretary of defense William J. Perry, a bipartisan group of national security experts with scientific, military, diplomatic, and political backgrounds that provides the secretary of state with independent advice on all aspects of arms control and international security, made what it termed "modest initiatives" for implementing additional nuclear-force reductions in the near term. This author was a member of the board and of the study group that prepared the report. The board recommended that the United States consider actions to

◉ Implement the New START reductions early and take off of operational states all of the strategic weapons it would be reducing

◉ Lay the groundwork for reducing nonstrategic weapons by working with Russia toward a shared definition of these weapons and working closely with allies to better understand the national security challenges that have led to the creating and retention of such large stockpiles of these weapons

◉ Implement mutual reductions with the Russians below New START, including nonstrategic weapons. "The United States could communicate to Russia," wrote the board, "that the United States is prepared to go to lower levels of nuclear weapons as a matter of national policy . . . if Russia is willing to reciprocate. This could improve stability by reducing Russia's incentive to deploy a new heavy ICBM."[38]

In March 2013, George Shultz, Henry Kissinger, William Perry, and Sam Nunn published the fifth in their series of op eds. Warning that "the continuing risk posed by nuclear weapons remains an overarching strategic problem, but the pace of work does not now match the urgency of the threat," the four urged bold actions to "reduce reliance on nuclear weapons, prevent their spread, and ultimately end them as a threat to the world."[39] As did the International Security Advisory Board, the four recommended speeding up the reductions planned under New START and exploring going below these levels with mutual, reciprocal, verifiable reductions with Russia. The four also urged the administration to "work with nuclear-armed nations worldwide to remove all nuclear weapons from the prompt-launch status" and to "establish a joint enterprise" with other key nations to implement these and other practical measures at an accelerated pace.

But neither the United States nor Russia will take even these modest steps if it believes that the global nuclear threat environment is increasing, that large nuclear arsenals are essential to security, or that decreasing its arsenals will encourage other states to increase theirs. It is thus vital to understand what history tells us about the relationship of U.S. and Russian arsenals on the nuclear decisions of other states. Chapter 9 attempts to do exactly that, but first there is one more nuclear nightmare to examine. And it may be the scariest of all.

EIGHT
THE MOST DANGEROUS COUNTRY ON EARTH

On any given week, there are several contenders for which country people might feel poses a great danger to global security. Though many, like Iran or Mali, Russia or China, may pose serious problems, the confluence of several disturbing trends make Pakistan the most dangerous country on earth. Pakistan has an unstable government, a fragile economy, strong extremist influences in its military and intelligence agencies, and enough nuclear material for 200 bombs. And al Qaeda and a half dozen similar groups operate inside the country. If terrorists ever detonate a nuclear device in America, they will likely have gotten the bomb or the material from Pakistan.[1]

It is not just a question of the security of the weapons; it is a question of the security of the government. If the government falls, if the army splinters, who gets the weapons? Who gets the nuclear materials for building these weapons? Where do the scientists and technicians who know how to make the material and build the weapons go? Pakistan could flip from a major non-NATO ally to our worst nuclear nightmare overnight. As the former CIA agent Valerie Plame Wilson said: "Here you have a nation-state that is essentially imploding. You have a very unstable nation-state that is nuclear-armed. Their intelligence service is deeply infiltrated with those that are antithetical to U.S. national security interests."[2]

Iran and North Korea, by comparison, are serious challenges but present far less of a threat. Iran does not have (and may never have) nuclear weapons, and North Korea has only a few. Both of these nations are more isolated and face more international pressure than ever before. This makes a negotiated solution to these programs more feasible or, failing that, their containment and deterrence. (Both nations are discussed in more detail in chapter 10.)

Pakistan also shares a border with another nuclear-armed nation, India, with which it has fought three major wars in sixty years. Yet the nuclear programs in India and Pakistan get little press or public attention. We are lulled into complacency by several factors. These programs are run by states that have close ties to the United States and its allies, including various forms of nuclear cooperation. Both are nominally democracies. The programs have grown slowly over several decades, with U.S. officials often looking the other way or justifying them to the American public. But these state-to-state relations mask a seething danger—conflicts between the two nations and within the two nations could lead to nuclear catastrophe.

Some in the popular media have picked up on these developments and tried to highlight them. One particularly good example came during the first season of the television series *The West Wing*, when the fictional president Josiah Bartlet, played by Martin Sheen, is confronted with an Indian invasion of Pakistan. Three hundred thousand Indian troops cross the border through the disputed territory of Kashmir to put a "final end" to the problem of Pakistani insurgents attacking Indian posts. The president's aides are deeply concerned that a conventional war will not stay conventional for long. All are worried that each side has several nuclear weapons (which is what each side had in January 2000 when the show aired) and will soon use them. Secretary of State Madeleine Albright was quoted as saying that the episode was one of the best expositions of foreign policy on television that she had seen.[3]

In the show, the British expert called in to advise the president, Lord John Marbury, tells them, "Your Congress has been pathetically inept at halting the proliferation of nuclear weapons in this region." (It was actually Congress that pushed reluctant presidents to finally resort to tougher actions, but too late to stop the programs.) The Pakistanis are said to be concerned that their army cannot stop the Indian forces and begin to give command and control of nuclear weapons to commanders in the field. This is precisely what worries real national security advisors today.

One concern is that terrorists could acquire an assembled nuclear warhead or enough fissile material to construct a bomb. A second is that terrorists operating from Pakistan could launch another attack on India, similar to the 2001 New Delhi attack and the 2008 Mumbai bombings, which would force India to retaliate, thrusting both nations into a military conflict that could escalate to nuclear use.

There is third scenario, combining these two concerns. Pakistan guards its nuclear weapons tightly, but it also plans to move these weapons into the field for possible use should a conflict with India develop. The MIT Professor Vipin Narang explains the risks of theft and use of the weapons in this case:

> Perhaps the scariest implication of these arrangements is that extremist elements in Pakistan have a clear incentive to precipitate a crisis between India and Pakistan, so that Pakistan's nuclear assets become more exposed and vulnerable to theft. Terrorist organizations in the region with nuclear ambitions, such as al-Qaida, may find no easier route to obtaining fissile material or a fully functional nuclear weapon than to attack India, thereby triggering a crisis between India and Pakistan and forcing Pakistan to ready and disperse nuclear assets—with few, if any, negative controls—and then attempting to steal the nuclear material when it is being moved or in the field, where it is less secure than in peacetime locations.[4]

These are not abstract concerns or implausible scenarios. There have been repeated instances that indicate militant groups could be much closer than most realize to getting their hands on a nuclear weapon. Extremist groups have staged major attacks on military bases, including ones suspected of housing nuclear weapons. There is no evidence that the attackers sought the nuclear weapons or information at these bases or were even aware of the possible nuclear functions at the bases. But the number of attacks is mounting. A suicide bomber killed eight air force personnel and wounded forty others at a Punjab air force base that housed the military headquarters for the control of Pakistan's nuclear arsenal; a suicide bomber attacked a bus at the Kamra Air Force Base in Peshawar province that includes facilities likely associated with the storage and maintenance of nuclear weapons; and militants launched a major attack on the Karachi Naval Base that killed ten and wounded forty in a sixteen-hour gun battle, as well as an August 2012 attack on Pakistan's main air force base near the capital, Islamabad.

The *Atlantic*'s Jeffrey Goldberg wrote after the last attack in an article, "Pakistan: Maybe Not the Best Country in Which to Store Nuclear Weapons":

> Here's the thing: If you were looking for a safe place to store nuclear weapons, would you choose a country that is the epicenter of global jihadism, and that sees its military bases, and even its military's general headquarters, attacked with some regularity, and some success? If you answered no, you are correct! Once again this week, we see Pakistani radicals having some measure of success attacking a base at the heart of the country's military-nuclear complex. . . .
>
> No nuclear material went missing this time. It is, however, only a matter of time before a more serious breach is made, with enormous consequences. Last year, Marc Ambinder and I wrote about Pakistani nuclear security in our Atlantic cover story "The Ally From Hell," and we provided some detail about previous attacks on Pakistani nuclear sites. We also conveyed Pakistan's assertions that, hey, everything is fine, no worries.[5]

This kind of "whistling past the graveyard" humor is common among experts trying to deal with the Pakistan problem. But this is no joke. These same experts agree that the profound nuclear risks cannot be adequately addressed without broad, sustained U.S. engagement on a number of interrelated issues.

PAKISTAN'S ARSENAL

Pakistan has the fastest growing nuclear arsenal in the world, with an estimated 90 to 110 warheads that could grow to 150 to 200 within this decade along with new production facilities and new nuclear-capable ballistic missiles.[6] The analysts Hans Kristensen and Robert Norris of the Federation of American Scientists provide the best independent estimates of national nuclear arsenals in their comprehensive "Nuclear Notebook" series in the *Bulletin of the Atomic Scientists*. They note that after Pakistan followed India and tested its first nuclear weapons in 1998, the U.S. Defense Intelligence Agency projected that by 2020 Pakistan would have between 60 and 80 warheads. But "Pakistan appears to have reached that level in 2006 or 2007. . . . With four new delivery systems and two plutonium production reactors under development," they note, "the rate of Pakistan's stockpile growth may even increase over the next 10 years."[7]

Most of Pakistan's weapons have been built using uranium enriched at its facilities at Kahuta and Gadwai. As of 2011, Pakistan was believed to have a stockpile of about 2,750 kilograms of highly enriched uranium.[8] Over the past few years, Pakistan has increased its ability to produce plutonium, adding in 2009 a second production reactor to its original 1998 Khushab reactor, then a third, and recently a fourth spotted by satellites under construction in 2011.[9] By the end of 2011, Pakistan likely had produced 135 to 145 kilograms of plutonium. Pakistan has enough uranium and plutonium to build 175–262 warheads.[10]

Pakistan's delivery systems have also been rapidly increasing in numbers and sophistication. It possesses nuclear-capable aircraft, most likely the F-16 A/B airplanes the United States sold the country in the mid-1980s, and perhaps also the Mirage V supplied by the French. The United States in 2001 also approved a Pakistani request to buy thirty-six F-16 C/D aircraft, eighteen of which had been delivered by 2012. These planes have a range of 1,600 kilometers (1,000 miles) and can likely carry one nuclear bomb each.

Pakistan has three types of nuclear-capable ballistic missiles currently in its arsenal and is developing three additional models. Operational short-range varieties include the Ghaznavi (also known as the Hatf-3) and Shaheen-I (Hatf-4). The Ghauri (Hatf-5) is its operational medium-range missile. Another medium-range missile is under development, the Shaheen-2 (Hatf-6), as are two additional short-range systems, the Abdali (Hatf-2) and the Nasr (Hatf-9). The new Nasr system will only travel 60 kilometers (37 miles) and is clearly a tactical weapon, meant for use on troops in the battlefield rather than strategic targets in India. Kristensen suggests that the Pakistan military sees this missile as a counter to India's conventional forces.[11]

Pakistan is also working to develop two types of cruise missiles, the Babur (Hatf-7) and Ra'ad (Hatf-8). Both missiles are designed with stealth capabilities to minimize their radar cross section and could deliver conventional or nuclear warheads. The Babur is ground-launched and has a range of 600 kilometers (370 miles) and the Ra'ad is air-launched and has a range of 350 kilometers (220 miles). When fully operational these missiles will improve Pakistan's strategic depth (the ability to strike at India from deep within its own territory) and signal a rapidly modernizing delivery capability.[12]

Finally, Pakistan might be working to develop a sea-based leg of its arsenal. In 2012, the Pakistan navy opened a new Naval Strategic Force Headquarters. In the press release announcing the inauguration, the navy hinted at nuclear capabilities, "The Force, which is the custodian of the nation's second strike capability will strengthen Pakistan's policy of credible minimum deterrence and ensure regional stability."[13]

SECURITY

Experts are divided on the security of this growing nuclear arsenal. Notably, experts at the International Institute for Strategic Studies (IISS), the Atlantic Council, and the Carnegie Endowment for International Peace have believed for years that Pakistan's nuclear weapons are secure and that the integrity of the military forces responsible for protecting those assets will not be compromised. The French analyst Bruno Tertrais succinctly summarizes this point of view in an IISS dossier from July 2012:

> In the past decade a robust set of institutions and procedures has been put in place, aimed at preventing the unauthorized use, theft or sale of nuclear and other WMD-related materials and related technology. There is no doubt that the Pakistan military has been taking nuclear and WMD security very seriously—first and foremost because it is in its own interest—and that it does so in a very professional way.
>
> Those who support this analysis believe that the main risks today are not those of 'weapons falling into the wrong hands' or an 'Islamist takeover of the country.' Rather, they are of the deliberate use of and perhaps partial loss of control of the nuclear complex in wartime, low-level leaks of WMD expertise or materials, or a radiological incident in peacetime.[14]

Shuja Nawaz of the Atlantic Council agrees, writing in August 2009, "Pakistan appears to be very serious about securing its nuclear assets."[15] Toby Dalton and George Perkovich, both of Carnegie, are perhaps the most unequivocal, stating in May 2011 that "Pakistan's nuclear weapons are probably quite secure from terrorists—the nukes are its crown jewels."[16]

Other well-respected experts are more concerned about the safety and security of the Pakistani nuclear complex. Their concerns have deepened with increasingly frequent reports, corroborating long-standing suspicions that Pakistan's military and intelligence services have been compromised by extremist elements.[17] In November 2007, former Pakistani prime minister Benazir Bhutto challenged President Pervez Musharraf's claim that the arsenal was secure, saying, "We have been facing chaos, growing chaos for some time.... We need to maintain Pakistan's stability. If there is no stability, then I'm afraid the [nuclear] controls could weaken."[18] In May 2009, former U.S. intelligence official Rolf Mowatt-Larssen argued that "the insider threat combined with outsiders" could take over a nuclear facility.[19]

A subgroup of experts is more worried about the security of the fissile material manufactured and stored in the sprawling complex. Shaun Gregory of the University of Bradford points to several high-profile, well-coordinated terrorist attacks on Pakistani military facilities as evidence that "the safety and security of nuclear weapons materials in Pakistan may very well be compromised at some point in the future."[20] David Albright of the Institute for Science and International Studies has put forth a likely scenario in which "militants or their sympathizers are able to divert nuclear material during the weapon-production process, where many more people come into contact with sensitive items."[21] Dalton, Hibbs, and Perkovich of the Carnegie Endowment for International Peace also have less confidence in the country's fissile material stocks: "As Pakistan's nuclear weapons program grows, so too will the amount of fissile material transiting between production and assembly facilities. This theoretically creates more opportunities for terrorist attack or diversion with the help of potential sympathizers within the nuclear program."[22] Tertrais acknowledges that the security of the weapons is highly dependent on the security of the government. "In the longer term, the legal and institutional barriers that have been put into place to protect the arsenal could erode," he says, "A weakening of the state and an increased sympathy for radical militants within the armed forces or the nuclear establishment would make for a dangerous combination."[23]

U.S. officials have consistently assured the public and Congress that the arsenal is secure, although there has been significant discussion over whether the Pakistani military services have been compromised by extremist elements and whether those elements could orchestrate a takeover of Pakistan's civilian government. In April 2009, Secretary of State Hillary Clinton said the security of Pakistan's nuclear arsenal is "an issue we have very adamant assurances about from the Pakistani military and Government.... The current thinking of our Government is that it is safe." She continued,

> But that's given the current configuration of power in Pakistan. . . . One of our
> concerns . . . is that if the worst, the unthinkable, were to happen, and this ad-
> vancing Taliban encouraged and supported by al-Qa'ida and other extremists
> were to essentially topple the Government for failure to beat them back—then
> they would have the keys to the nuclear arsenal of Pakistan.[24]

In November of that year, Secretary Clinton seemed more confident: "The nuclear arsenal that Pakistan has, I believe is secure. I think the government and the military have taken adequate steps to protect that."[25] Assistant Secretary of State Robert Blake later added, "We don't think there is any renewed concern . . . those assets remain under much tighter security than what we saw in Pakistan's naval base" (referring to the May 2011 militant attack on Pakistan's Karachi Naval Station).[26] Joint Chiefs Chairman Adm. Mullen said in July 2011 that Pakistan's nuclear arsenal has become "physically more secure."[27]

With the rare exception of individuals like the late Benazir Bhutto, current and former Pakistani officials have also said that their nuclear assets are safe, and, moreover, that the ranks of the military divisions charged with protecting those assets remain intact and have not been infiltrated by extremist elements. Former Pakistani prime minister Yousaf Raza Gilani said in 2010 that Islamabad had "laid to rest" any alarm about its nuclear security.[28] Former Pakistani president Pervez Musharraf was more candid in 2011 but similarly confident: "If Pakistan disintegrates, then it can be dangerous. Otherwise, if Pakistan's integrity is there, and which I'm sure it will be there as long as the armed forces of Pakistan are there, there is no danger of the nuclear assets or strategic assets falling in any terrorist hands."[29]

There is a pervasive view among Pakistanis that the United States is planning to raid Pakistan in order to take its nuclear arsenal. Tom Hundley writes that this fear could be lead to dispersed storage of the arsenal:

> The United States, which is duly concerned that Pakistan's nukes could fall
> into the wrong hands, almost certainly does have a plan to neutralize those
> weapons in the event of a coup or a total state collapse. When the question was
> put to Condoleeza Rice during her 2005 confirmation hearings to become sec-
> retary of state, she replied, 'We have noted this problem, and are prepared to try
> to deal with it.' *Try* is the key word. Military experts—American, Pakistani and
> Indian—agree that grabbing or disarming all of Pakistan's nukes at this stage

would be something close to mission impossible. As one senior Pakistani general told me, 'We look at the stories in the U.S. media about taking away our nuclear weapons and this definitely concerns us, so countermeasures have been developed accordingly.' Such steps have included building more warheads and spreading them out over a larger number of heavily guarded locations. This, of course, also makes the logistics of securing them against theft by homegrown terrorists that much more complicated.[30]

A TROUBLED PAST

Relations between Pakistan and India are among the most hostile on earth. Tensions date back to the birth of the two countries. When Britain pulled out of its Indian colony in 1947, it partitioned its former possession into two nations. The new Muslim state, Pakistan, comprised eastern and western territories separated by 1,000 miles of Indian territory. Partitioning was traumatic for both countries as 10 to 12 million refugees relocated across the new border. It was a bloody affair. The U.S. embassy in Karachi reported "appalling stories of murder and atrocities, which served to inflame the minds of the masses whether Muslims, Hindus or Sikhs with a sense of grievance and a not unnatural desire for revenge."[31] Conservative estimates put the death toll from the migration between 200,000 and 500,000.[32]

Adding to the turbulence, Mohammed Ali Jinnah, a champion for an independent Pakistan, died just one year after the country was formed, leaving the nation without its visionary leader. Some argue that this lack of a core identity elevated the conflict with India as the main factor legitimizing the Pakistan state.[33] The late prime minister Benazir Bhutto said:

> The 1948 war with India made Pakistan feel vulnerable to the Indian threat. Consequently, a large portion of the budget was spent on defense to counter India's military. India's military, of course, was backed by a much larger population and economy. Between 1947 and 1950 approximately 70 percent of the Pakistani budget was spent on defense. As Liaquat Ali Khan, Pakistan's first prime minister put it, 'The defense of the State is our foremost consideration . . . and has dominated all other government activities.' This began the process of giving the military inordinate stature and influence in Pakistani society, while diverting money away from economic and social development. Its political

effect was dramatic. Instead of strengthening democratic institutions and infrastructure, unelected institutions such as the army and the intelligence agencies took precedence. They became the central institutions of the new Pakistan.[34]

Many issues between the two countries were left unresolved with the partition, but foremost was a territorial dispute over the states of Jammu and Kashmir. At partition, the princely maharaja ceded the two states to India, but the Muslim majority population rebelled, leading to the first Indo-Pakistani War. The United Nations brokered a ceasefire in 1949, which ended the fighting but did not resolve the dispute. Kashmir continued to seethe, and war broke out again in 1965. The UN again stepped in and pushed both countries to sign the Tashkent agreement, which stipulated a return to the prewar cease-fire line.[35]

The third major conflict with India led to the humiliation of the Pakistani army and the loss of East Pakistan. East Pakistan was predominantly ethnic Bengali, a part of the Pakistani population who felt increasingly maligned by the government. Bengali grievances coalesced into a separatist movement in 1971, which triggered a harsh crackdown by the Pakistani army. Atrocities and mass killings were so egregious that twenty U.S. State Department officials in East Pakistan sent a telegram of dissent back to Washington, calling the events genocide and chastising the U.S. policy of nonintervention as "moral bankruptcy."[36]

India stepped in after 10 million refugees poured across the border and in a matter of six months had completely routed the Pakistani army in East Pakistan, which then declared itself the independent nation of Bangladesh. Indian military superiority on the subcontinent was now well established. Experts agree that this war was the most traumatic event in Pakistan's brief history, spurring many decisions with a decidedly negatively impact on the South Asian security situation. Pakistani leaders often cite the defeat as convincing proof that they need nuclear weapons—as well as private justification for beginning a low-level insurgency as a tool against India.

Not long after the war, in 1974, India conducted its first, allegedly "peaceful" nuclear test. Pakistan had already begun a secret program to develop a nuclear weapons capability, but "that test was the tipping point that transformed the 1972 'capability decision' into a 'proliferation decision.' "[37] Pakistan revved up its program, led by scientist A. Q. Khan, and by the mid-1980s probably had the ability to build a nuclear bomb.[38] In 1998, India's newly elected conservative government shocked the world with its first overt nuclear weapons test. Despite intense international pressure Pakistan followed suit, testing a weapon a mere two weeks later.[39]

With the dangers of conflict heightened by nuclear capability, Pakistan and India fought again in 1999, a conflict often referred to as the Kargil crisis though some cite it as a fourth war. Fighting had again erupted in Kashmir when Pakistani troops occupied territory across the line of control. India responded by mobilizing 200,000 troops and the Indian air force, recapturing the land within a few months. Owen Bennett Jones documents several instances during the crisis when Pakistani leaders considered the use of its nuclear arsenal.[40] They did so again during another crisis in 2002, where both militaries were on high alert at the border when India mobilized after a terrorist attack on its New Delhi parliament building. According to Jones, General Musharraf said, "If Indian troops moved a single step across the international border or the Line of Control, they should not expect a conventional war from Pakistan."[41]

DOOMSDAY DOCTRINES

As nuclear arsenals in India and Pakistan grow, so do the risks of war by design, miscalculation, or accident. Neither country's declared nuclear strategy alleviates these concerns; they exacerbate them.

India has officially adopted a policy of "Cold Start." This is not a new kind of arms-control agreement but a plan to mass troops along the Pakistan border within days of an order. Pakistan, in turn, publicly plans to use short-range (tactical) nuclear weapons against any Indian troops that cross its border, in the belief that India will not respond as long as the weapons are not used on Indian territory. India does plan to respond, however. Walter Ladwig, a visiting fellow at the Royal United Services Institute in London, wrote:

> Limited war on the subcontinent poses a serious risk of escalation based on a number of factors that are not necessarily under the control of the policymakers or military leaders who would initiate the conflict. A history of misperception, poor intelligence, and India's awkward national security decision-making system suggests that Cold Start could be a risky undertaking that may increase instability in South Asia.[42]

The Indian strategy developed after an attack by five gunmen on the Indian Parliament building in December 2001. The terrorists, who killed twelve people and injured twenty-two others, were quickly linked to Pakistani extremist groups, Laskkar-e-Taiyyaba and Jaish-e-Mohammad. After Pakistan refused Indian demands to arrest and extradite suspected militants, India sent armored troops toward the border, but it took them three weeks to get there. The United States and other nations intervened to prevent an invasion. "The result was a ten-month standoff that ended with India's quiet withdrawal," says Ladwig. "In the eyes of many senior Indian officers, Pakistan had outplayed them. It had managed to inflict a high-profile attack on the Indian capital via its proxies and then exploited the Indian Army's long deployment time to internationalize the crisis in a manner that allowed Pakistan to escape retribution."[43]

India now plans, at least theoretically, to respond to the next terrorist attack with a rapid conventional strike against Pakistan, driving deep into its national territory. The aim "would be to make shallow territorial gains, 50–80 kilometers deep, that could be used in post-conflict negotiations to extract concession from Islamabad."[44]

But Pakistan would compensate for the inability of its own tanks, troops, and planes by firing nuclear weapons to stop the Indian invasion. Although the precise conditions under which Pakistan would use nuclear weapons are not clear, many experts, including Ladwig, cite the statements of Lt. General Khalid Kidwai of Pakistan to an expert delegation of Italian scientists.[45] Kidwai, then the head of the Strategic Plans Division, detailed for the group the situations in which Pakistan would use nuclear weapons: if India attacks Pakistan and conquers a large part of its territory; if India destroyed significant part of Pakistan's military forces; if India blockaded Pakistan; or, if India tried to destabilize Pakistan politically.[46]

In an article on Pakistan's tactical nuclear build-up, Tom Hundley concludes that an escalation to full-scale nuclear war developing from "miscalculation, miscommunication or panic," is more likely than terrorists stealing a weapon: "As these ready-to-use weapons are maneuvered closer to enemy lines, the chain of command and control would be stretched and more authority necessarily delegated to field officers. And, if they have weapons designed to repel a conventional attack, there is obviously a reasonable chance they will use them for that purpose."[47]

The situation is not entirely bleak. India's doctrine may be more talk than capability. A leaked 2010 cable from the U.S. Mission to India calls Cold Start "a mixture of myth and reality." The cable from the embassy concluded:

> If the GOI [Government of India] were to implement Cold Start given present Indian military capabilities, it is the collective judgment of the Mission that India would encounter mixed results. The GOI failed to implement Cold Start in the wake of the audacious November 2008 Pakistan-linked terror attack in Mumbai, which calls into question the willingness of the GOI to implement Cold Start in any form and thus roll the nuclear dice. At the same time, the existence of the plan reassures the Indian public and may provide some limited deterrent effect on Pakistan. Taken together, these factors underline that the value of the doctrine to the GOI may lie more in the plan's existence than in any real world application.[48]

If India did mobilize its forces for attack, it might take Pakistan days, perhaps weeks, to ready its nuclear forces. Analysts at the London-based International Institute for Strategic Studies say that unlike U.S. or Russian weapons, thousands of which are ready to launch within tens of minutes, Pakistani nuclear systems are kept "in a low-alert form." This means that the weapon cores are not actually in the warheads and the warheads are not mated with delivery vehicles. "According to the Defense Ministry, the launch mechanism, the device and other mechanisms are kept at different places. Nuclear safety, physical security and access (maintenance) reasons all argue for separating the fissile cores from the warheads."[49]

India's new doctrine was severely tested by another brazen terrorist attack in November of 2008. On live news, the world watched a group of armed gunmen hold several civilian locations in Mumbai hostage in a coordinated four-day attack that killed 172 people and wounded 308. The perpetrator was again Lashkar-e-Tayyiba, based in Pakistan. Bruce Riedel believes that one objective of the attacks was to derail a peace process that was beginning to look optimistic with the rise of a new civilian government in Pakistan.[50] In the aftermath of the attack, India, under intense international pressure, did not pursue a military response. They demanded that Pakistan ban the non-state actors involved and focused on improving the response times of their police and other internal security mechanisms. But this restraint is scant reassurance for the future. If there were another large-scale terrorist attack within India, the Indian government would be under tremendous domestic pressure for a fast, firm response. Riedel notes:

> Should another attack occur, the United States and the rest of the international community would undoubtedly urge restraint on India and try to press Pakistan to "do more." But that tactic will not work forever. It amounts to playing Russian roulette in South Asia. Sooner or later a Pakistan-based terror attack on India is going to lead to Armageddon.[51]

These are strong words but they are not hyperbole. It may be worse than perhaps Reidel himself realizes. A South Asian nuclear war would destroy the subcontinent, perhaps the most heavily populated region on Earth. But the catastrophe would also have global climate consequences. As detailed in chapter 5, the use of just one hundred nuclear weapons would generate smoke and clouds that would blanket the planet, decreasing global temperatures, killing food crops, and triggering worldwide famine. Could that many weapons possibly be used? Yes. Pakistan's capabilities and doctrines are unclear, but at least one former nuclear official, giving an example of the type of calculations that Pakistani planners might make, said that for a set of ten possible targets, a country might need sixty-eight to seventy warheads (without taking into account the risk of a preemptive strike).[52] And that does not count the warheads that might be used by India.

India is actively building up its military, which some experts see as a strategic shift to compete with China rather than Pakistan.[53] India likely has eighty to one hundred plutonium-based nuclear weapons, which could be delivered by a triad of delivery vehicles: bombers, land-based missiles, and fairly new submarines.[54] Aircraft are the strongest leg of the triad. India has nuclear-capable Mirage 2000H/Vajra and Jaguar IS/IB/Shamsher fighter-bombers with a range of up to 1,800 km.[55] In 2011, India completed a $15 billion deal with France to purchase 126 nuclear-capable Rafale fighter jets to modernize its bomber capabilities.[56] The country has a range of options for its land-based missiles. The short range Prithvi I only travels 150 kilometers; the Agni I has a range of 700 kilometers; the Agni II, 2,000 kilometers; and the Agni III, 3,000 kilometers. In 2012, missile tests were successfully conducted for the Agni V, making India one of the few countries with missiles that can reach 5,000 kilometers.[57] Finally, India has launched the indigenously built Arihant submarine, which is slated to become fully operational in early 2013. The submarine will be capable of carrying twelve missiles with a range of 750

kilometers. There are plans to build at least two more Arihant-class submarines in the future.[58]

One problem with India's nuclear arsenal is its lack of transparency,
which greatly heightens tensions in the region. Hans Kristensen writes:

> All Indian nuclear systems are dual-capable (they can carry either nuclear or
> conventional warheads), and the operational status of these systems is am-
> biguous. This not only makes the size, composition and readiness of India's
> nuclear arsenal difficult to determine, but it also has troubling implications
> for stability on the subcontinent, especially in the case of a war with Pakistan;
> for example, preparations for an Indian launch of a conventionally armed nu-
> clear-capable ballistic missile could be misidentified by Pakistan as a pending
> nuclear attack, triggering nuclear escalation of the conflict.[59]

Pakistan's other neighbor, China, also exacerbates the problem. China
and Pakistan developed diplomatic ties shortly after Pakistan's independence
and continue to be allies today. China has consistently supplied Pakistan with
missile, aircraft, and nuclear technology and allegedly had ties to the A. Q.
Khan network. China also finances significant infrastructure projects in Pakistan for the energy, engineering, mining, and telecommunications sectors.[60]
Also raising eyebrows is China's plan to build two new nuclear reactors at
Chashma despite pressure from the international community, which maintains that this would violate international nonproliferation rules.[61] The worse
U.S.-Pakistan relations get, the more Pakistani leaders threaten to move
closer to China. After the 2011 U.S. raid that killed Osama bin Laden, China's
prime minister responded that Pakistan and China "will remain forever good
neighbors, good friends, good partners and good brothers."[62]

WHAT WE CAN DO

U.S. policy options for Pakistan are limited. Previous administrations—
Republican and Democrat—have so badly mismanaged relations with Pakistan that it will take years to get in a position where we might be able to seriously reduce the nuclear risks. There is no silver bullet. The Eighty-second
Airborne cannot be sent in to secure or destroy Pakistan's nuclear weapons
in case of a government collapse. Even if we knew where all of them were—
which we do not—U.S. troops would have to fight the Pakistan Army to get to
the storage locations.

As I wrote for the 2008 paperback edition of *Bomb Scare: The History and Future of Nuclear Weapons,*

> Past Democratic and Republican administrations have constantly placed pro-
> liferation and democracy concerns second to other geopolitical aims. Officials
> who regarded Pakistan as an ally needed to rout Soviet troops (and later the
> Taliban) from Afghanistan, or wanted the country as a balance to India or
> China, then looked the other way as Pakistani scientist A. Q. Khan developed
> a network to import technology and materials for Pakistan's nuclear weapons
> program, even when he began exporting the technology to other countries. The
> nuclear chickens may be coming home to roost, reminding everyone that nu-
> clear weapons are a danger wherever they exist and terrorists who are intent
> on acquiring them will go to the most vulnerable sites, regardless of the politi-
> cal orientation of the state.[63]

The majority of Pakistan's security establishment and general population seem convinced the United States intends to take over its nuclear weapons, thereby stripping Pakistan of its supposed guarantor of security and its most potent bargaining chip. After the May 2011 bin Laden raid in Abbottabad, U.S.-Pakistani relations went into free fall. Rather than investigating how bin Laden was living undetected in a town full of military establishments, the Pakistani government arrested the doctor who helped the CIA find bin Laden and sentenced him to thirty-three years in prison.[64] Disputes over the use of U.S. drones to target suspected terrorists escalated; Pakistan officials can-celed trips to Washington; and poll numbers showed that the Pakistani popu-lation hated America more than India.[65]

Pakistan also closed the ground routes crucial to resupplying NATO troops in Afghanistan after a clash with NATO forces killed twenty-four Pa-kistani soldiers in November 2011. After several rounds of acrimonious nego-tiations, the routes were reopened in July 2012. The seven months of using alternate routes through Russia and Caucusus states cost the Pentagon $2.1 billion dollars.[66] Vali Nasr, hoped this might pave the way to better relations:

> The U.S. should adopt a long-term strategy that would balance U.S. security
> requirements with Pakistan's development needs. Managing relations with Pa-
> kistan requires a deft policy—neither the blind coddling of the George W. Bush
> era nor the blunt pressure of the past year, but a careful balance between pres-
> sure and positive engagement. This was Clinton's strategy from 2009 to 2011,

when U.S. security demands were paired with a strategic dialogue that Pakistan coveted. That is still the best strategy for dealing with this prickly ally.[67]

Others are more skeptical, particularly as the United States continued its policy of drone strikes against suspected terrorist targets. "You can't undertake unilateral attacks on Pakistan's soil and say that you are friends of Pakistan," retired Pakistani general Saleem Haider told NPR in July 2012. "There's a contradiction in this." These disagreements have "given rise to intense anti-Americanism," reported NPR's Mike Shuster, evident at protests in Pakistani cities in July where "many banners called for closing the border to NATO resupply convoys once again and for jihad against the U.S."[68]

In the United States, Congress is wary of adding to the billions of dollars in military aid and nonmilitary assistance given to Pakistan over the past decade. Lawmakers withheld nearly 40 percent of U.S. military aid to Pakistan for fiscal year 2012. This might be a good sign. For decades, U.S. policy makers have put geopolitical considerations ahead of proliferation concerns, human rights, and democracy (certifying to Congress, for example, that Pakistan did not have a nuclear weapons program when all U.S. intelligence showed that it could already build a bomb). This has only increased the role of the military in Pakistan, alienated the Pakistani people, increased extremist influences, and allowed Pakistani scientist A. Q. Khan to spread nuclear technology around the globe. Indeed, if it were not for Pakistan, we might not have an Iranian nuclear program to worry about, at least not on the scale Iran achieved by 2012. Khan is heralded in his country as the "father of the atomic bomb," but he made millions selling Iran the design and parts for its first generation of centrifuges for enriching uranium, may have given Iran a working design for a nuclear weapon, and arranged a steady stream of assistance for Iran's nuclear scientists and technicians.[69]

Decreasing aid to Pakistan's military is a reasonable first step, but far more is needed: a comprehensive reorientation of the strategic relationship. In October 2012, the International Security Advisory Board presented its recommendations to the secretary of state on such a reorientation. I was a member of the board and of the Pakistan Study Group chaired by MacArthur Foundation president Robert Gallucci that prepared the report. "The situation in Pakistan today poses certain risks for our security and international security generally," the board warned. "That situation, quite likely, will deteriorate in the coming months and years, posing grave threats to American interests."[70]

Our national security interests are clear, said the board, and they include "an over-riding national interest in preventing nuclear weapons or fissile material from being transferred, lost, or stolen from Pakistani authorities. This risk will only increase as Pakistan begins to operate more and larger nuclear facilities." The United States, of course, is also interested in "preventing a South Asian nuclear war, slowing the Pakistani nuclear weapons program and avoiding a nuclear arms race with India. These goals will be served by reduced tension and increased confidence between India and Pakistan, and the U.S. should clearly work to promote this movement."[71]

The board recognized that our immediate national-security interests in Pakistan, as pointed out early in this chapter, could only be realized if the United States has a coherent global and regional strategy. Specifically, the board noted,

> The long-term interests of the U.S. vis-à-vis Pakistan should be a major part of our national strategy towards the region, broadly defined. These long-term interests can be ignored only at our peril and can be damaged if we focus exclusively on short-term dangers. These long-term interests are:
>
> ⊙ To influence to the best of our ability the gradual evolution of all elements of the Muslim world toward more tolerant, democratic and modern societies, integrated with the rest of the world, and providing little encouragement for Islamist extremism and terrorism.
> ⊙ To accommodate the rise of China and of India to major power status in a way that results in a stable international system in the Asia-Pacific region.
> ⊙ To encourage India and Pakistan to resolve their differences over Kashmir and other disputed areas, and to develop mutually beneficial economic relations.
> ⊙ To promote conditions that permit the strengthening of Afghanistan's governmental and civil society institutions so that Afghanistan can maintain its independence and enjoy mutually beneficial relations with its neighbors.
> ⊙ To prevent the proliferation of nuclear weapons capabilities beyond those nations that now possess them, to discourage the use of nuclear weapons, and eventually to roll back the nuclear weapons arsenals of all states that currently possess them.
> ⊙ To develop regional strategies and relations even farther afield, to include Iran and the region of the Persian Gulf.[72]

Some elements of such a comprehensive strategy have been detailed in previous chapters. The specific policies that could lead to a more stable, truly democratic, and less nuclear Pakistan must start with one essential truth: though Pakistan and the United States are clearly uneasy allies, neither can afford to walk away from the other. The United States and Pakistan need to cooperate if there is to be any hope of reducing the urgent threats outlined in this chapter. Despite the bleak rhetoric between the countries, experts agree that there are steps that the United States could and should take to improve relations. The ultimate goal of these intermediary steps should be to empower Pakistan to stabilize internally and strengthen its civilian institutions, guarantee the safety of Pakistan's nuclear assets, prevent nuclear terrorism, and avoid an India-Pakistan nuclear exchange on the subcontinent. Pakistan should be brought into talks with the other nuclear-armed states to reduce and eventually eliminate their nuclear arsenals.

IMPROVE THE ECONOMY

The United States is Pakistan's top export market, and a full one-third of Pakistani foreign direct investment comes from the United States.[73] This is to the U.S. advantage, and experts almost unanimously agree that encouraging stronger trade ties by offering Pakistan preferential trade status and lowering tariffs, particularly in the textile sectors, will help the relationship at no cost to the American economy.[74] This would help strengthen the private sector and would help combat chronically high unemployment rates.

Another productive step would be for the United States to quietly encourage expanded trade between Pakistan and India. In 2011, there was a mere $2.6 billion worth of trade between the two countries, compared with almost $100 billion in trade between India and China.[75] There is much opportunity for greater prosperity on both sides of the border and increased bilateral dialogue along with it.

Pakistan has already taken some steps in this direction. In 2011, the government decided to offer India favored-nation status and is currently revising some customs restrictions.[76] Both countries also relaxed visa requirements for businesspeople and tourists traveling across the border with an agreement signed September 8, 2012.[77] The United States would be wise to make the most of this momentum, says Moeed Yusuf, a Pakistan expert at the U.S. Institute for Peace. He says that the United States could encourage this transaction by offering to compensate Pakistan for any initial losses occurred from importing Indian goods.[78] These simple reforms would stimulate Pakistan's economy, employ millions of young and economically displaced Pakistanis who otherwise might be prime targets for recruitment by terrorist organizations, and put more money in the pockets of the Pakistani consumers—all without putting U.S. producers at risk.

A more productive economy would potentially wean Pakistan off of American aid that is already beginning to be withheld in a U.S. domestic environment of tight budgets and hostile public opinion. Although America has consistently given Pakistan aid through the years, the amount varies greatly according to American objectives in South Asia. The invasion of Afghanistan by the Soviets during the 1980s brought a large stream of security assistance, which dried up after the end of the Cold War. The next influx of aid came for counterterrorism efforts after 9/11. As the United States pulls out of Afghanistan in the next few years, aid is almost certain to decrease. Whatever the aid level, the practice of sending the overwhelming majority of the aid to Pakistan's military should end. Reduced military funding seems inevitable and wise, but Council on Foreign Relations senior fellow Daniel Markey warns:

> Alone, cutting U.S. military assistance will not force Pakistan to reassess its strategic posture. Pakistan's generals probably benefit from the assistance more than they claim, but they can also do without it. And anti-American sentiment in Pakistan is so intense at the moment, including within the ranks of the army, that Pakistan's generals can hardly appear to bow before U.S. pressure. So if Obama administration officials believe that assistance cuts and public rebukes [alone] offer enough leverage to coerce a Pakistani about-face, they will be sorely disappointed.[79]

Diversifying and targeting the aid will help. In 2009 Senators John Kerry (D-MA) and Richard Lugar (R-IN) introduced legislation to increase aid to the civilian sector of Pakistan. Education in particular has been called "the single most important long-term issue facing the country."[80] Pakistan faces a 50 percent illiteracy rate and an education system ranked among the worst in the world. Pakistani teachers rarely show up, and the available textbooks contain material that encourages extremist views toward India, women, and other religions and countries.[81] The Enhanced Partnership with Pakistan Act of 2009 (also known as the Kerry-Lugar-Berman bill) provided $7.5 billion in nonmilitary aid to Pakistan from 2010 to 2014,[82] which triples the amount of

U.S. assistance from previous years and, as of 2009, made the United States the largest source of bilateral aid to Pakistan.[83]

So far, implementation has been slow. A March 2011 USAID report on implementation of nonmilitary aid under the Kerry-Lugar-Berman bill said: "For fiscal year (FY) 2010, Congress appropriated more than $1.5 billion but by 30 June 2010 much of the money had yet to reach the field."[84] Nonetheless, Robert Lamb and Sadika Hameed of the Center for Strategic and International Studies recommend giving this aid package more time for the results to manifest: "It is difficult to see how cutting aid to Pakistan would contribute to the U.S. interest in a capable Pakistani state. Any changes to Kerry-Lugar should be designed to strengthen capacity or reduce contributors to instability—not remove the possibility to strengthen capacity."[85]

Most aid to Pakistan is still in the form of military assistance meant to support Pakistan's effort to combat extremists in the tribal areas. Two funds established in 2009, the Pakistan Counterinsurgency Fund and the Pakistan Counterinsurgency Capability Fund, go directly to security measures in addition to reimbursements from the coalition support fund. From 2002 through 2012 this aid has totaled about $15.8 billion.[86]

There are steps that can be taken to improve this security aid. Several Pakistan experts have highlighted a deficiency in helicopters, which a report by the Council on Foreign Relations notes are essential to transporting troops for counterinsurgency operations in mountainous terrain.[87] Although there would be well-founded concerns over how Pakistan would actually use those helicopters (for example, as weapons against India) Bruce Riedel and Shuja Nawaz agree that this may be the single most useful thing the United States could do. "It may not be out of the box [thinking], but it is the right answer. Advice and expertise are helpful, but the real sign of support is equipment, especially for air mobility," Riedel said. Nawaz makes the crucial point that Pakistani officials need to be involved in planning for aid targets and establishing performance indicators.[88] This will invest them in the process and improve aid effectiveness for both military and nonmilitary goals.

DIPLOMACY

The United States should continue to encourage Pakistan and India to maintain their bilateral dialogue. Although there have been bilateral talks on trade, water security, and other issues, the major problem continues to be Kashmir. Kashmir issues caused three of the four wars between the countries and inspired the Pakistani government to support a low-level insurgency that has had disastrous consequences for relations. Resolution of this long-held hostility "remains the ultimate game changer," as the expert Moeed Yusuf puts it.[89]

First, the United States should certainly encourage both sides to engage in bilateral talks on the issue while staying mindful that both sides face entrenched domestic opposition on Kashmir.[90] New Delhi would almost certainly resist any public pressure; however, experts agree that the United States should be actively but discreetly encouraging both sides toward talks. Even slow motion on Kashmir is better than no motion. The potential for conflict leading to a nuclear exchange is best mitigated through open lines of communication, which encourage crisis-escalation control during times of heightened tensions. The United States should ensure that bilateral efforts are not derailed despite terrorist provocations and mutual suspicion.

There are fragile signs of progress. In 2012, Pakistan and India held talks on demilitarization of the Siachen glacier in Kashmir, often called the "highest battlefield in earth." India captured the mountains in 1984, and both sides have stationed troops in the snowy peaks ever since. More soldiers die from the harsh conditions than the fighting, however.[91] In April 2012, a massive avalanche killed 140 Pakistani Army troops encamped there. Although the talks are moving slowly—they were in their thirteenth round at the time of this writing in July 2012—it is confidence-building measures like these that are vital to defusing regional tensions.[92]

Michael Krepon at Stimson Center kept a database detailing confidence-building measures (CBMs) between India and Pakistan over the past twenty years. He finds that measures that require little political capital (such as the release of fisherman captured in disputed waters) happen often but rarely lead to more formal military or nuclear confidence-building measures. Only six formal CBMs have been counted since the mid-1980s. Krepon notes:

> This is a meager list of accomplishments for a quarter-century of diplomatic engagement. In the same timeline, the United States and the Soviet Union went from a fierce nuclear arms competition to deep cuts in nuclear forces. Other military-related CBMs between Pakistan and India can easily be envisioned— such as a cruise missile flight test notification agreement, an incidents at sea agreement, and a withdrawal from current positions on the Siachen Glacier— but the timing is not yet ripe for these accords.[93]

Second, the U.S. government should reassess how it pursues its own dialogue with Pakistan. There is little question that the United States should lend more support to the civilian leadership of the Pakistani government and be firmer when dealing with the military leadership so that recognition of and long-term support for the civilian government is not undermined. Although ostensibly a democracy, Pakistan has bounced back and forth between civilian and military leadership since its creation. The military often acts without the knowledge of elected officials and vice-versa.

Historically, America has close ties to the military because of close collaboration against the Soviets in the 1980s. Bruce Riedel and other experts agree that going straight to the military with American concerns—even if there is a more productive relationship there—damages civilian institutions and severely undermines the legitimacy of the elected government.[94] The International Crisis Group says, "The interests of the international community, the U.S. and EU in particular, are best served by a politically stable, democratically-governed state, and not a military-backed government with a civilian façade."[95] This should be foremost in the U.S. mindset when dealing with Pakistan. Experts recognize that the United States won't be able to solve this problem completely but should work with both sides to create tools to prevent crisis. The Council on Foreign Relations Task Force suggests:

> The United States cannot rectify the civil-military power imbalance that plagues the Pakistani state. It can, however, regularly reiterate its preference for democratic rule and take pains to involve Pakistan's civilian leaders in all major bilateral dialogues. Washington should target support to partners and institutions that share common goals.[96]

It is of foremost importance that America stays engaged with Pakistan despite difficulties in the relationship. As Daniel Painter at the American Security Project wrote, "In the frustrating, complex process of working with Pakistan, it is tempting to simply walk away, writing Pakistan off as rogue state. This would be a mistake. National security demands the U.S. continue to engage Pakistan to address these nuclear threats."[97]

SHORT-TERM NUCLEAR FIXES

These recommendations would improve general relations between the United States and Pakistan as well as between Pakistan and India. These are necessary but not sufficient conditions for addressing the dangerous nuclear posture India and Pakistan maintain. Many of the experts mentioned in this chapter, and others, have put forward a number of policy recommendations for the two nations. Most of these recommendations also factor in China, which India considers its principle rival. These should be considered integral to any U.S. involvement in maintaining the bilateral India-Pakistan dialogue.

First, India and Pakistan could become more transparent on fissile material stocks. As Moeed Yusuf of the U.S. Institute of Peace suggested in January 2011, "both sides need to discuss the logic of their fissile missile stockpile trajectories."[98] Declarations of un-reprocessed rather than reprocessed spent-fuel stocks would be more technically ambiguous and, therefore, more politically digestible to both because sharing the amount of spent fuel that has been reprocessed would reveal the size of each country's plutonium stocks, which certainly is a matter of national security and a closely guarded secret. Nonetheless, sharing information on un-reprocessed spent fuel would allow each country to extrapolate from gathered data the other's potential for plutonium stockpiling, which would increase transparency in the near term and build confidence in the long term, creating space for India and Pakistan to discuss additional nuclear-related confidence-building measures.

Second, India and Pakistan should establish a direct executive hotline similar to the Moscow-Washington hotline that was born of the lessons learned from the 1962 Cuban Missile Crisis. India and Pakistan can create a similar direct connection that links together the prime ministers of both countries for immediate and direct communications during periods of crisis escalation. A similar hotline was set up in March 2011 between the Pakistani Interior Ministry and the Indian Home Ministry to share terrorist-related information in real time, and before that a hotline was agreed upon between the Foreign Ministries, though whether it has been operational is unclear. A direct executive-branch-level hotline that follows these templates would, as Moeed Yusuf writes, "force the two sides to communicate directly during crises instead of relying on a third party."[99]

Third, India and Pakistan should set up nuclear-risk-reduction centers. Such centers could follow the U.S.-Russia model, facilitating data and information sharing and lowering the potential for escalation during a crisis. Mohammed Badrul Alam of the Institute of Peace and Conflict Studies in New Delhi notes: "The idea of having a nuclear risk reduction center in each country has received favorable reactions both within and outside of South Asia, including from skeptics who had felt such a proposal to be too unrealistic."[100]

Fourth, India and Pakistan should engage in exchanges between the authorities in both countries who are responsible for managing the civilian uses of nuclear energy to share best practices. Immediately after the disaster at Fukushima, Japan, in 2011, Pakistan raised concerns about nuclear safety at its Chashma site.[101] As A. H. Nayyar, M. V. Ramana, and Zia Mian write, "The first lesson for South Asian publics and decision-makers is that nuclear establishments underestimate the likelihood and severity of possible accidents."[102] Both India and Pakistan have an opportunity to share best practices and learn from each other.

The Track II Ottawa Dialogue that took place in July 2011 between current and retired Indian and Pakistani government officials yielded some concrete recommendations,[103] including an endorsement of nuclear-risk-reduction centers. Additionally, the Ottawa Dialogue participants recommended that officials and scientists from the Indian and Pakistani civilian nuclear programs convene to share their regulatory experiences and discuss nuclear safety.

Finally, the United States should rule out any U.S-Pakistan nuclear-cooperation agreement under current conditions. This issue is divisive among Pakistan experts. Moheed Yusuf points out that the Pakistanis feel the United States discriminates against them. The United States, after all, negotiated and signed a Civil Nuclear Agreement with India that gave India generous conditions for nuclear trade while requiring few real concessions. This agreement undermined the credibility of the United States as an objective proponent of bilateral efforts between Pakistan and India. Yusuf argues for a similar deal with Pakistan, a process that could begin he says, by "reassuring Pakistan by setting preconditions for initiation of talks on a nuclear deal and finding ways to bring Pakistan and India into the legal ambit of the non-proliferation regime, with all its responsibilities."[104] An agreement could bolster energy security and perhaps establish some IAEA safeguards on nuclear facilities, says Shuja Nawaz.[105] Finally, some argue that even if it is unlikely that a deal would be signed, the process would still have value. Bruce Riedel argues that the process would "open the door to greater dialogue on Pakistan's past and to more transparency about where it is going." He warns, "If the United States does not [offer Pakistan a nuclear cooperation deal], China will."[106]

But compounding one bad decision with another is not the way to improve U.S.-Pakistan ties or encourage reduction in Pakistan's nuclear weapons. Indeed, there is evidence that the U.S.-India nuclear deal stimulated Pakistan's desire to increase its nuclear arsenal. A 2012 Congressional Research Service report cited Pakistani air commodore Khalid Banuri, director of arms control and disarmament affairs, who listed the India deal along with India's conventional build-up and missile-defense research as reasons Pakistan decided "to make qualitative and quantitative adjustments."[107]

Many experts believe a Pakistani nuclear deal would further undermine the Nuclear Non-proliferation Treaty on a global scale. Moreover, a U.S.-Pakistan nuclear cooperation agreement lacks support, both internationally and domestically in Congress. Experts at the Carnegie Endowment for International Peace point out that Pakistan lacks the necessary lobby in Washington to get an agreement passed and that nuclear companies would be hesitant to invest in Pakistan because of terrorism concerns.[108] The Council on Foreign Relations Task Force agrees that seeking an agreement "would only serve to frustrate both sides by raising false hopes and diverting attention from other pressing issues. But the Obama administration should do more to help tackle Pakistan's serious energy needs by nonnuclear means."[109]

None of these steps by itself will solve the Pakistan problem. But together they can reorient U.S. policy, improve Pakistan-India relations, improve Pakistan's economy, reduce incentives for violent upheaval, decrease misunderstanding during crisis, and begin a more hopeful trajectory for the subcontinent. While Pakistan will likely remain the most dangerous country on earth for many years, these are actionable steps the U.S. and others can pursue to steadily reduce the risks of a nuclear catastrophe and allow Pakistan to one day realize its enormous potential.

PART III
SOLUTIONS

NINE
POSTURE AND PROLIFERATION

The nuclear posture and strategic decisions of nuclear-armed nations have a significant, often immediate impact on the nuclear-acquisition decisions of other nations.[1] A decision by a state to acquire nuclear weapons can trigger a similar decision in a rival state. Conversely, the commitment not to acquire or maintain nuclear weapons by one state or group of states can foster similar commitments regionally or globally.

This relationship is contested. Those who favor maintaining a large number of nuclear weapons argue that it is naïve, even arrogant, to believe that reducing the role and numbers of nuclear weapons in the United States will have any impact on a decision by, say, Iran and North Korea on whether they will build their own weapons. They hold that U.S. (and Russian) nuclear policy is irrelevant to other nations, who will make decisions based on their own security calculations, not the postures of other nuclear-armed states.

For example, former senator Jon Kyl (R-AZ) opposed the New START treaty in part by mocking the idea that U.S. actions influence others:

> A central tenet of the Obama Administration's security policy is that, if the U.S. 'leads by example' we can 'reassert our moral leadership' and influence other nations to do things. It is the way the President intends to advance his goal of working toward a world free of nuclear weapons and to deal with the stated twin top priorities of the Administration: nuclear proliferation and nuclear terrorism.[2]

There is, however, a solid, historical record showing that U.S. and Russian nuclear policies have a profound impact on other nations' policy choices. This relationship was recognized in U.S. national intelligence assessments in the 1950s and 1960s and informed the U.S. decision to negotiate the Non-Proliferation Treaty. The new international norm established by the NPT and related agreements—that the world was moving toward the elimination of nuclear weapons—helped prevent, and in some cases reverse, the acquisition of nuclear weapons by new states.

Even as the nuclear-armed nations increased and improved their nuclear weapons in the 1970s and early 1980s, the process of negotiation of new arms-control treaties maintained the deterrent effect of the NPT. Nations and publics saw the arms race as a violation of disarmament commitments and sought to bring the violating states back to the established norm. When the United States and Russia negotiated sharp reductions in nuclear arsenals in the late 1980s and early 1990s, they reaffirmed this norm and substantially enhanced nonproliferation efforts, including the decisions by Ukraine, Belarus, and Kazakhstan to give up the nuclear weapons—inherited from the break-up of the Soviet Union in 1991—and the successful indefinite extension of the NPT at a crucial conference in 1995.

The United States briefly ended the negotiated reduction process in the early 2000s, and both the United States and Russia again emphasized the importance of modernizing and maintaining nuclear weapons and expanded their use to additional nonnuclear missions. As some nations concluded that the nuclear-weapon states had no intention of eliminating their nuclear weapons, and as India and Pakistan seemed to win acceptance as new nuclear nations, the antiproliferation impact of the NPT waned. When new states began to develop nuclear weapon technologies, the international cooperation needed to prevent this development became harder to muster.

Reestablishing the commitment to the elimination of nuclear weapons by the United States and other nuclear-armed states coupled with practical steps toward that goal would be a powerful barrier to the spread of nuclear weapons to other states. The interim report of the Commission on the Strategic Posture of the United States, chaired by William J. Perry and James R. Schlesinger, correctly notes: "If the U.S. by its actions indicates to other nations that we are moving seriously to decrease the importance and role of nuclear weapons, we increase our chance of getting the kind of cooperation we need to deal effectively with the dangers of proliferation." As the commission found:

> What we do in our own nuclear weapon program has a significant effect on (but does not guarantee) our ability to get that cooperation. In particular, this cooperation will be affected by what we do in our weapons laboratories, what we do in our deployed nuclear forces, what kind of nuclear policies we articulate, and what we do regarding arms control treaties (e.g., START and CTBT).[3]

The historical record strongly supports this conclusion.

HISTORIC LINKAGE BETWEEN U.S. NUCLEAR POSTURE AND PROLIFERATION

Nonproliferation has been a declared part of U.S. national security strategy since 1945. President Harry Truman said in his message to Congress in October 1945, "The hope of civilization lies in international arrangements looking, if possible, to the renunciation for the use and development of the atomic bomb." From the beginning, officials recognized the linkage between the U.S. nuclear posture and proliferation. They detailed this linkage in successive official assessments. In 1958, when only three countries had nuclear weapons, a now declassified National Intelligence Estimate (NIE), the first exclusively devoted to proliferation, noted:

> A U.S.-USSR agreement provisionally banning or limiting nuclear tests would have a restraining effect on independent production of nuclear weapons by fourth countries. However, the inhibiting effects of a test moratorium would be transitory unless further progress in disarmament—aimed at effective controls and reduction of stockpiles—were evident.

Specifically, the agencies concluded:

In the interest of encouraging progress in disarmament among the major powers, there is popular support throughout most of the world for a ban on tests.
Hence, a U.S.-USSR agreement provisionally banning or limiting tests would
bring into play strong public pressures against testing by fourth countries,
even though such countries might not initially be parties to the agreement.

The test ban might not stop some countries, such as France, from testing,
said the report. "Nevertheless, popular pressure, among other reasons, would
probably force the Government to postpone further tests." In the longer run,
France would likely restrict its right to make weapons "only as part of an ar-
rangement which required reduction of the stockpiles of the major nuclear
powers." Similarly, international agreements would help deter Japan from
acquiring weapons, even if it were close to nuclear capability, as "not only
the public but the government as well would welcome any agreement which
promised to be effective . . . although they would be reluctant to accept re-
striction greater than those accepted by other fourth countries, notably Communist China."[4]

International agreements have their limits, the NIE noted: "The Chinese
Communists probably would not be deterred from nuclear weapons production by a limited disarmament agreement, except insofar as they might
be prevented by Soviet adherence and Soviet withholding of assistance from
China for development of a weapons program."[5]

Subsequent NIEs reaffirmed this linkage. The first assessment done
during John F. Kennedy's presidency, in September 1961, reviewed the capabilities of fourteen countries believed capable of developing an operational
nuclear weapon but noted that having the capability "does not answer the
question whether they will actually do so." The decision to go ahead with
a program "will depend on a complex of considerations both domestic and
international."[6]

Domestic considerations other than technical capabilities include cost,
security requirements, the desire to increase prestige, and domestic opposition to a program. International factors include the nature of relations with
other states and the international security climate. Significantly, the estimate
found:

The prospect of an agreement among the major powers for a nuclear test ban,
for example, especially if it were viewed as a forerunner to broader disarma-

ment steps, would undoubtedly strengthen force opposed to the spread of nuclear capabilities. Growing pessimism as to the likelihood of any realistic disarmament agreement could in some cases (e.g., Sweden, India) tend to undermine opposition to the acquisition of a national nuclear capability.[7]

These early NIEs were as concerned with the nuclear weapon decisions of U.S. friends and allies as they were with potential adversaries. They remind us that the proliferation problem has never been confined to hostile states. The considerations many U.S. allies had then mirror considerations these allies have today. The 1961 NIE examined each specific case, judged France and Israel as likely to develop weapons (France had tested in 1960; Israel would have a bomb by 1968), and found other likely cases were significantly dependent on international disarmament efforts. Specifically, Sweden would be technically capable of making a nuclear weapon by 1963.

> If at that time the international climate appeared to be calm, especially if positive steps toward disarmament had been agreed upon by the major powers—or there were reasonable hopes that one would materialize—it is unlikely that the Swedes would decide to undertake a nuclear weapons program. In the absence of such reassuring factors and especially if other countries had already decided to produce nuclear weapons, the pressure to initiate a nuclear weapons program would probably grow sharply.[8]

India, the estimate said, would be under great pressure to develop a nuclear weapon if China exploded a nuclear device; "even so, we believe India would not decide to devote its nuclear facilities to a weapons program unless its leaders were firmly convinced that no broad disarmament agreements were possible." Overall, the agencies judged the seven nations capable of developing nuclear weapons as unlikely to do so in the next few years but warned, "These attitudes and views could change in the coming years with changing circumstances, e.g., if it became increasingly clear that progress on international disarmament was unlikely."[9]

GILPATRIC COMMITTEE CONCLUDES WEAPON STATES MUST LEAD BY EXAMPLE

In January 1965, a report from President Johnson's Committee on Nuclear Proliferation, chaired by Roswell Gilpatric, concurred with the analysis of the earlier NIEs: "It is unlikely that others can be induced to abstain indefinitely from acquiring nuclear weapons if the Soviet Union and the United States continue in a nuclear arms race."[10] The first page of the report summarized:

> The Committee is now unanimous in its view that preventing the further spread of nuclear weapons is clearly in the national interest. . . . [T]he United States must, as a matter of great urgency, substantially increase the scope and intensity of our efforts if we are to have any hope of success. Necessarily, these efforts must be of three kinds:
>
> (a) negotiation of formal multilateral agreements;
> (b) the application of influence on individual nations considering nuclear weapons acquisition, by ourselves and in conjunction with others; and
> (c) example by our own policies and actions.[11]

The committee detailed necessary steps, including tougher export controls, stricter safeguards on civilian nuclear programs, and increased budgets for the IAEA, and it acknowledged the importance of the participation by the Soviet Union in efforts to stop proliferation. It warned: "Lessened emphasis by the United States and the Soviet Union on nuclear weapons, and agreements on broader arms-control measures must be recognized as important components in the overall program to prevent nuclear proliferation."[12] Its primary recommendation stressed the importance of multilateral agreements: "Measures to prevent particular countries from acquiring nuclear weapons are unlikely to succeed unless they are taken in support of a broad international prohibition applicable to many countries."[13] These agreements should include a global nonproliferation agreement (President Johnson concluded the Non-Proliferation Treaty in 1968 and President Richard Nixon secured its ratification in 1970); nuclear-free zones, particularly in Latin America and Africa (both have such treaties in effect today); and a comprehensive test ban (concluded in 1996 but yet to enter into force).

After noting specific recommendations for policies toward individual nations and increased safeguards, the committee concluded: "If we are to minimize the incentives for others to acquire nuclear weapons, it is important that we avoid giving an exaggerated impression of their importance and utility and that we stress the current and future important role of conventional armaments."[14]

DISARMAMENT AS PART OF A WEB OF RESTRAINTS

While progress toward disarmament is important, no assessment ever found that it was the only factor in nonproliferation. NIEs usually included a web of issues influencing the decisions of individual nations on nuclear weapons programs. A December 1975 estimate summarized: "Threshold-crossers' decisions will be strongly affected by what happens in the whole complex web of international relations—North-South disputes, East-West relations, economic, technological and military developments."[15] The main reasons that states acquire nuclear weapons are security, prestige, domestic politics, and, to a lesser degree, technology and economics. The reasons states do not develop nuclear weapons can be grouped into the same set of factors: security, prestige, domestic politics, technology, and economics.

Each driver for acquiring nuclear weapons has a matching barrier. That is, states decide not to build nuclear weapons—or, in some cases, give up weapons they have acquired or programs they have started—because they decide that the security benefits are greater without nuclear weapons or that prestige is enhanced by non-nuclear-weapon status, because domestic politics convince leaders not to pursue these programs, or because the technological and economic barriers are too significant to overcome.

An effective nonproliferation policy will minimize the drivers and maximize the barriers. A recent example of this approach is found in the 2007 NIE on Iran. The assessment concluded, "Tehran's decisions are guided by a cost-benefit approach rather than a rush to a weapon irrespective of the political, economic, and military costs." It found that "some combination of threats of intensified international scrutiny and pressures, along with opportunities for Iran to achieve its security, prestige, and goals for regional influence in other ways" might convince Tehran to halt its nuclear program.[16]

The United States on its own or through its alliances could influence some of these factors in the case of Iran or other states. But the global nonproliferation regime has proved a formidable barrier. Since the signing of the NPT, many more countries have given up nuclear weapon programs than have begun them. In the 1960s, twenty-three states had nuclear weapons, were conducting weapons-related research, or were actively discussing the pursuit of nuclear weapons. Today, only ten states have nuclear weapons or are believed to be seeking them.[17] Before the NPT entered into force, only six nations abandoned indigenous nuclear weapon programs that were under way or under consideration: Egypt, Italy, Japan, Norway, Sweden, and West Germany. Since then, Argentina, Australia, Belarus, Brazil, Canada, Iraq, Kazakhstan, Libya, Romania, South Africa, South Korea, Spain, Switzerland, Taiwan, Ukraine, and Yugoslavia have all abandoned nuclear weapon programs or nuclear weapons (or both). Now North Korea, Iran, and Pakistan are the only three states in the world that began acquiring nuclear capabilities after the NPT entered into force and have not ceased their efforts.

In other words, the reason that more states do not have nuclear weapons is because many nations, working together, have implemented polices to steadily reduce the role and numbers and desirability of nuclear weapons in the world. The reason that there are still nine nations with 17,000 weapons is that these policies have not gone further, faster. These policies are institutionalized in a global nonproliferation regime composed of treaties, security assurances, export restrictions, inspections and disarmament agreements. This regime will crumble if the consensus built on disarmament and nonproliferation commitments is not restored.

HISTORY'S VERDICT

History has borne out U.S. assessments of the essential connection between controlling existing arsenals and preventing new ones. These previous national estimates can assist today's officials in efforts to apply the same logic to current threats. The Strategic Posture Commission's interim report recognized this connection, noting, "The fact that other states possess nuclear weapons continues to affect decisions about the needed U.S. strategic posture." The reverse is also true: The fact that the United States and other nations possess nuclear weapons continues to affect other states' decisions about nuclear strategies. The interim report's Finding 10, that "other nations are unlikely to eliminate their nuclear weapons just because the United States does so," is true, but they are also unlikely to eliminate their weapons if the United States does not. A negotiated process of nuclear reductions and restraints has proven to be an essential element for convincing states to limit or eliminate their weapons and weapon programs.

The final report of the commission indicates the delicate balance that must be struck in these policies.

Programs to maintain the deterrent force are largely national programs, although their implementation involves a substantial international component with allies. In contrast, arms control and nonproliferation and associated activities are inherently international in character and their success requires the broadest possible international support.

This can become important when there are conflicts or trade-offs between the two. For example, a U.S. policy agenda that seems to stress unnecessarily our nuclear weapon posture could erode international cooperation to reduce nuclear dangers. Conversely, a policy agenda that emphasizes unilateral reductions could weaken the deterrence of foes and the assurance of allies. It is necessary to strike a balance in meeting these two imperatives.[18]

That is why the primary recommendation of the commission (for which I served as an expert advisor) was: "The United States should continue to pursue an approach to reducing nuclear dangers that balances deterrence, arms control, and non-proliferation. Singular emphasis on one or another element would reduce the nuclear security of the United States and its allies."[19]

Recognizing the enduring relationship between the reduction of existing nuclear arsenals and the prevention of new ones, the 2010 Nuclear Posture Review found: "By demonstrating that we take seriously our NPT obligation to pursue nuclear disarmament, we strengthen our ability to mobilize broad international support for the measures needed to reinforce the non-proliferation regime and secure nuclear materials worldwide."[20] These findings are correct, if regularly contested by supporters of the nuclear status quo. History provides ample evidence that a steady, determined commitment by the United States and other nuclear-armed nations to eliminate nuclear weapons and to take practical, immediate steps toward that goal will improve U.S. security and substantially enhance prospects for preventing the acquisition of nuclear weapons by new states and by terrorist groups.

TEN
THE END OF PROLIFERATION

It is common to hear people talk about "states like Iran and North Korea." But there are no states like Iran and North Korea. These states are really the last of their kind. Apart from the eight nations with established nuclear weapons programs, there are no other nations racing to establish the capability to build nuclear weapons and certainly none with the hostility and disdain for the international system exhibited by North Korea and Iran. If both programs can be contained, curtailed, and ultimately rolled back, it then becomes possible to talk about the end of proliferation.

There would remain, of course, the threshold problem presented by states with advanced nuclear power programs. Any state with nuclear reactors can, theoretically, evolve that program into a nuclear weapons capability. Any state with the ability to enrich uranium for fuel rods, like Brazil, could theoretically use those facilities to enrich uranium for weapons.

Any state that extracts plutonium from spent fuel rods, like Japan, could fashion that plutonium into bombs. There are a few states, like South Korea, that seek to acquire uranium-enrichment or plutonium-reprocessing capabilities as part of their civilian fuel-production enterprises. But this is a categorically different problem. It is a problem inherent in the spread of nuclear technology for civilian use. All such technology could be applied to future military purposes.

Over the course of the nuclear age, perhaps thirty nations have gone down this path, or at least explored it. More nations abandoned their programs than consolidated as nuclear weapon powers. No other nation today—not Syria, whose nuclear reactor was bombed by Israel and never replaced, nor Burma, which does not appear to have gotten far with some rumored nuclear trade with North Korea—comes close to the scale and sophistication of the programs in Iran and North Korea. In other words, no other nations are looming on the new-nuclear-state horizon.

It is true that if North Korea consolidates as a nuclear weapon state, with new nuclear tests and a growing arsenal, or if Iran crosses the nuclear Rubicon and declares itself a nuclear weapon power, then pressures will grow on some of their neighbors to seek to match their capability. North Korea's nuclear test in 2013 stirred conservatives in South Korea to openly call for the South to develop its own weapons. Though this is unlikely in the near future, this debate could move other nations to begin to hedge their bets by seeking their own enrichment or reprocessing capabilities, and those with it may move ever closer to the development of nuclear weapons. We could see the cascade of proliferation that many experts have predicted, a new wave of nuclear weapon programs similar to the wave that rose then receded in the 1960s.

But there is nothing automatic about this process; there are powerful counterpressures and barriers to the spread of nuclear weapons. Colin Kahl, Melissa Galton, and Matthew Irvine argue in a 2013 study that

> predictions of inevitable proliferation cascades have historically proven false.... In the six decades since atomic weapons were first developed, nuclear restraint has proven far more common than nuclear proliferation, and cases of reactive proliferation have been exceedingly rare. Moreover, most countries that have started down the nuclear path have found the road more difficult than imagined, both technologically and bureaucratically, leading the majority of nuclear-weapons aspirants to reverse course.[1]

Indeed, even though North Korea has tested nuclear weapons three times and has medium-range missiles that could deliver nuclear warheads to the surrounding states, none of its nuclear-capable neighbors has actually begun a weapon program of its own. Kahl and his colleagues argue persuasively that Iran's neighbors would be similarly unlikely to race to get nuclear weapons even if Iran did. They would be limited both by their own technological, economic, and political realities (Egypt and Turkey) and by solid security calculations. "The Saudis are unlikely to engage in a race to indigenously produce the bomb because doing so could make the Kingdom's strategic predicament worse, not better," they write. "It would complicate the Kingdom's national security, risk a strategic rupture with the United States, do great damage to Saudi Arabia's international reputation and potentially make Riyadh the target of international sanctions. Furthermore, technical and bureaucratic constraints make a Saudi dash to nuclear weapons implausible."[2] But dramatic progress by North Korea or Iran would certainly increase proliferation incentives, requiring a major effort by the United States and other nations to establish new security assurances in the regions and new methods of isolating and punishing the proliferators.

THE PYONGYANG PUZZLE

Effective diplomacy has constrained but not ended the program in North Korea. As much as some would wish, there is no viable military option that could end the nuclear program or topple the dictatorial regime. Korea remains the most heavily militarized region on earth. An attack on North Korea could trigger a conventional war that would kill hundreds of thousands of South Koreans in the first few hours. Trying to run out the clock on the regime is risky as well. History shows that this hermit kingdom cannot be contained or ignored indefinitely. Philip Yun, a North Korea expert and the executive director of Ploughshares Fund, warns:

> Just as a policy of fostering regime change is not tenable, a seemingly reasonable wait-and-see/status quo approach is also inadequate. It could sow the seeds for yet another nuclear test in 2013, which could lead to engineering advances that allow the totalitarian North to produce smaller (and more) nuclear warheads. And what better way for a determined North Korea to "market" its nuclear know-how for export?[3]

Diplomatic efforts have made it increasingly difficult for North Korea to engage in the kind of nuclear and missile trade that proved lucrative in the past.
The Carnegie Endowment senior associate Mark Hibbs notes that cooperat-
ing member states of the United Nations "have increased their surveillance of
North Korea's shipping fleet." As a result, "more than ever before, the number
and whereabouts of North Korean vessels is understood and tracked in real
time, assisting efforts to interdict suspicious cargo."[4]

Narrowing North Korea's options, restricting its ability to trade technology for cash, and tightening financial sanctions on the regime are all necessary steps as is continued engagement to seek a negotiated solution. Unfor-
tunately, none of the nations pressuring and engaging North Korea has put in
place a coherent, sustained, or successful effort. Paul Carroll of Ploughshares
Fund, who has visited North Korea more times than most people would care
to, summarized the problem in a 2012 article for the *Yale Journal of International Affairs*:

> Both the United States and China have been thoroughly engaged with North
> Korea, but the *nature* of that engagement has been flawed. For China, its de-
> fault position has been to provide aid and political cover when most of the rest
> of the world is turning the screws in response to misbehavior. China ultimately
> provides enough food and other assistance to keep the regime in power and
> the state intact. But that is all it has done. The United States has also paid
> plenty of attention to the DPRK. But that attention has almost always been
> punitive: unilateral or UN-sponsored sanctions as a reaction to provocative ac-
> tions taken by the North. Neither China's propping up nor the United States'
> beating down is sufficient to achieve the security aims each has with respect
> to Pyongyang.[5]

David Albright and Christina Walrond of the Institute for Science and International Security estimate that North Korea has produced enough plutonium for six to eighteen nuclear weapons.[6] Others put the figure lower. Siegfried Hecker, a Stanford University senior fellow and former director of Los
Alamos National Laboratory, estimates the North Korean stockpile might be
enough for four to eight "primitive nuclear devices."[7] But clearly North Korea
has enough material for several bombs.

Negotiated agreements shut down North Korea's production of plutonium, and these have not restarted. The country is believed to be building a
new nuclear reactor that could produce plutonium, but the grade produced

would not be ideal for nuclear weapons. The North Korean regime admits it has begun a centrifuge program to produce, it says, enriched uranium for this new reactor. These centrifuges could be used to enrich uranium to weapons grade, but it is not believed to have done so as of early 2013. Any negotiated deal with North Korea would have to bring an end to both production programs.

As difficult as talks with North Korea have proven, there is no viable alternative. Efforts to coerce North Korea into compliance or collapse have failed. As I detailed in *Bomb Scare*, Bush-administration policies vacillated between negotiations and regime change. After emphasizing regime change during the first Bush term, the policy swung back to negotiations through the Six-Party talks involving the United States, North Korea, South Korea, Japan, China, and Russia. In September 2005 the parties announced an agreement wherein the United States reaffirmed its desire for peaceful relations with North Korea; the United States and North Korea agreed in principle to work toward the normalization of relations; and North Korea pledged to walk back its nuclear program, readmit international inspectors, and adhere to the Non-Proliferation Treaty. But the agreement was torpedoed by a U.S. Treasury Department announcement the next day of strong new sanctions on the bank, Banco Delta Asia, a major financial conduit for North Korea and for North Korean leaders.

The intent may have been to increase pressure to get a deal, but it appears more likely to have been part of the effort by some in the administration to strangle North Korea as the sanctions hit *after* the agreement was reached. As Michael Mazarr and James Goodby document:

> The Treasury Department's BDA scheme crashed into this strategy like an unguided missile. Those who credit the BDA scheme with "getting the North back to the table" therefore misunderstand the chronology: a major deal was in the offing when the BDA charges drove the North *away* from the Six Party Talks. Some State officials have claimed that they were not warned of the BDA sanctions in advance; others, and Treasury officials, dispute this contention. What is not in dispute is Pyongyang's reaction: it was immediate and furious. In bilateral meetings, North Korean officials harped on the subject, demanding return of their funds as a precondition for further progress in negotiations.[8]

It was not that the sanctions were not effective; they were. Banco Delta Asia suffered a major loss of funds; other banks backed away from doing business with North Korea; North Korea's ability to conduct business with other nations was seriously constrained. But the economic pressure failed to achieve either a collapse of the regime or an end to the nuclear program. Quite the opposite: the nuclear program expanded. By 2007, the administration was forced to back down, returning Pyongyang's sequestered BDA funds. Talks resumed, but with North Korea now convinced that the United States could not be trusted and real purpose of U.S. actions was not to end the nuclear program but to end the regime. The election of a new president in 2008 did not change North Korean views as they, like Iran, believe that U.S. strategy is little affected by a change in parties; it is the same policy with a different face.

The lesson, proven once again in this case, is that the point of sanctions is to drive toward a negotiated deal. Sanctions alone can never work to force compliance or a change in regime. They must be part of an integrated strategy that combines pressures with incentives, culminating in a negotiated compromise that serves both parties' interests and allows leaders on all sides to claim victory. Siegfried Hecker argues that however difficult it may be, the United States must engage North Korea as well as pressure it. "The fundamental and enduring goal must be the denuclearization of the Korean peninsula," he writes, "However, since that will take time, the U.S. government must quickly press for what I call 'the three no's'—no more bombs, no better bombs, and no exports—in return for one yes: Washington's willingness to seriously address North Korea's fundamental insecurity along the lines of the joint communiqué."[9] Very similar dynamics are present when trying to deal with the thorny issue of Iran.

TROUBLES WITH TEHRAN

On the morning of June 14, 2012, American negotiators were sitting across a table in Moscow facing Iranian representatives as part of the "P5+1" talks, convened to try to find a compromise solution to the nuclear standoff with Iran. Back in the United States, TV viewers heard an ominous voice warn, "It's time to act!" as a fiery ballistic missile launched across their screens in New York and Washington, D.C. The voice was narrating a commercial, produced by the neoconservative organization the Emergency Committee for Israel that made a not-so-subtle case to strike Iran:

> President Obama says we must prevent the Iranian regime from getting nuclear weapons. Yet talking isn't accomplishing this goal. Today, Iran has six

times more enriched uranium than when President Obama came into office—enough for five nuclear bombs. We fear that the Obama administration is now intent on kicking the can down the road past the election. The Emergency Committee urges the president to live up to his promise to stop Iran. Don't delay. Don't ask others to do our job for us. It's time to act.

In 2012, there was little appetite in the United States for another war. U.S. combat troops had just pulled out of Iraq and are slated to come out of Afghanistan by 2014. The public was almost completely focused on domestic problems—a recovering economy, high unemployment, and a sluggish housing market. There was enormous pressure on the Defense Department to cut its budget. A survey of public opinion by the Chicago Council on Global Affairs released in September 2012 found that while Americans saw the Middle East "as the greatest source of future threats, they are gradually shifting their foreign policy focus towards Asia and a rising China." The survey found a decidedly antiwar public. Just over half of those surveyed (51 percent) opposed a military strike on Iran, even if the United Nations authorized one. A whopping 70 percent opposed a U.S. strike on Iran, and 60 percent did not want the United States to get involved in any war between Israel and Iran.[10]

Iran's slow but relentless expansion of its nuclear program, however, combined with the insistence by some inside and outside America that military action was the only way to stop the program and a media whose drive for viewers and readers encourages breathless speculation about imminent war, made Iran the dominant nuclear policy and national security issue for most of 2011 and 2012. This was not because Iran had a nuclear bomb, was close to making a nuclear bomb, or, according to the best U.S. and allied intelligence, had made a decision to build a nuclear bomb. Iran's nuclear capabilities were thus far confined to the fuel cycle, which was the major topic of negotiation in the P5+1 talks. Iran holds that it is guaranteed access to the peaceful uses of nuclear technology—including the right to enrich uranium—as a member of the nuclear Non-Proliferation Treaty. Iran's neighbors and most of the West are wary that Iran is hedging for the capability to "sprint to the bomb" if it chooses to do so. Experts at the International Institute for Strategic Studies note:

> Iran's nuclear effort is designed to support an independent nuclear-power program. But the still secretive nature of the program, its economic inefficiency and inconsistencies, and the substantial evidence that has emerged of nuclear

weapons-related research raise questions about Iran's actual purpose. The nation is investing vast resources in a complete nuclear fuel-cycle, which, without significant improvements in centrifuge power and foreign supply or new discoveries of uranium, would barely be able to sustain a single Bushehr-type reactor. The evidence leads to a conclusion that the program is also intended to give Iran a nuclear weapons capability.[11]

Iran is working to master all stages of the nuclear fuel cycle, including mining, milling, enrichment, fuel fabrication, and conversion. It is furthest along on enrichment, thanks, in part, to centrifuge designs and components Iran illegally bought from the A. Q. Khan network.[12] It is enriching uranium at two sites. The major site, the Natanz Fuel Enrichment Plant, is under IAEA safeguards, meaning inspectors regularly visit the plant and report on production and other activities. The majority of the Natanz centrifuges enrich the uranium to 3.5 percent, supposedly as fuel for the country's power reactor. However, a smaller facility at the site enriches to close to 20 percent, supposedly as fuel for Iran's research reactor. Fordow, a previously clandestine facility tunneled into the mountains near the holy city of Qom, began enriching to close to 20 percent in 2011.[13] Iran steadily increased the number of centrifuges at Fordow during 2011 and 2012.

Much analysis is centered on "breakout" scenarios—different pathways Iran could take to build a nuclear weapon. According to David Albright, it would take Iran four to twelve months to make enough uranium for nuclear weapons.[14] That is, Iran could take the low-enriched uranium (LEU) and feed it back into its centrifuges to quickly enrich it to the approximately 90 percent grade (high-enriched uranium or HEU) needed for a nuclear weapon. The world would almost certainly see this happening:

> In order to conduct a dash using LEU at Natanz, Iran would need to visibly violate its commitments under the NPT, including diverting the LEU from IAEA safeguards and likely ejecting IAEA inspectors from the country. Although only minor modifications may be necessary in the Natanz FEP infrastructure before Iran could start to enrich to weapon-grade levels, any dash using the FEP would not proceed quickly. Based on ISIS's most recent calculations, reflecting reduced performance of the centrifuges in the FEP over the last year, but more enriching centrifuges, Iran would need about four months to produce enough weapon-grade uranium for just one bomb. And in undertaking such a

risky effort in which its facilities could be destroyed by military strikes, Iran would likely want to be able to produce enough weapon-grade uranium to make several weapons.[15]

It would take Iran an additional one to three years to turn this uranium into a warhead for a ballistic missile.

Given these growing capabilities, there is a desire by some in the United States to push for a military attack on Iran's facilities. This has the support of some of Iran's not-so-friendly neighbors. Iran's Arab rivals in the Gulf would like the United States to "cut off the head of the snake," as one leader famously put it in a conversation with U.S. officials later disclosed by one of the WikiLeaks cables. Given the strident rhetoric from the Iranian regime, some Israeli leaders understandably view an Iranian nuclear weapon as a grave threat. Speaking at the American Israeli Public Affairs Committee in March 2012, Prime Minister Benjamin Netanyahu issued a ringing warning: "Israel has waited patiently for the international community to resolve [Iran]. We've waited for diplomacy to work. We've waited for sanctions to work. None of us can afford to wait much longer."[16]

Would a military strike actually slow the program down? Some conservative politicians in both the United States and Israel viewed a military strike as the best solution to Iran's nuclear ambitions and urged a strike before Iran entered what Israeli officials called "a zone of immunity," where Iran could enrich uranium for a bomb quickly in mountain redoubts safe from aerial bombardment. U.S. officials repeatedly declared that a military option was not off the table, but many military leaders and experts doubted the benefits of a military strike and feared the unintended consequences. Colin Kahl at the Center for New American Security, a former deputy assistant secretary of defense for the Middle East, spoke for many when he rebutted calls for war in his March 2012 *Foreign Affairs* article:

> The lesson of Iraq, the last preventive war launched by the United States, is that Washington should not choose war when there are still other options, and it should not base its decision to attack on best-case analyses of how it hopes the conflict will turn out. A realistic assessment of Iran's nuclear progress and how a conflict would likely unfold leads one to a conclusion . . . now is not the time to attack Iran.[17]

A military strike on Iran would not be a trivial affair. If conducted by the United States it would involve hundreds of air strikes over many days or weeks. Secretary of Defense Leon Panetta warned, "The consequence could be that we would have an escalation that would take place that would not only involve many lives, but I think it could consume the Middle East in a confrontation and a conflict that we would regret."[18]

The former commander in chief of the Central Command, General Anthony Zinni, was more blunt, saying that he liked to respond to advocates of attacking Iran with "And then what?"

> After you've dropped those bombs on those hardened facilities, what happens next? What happens if they decide, in their hardened shelters with their mobile missiles, to start launching those? What happens if they launch them into U.S. bases on the other side of the Gulf? What happens if they launch into Israel, or somewhere else? Into a Saudi oil field? Into Ras Laffan, with all the natural gas? What happens if they now flush their fast patrol boats, their cruise missiles, the strait full of mines, and they sink a tanker, an oil tanker? And of course the economy of the world goes absolutely nuts. What happens if they activate sleeper cells? . . . What happens if there's another preemptive attack by the West, the U.S. and Israel, they fire up the streets, and now we've got problems. Just tell me how to deal with all that, OK?
>
> Because, eventually, if you follow this all the way down, eventually I'm putting boots on the ground somewhere. And like I tell my friends, if you like Iraq and Afghanistan, you'll love Iran.[19]

Kahl wrote, "While the potential costs of attacking Iran are fairly clear, the potential benefits are uncertain."[20] Even though a strike could damage current operations, Iran already has the know-how to restart its nuclear program, probably at a faster pace. Iran would officially withdrawal from the NPT and kick out IAEA inspectors, creating more uncertainty about the progress of a restarted program. A preemptive strike on Iran would likely rally the country around an otherwise unpopular Iranian regime. Secretary of State Hillary Clinton outlined this concern in June 2012:

> There are those [in the Iranian government] who are saying, "The best thing that could happen to us is be attacked by somebody. Just bring it on because that would unify us." It would legitimize the regime. [The regime] doesn't represent the will of the people. It's kind of morphed into kind of a military theoc-

racy. And, therefore, an argument is made constantly on the hard-line side of the Iranian government that, you know, "We're not going to give anything up. And in fact we're going to provoke an attack because then we will be in power for as long as anyone can imagine."[21]

Many officials in the Israeli security establishment were also vocal in their concerns. Meir Dagan, former head of the Mossad, the national intelligence agency of Israel, called an attack on Iran "stupid" and a surefire way to start a Middle East war.[22] By the end of 2012, elite and popular opinion appeared to be strongly against a military strike on Iran. Many experts agreed with Bill Keller of the *New York Times*, who argued that if the worst happened, a nuclear-armed Iran could be contained and deterred:

> Despite the incendiary rhetoric, it is hard to believe the aim of an Iranian nuclear program is the extermination of Israel. The regime in Iran is brutal, mendacious and meddlesome, and given to spraying gobbets of Hitleresque bile at the Jewish state. But Israel is a nuclear power, backed by a bigger nuclear power. Before an Iranian mushroom cloud had bloomed to its full height over Tel Aviv, a flock of reciprocal nukes would be on the way to incinerate Iran. Iran may encourage fanatic chumps to carry out suicide missions, but there is not the slightest reason to believe the mullahs themselves are suicidal.[23]

Former national security advisor Zbigniew Brzezinski, speaking at a conference sponsored by the Arms Control Association and the National Iranian American Council on November 27, 2012, warned that "some of the energy for sanctions is driven simply by a kind of almost fanatical commitment to a showdown with the Iranians." If the pressure from existing sanctions and negotiations efforts do not yield results, he counseled, the best option would not be war but a mix of enhanced sanctions and deterrence. "Deterrence has worked against a far more powerful, far more dangerous, and indeed, objectively, more aggressive opponents in years past," he said. U.S. policy should be to prevent Iran from getting "a significant military nuclear capability," he said, and not focus on "a hypothetical, imaginary, non-credible notion that the moment they have one or two bombs they'll eagerly rush into national suicide."[24]

In much of the debate over Iran policy in 2011 and 2012, however, there was a steady current of commentary from those, like the columnist Charles Krauthammer, who argued the Iranian leadership cannot be deterred because they are not like other people. They are irrational, operating on a different level, more concerned with the Islamic afterlife than material concerns such as their nation, fortunes, families, or even their own lives. While the leadership has made many incendiary statements, there is little in the historic record of the regime to indicate that they are irrational. Chairman of the Joint Chiefs General John Dempsey declared flatly in March 2012, "The Iran regime is a rational actor."[25]

"Iran has been very calculating in its behavior, far more so than other so-called radical, revolutionary regimes," said CNN anchor Fareed Zakaria, on whose program Gen. Dempsey made his remarks. "If you look at Mao's China, he talked openly about destroying the world and about sacrificing half of China so that global communism could survive. The Iranians never talk like that and they certainly don't do things like that. Their behavior for 30 years has been calculating. They respond to inducements and pressures in ways that are completely understandable."[26] Bill Keller noted, "The religious-military-political conglomerate that rules Iran have a powerful instinct for self-preservation."[27]

In short, Iran and North Korea are difficult, idiosyncratic regimes skirting on the edge of the international system. But they are not unstoppable threats beyond the capabilities of the United States and its allies and partners. It is possible—and I have long argued—that the nuclear threats presented by North Korea and Iran can be isolated and deterred by the right combination of pressure and incentives. The major powers must constantly remind these nations of the potential benefits of rejoining the community of nations and complying with their international treaty obligations as well as the continued and escalating costs of their failure to do so. Coercive measures alone have never forced a nation into capitulation or compliance. A strategy that couples the pressures of sanctions, diplomatic isolation, investment freezes, travel restrictions, and other economic measures with practical compromises and realizable security agreements can, over the long run, encourage both these nations that they can realize their security, prestige, and regional goals more assuredly through a non-nuclear-weapons path.[28]

This path is not easy, but there are no alternatives. Those offered have failed the test of history, both recent and long term. Forcible regime change in Iran or North Korea, for example, is infeasible, given it would require a military effort larger than the wars in Iraq and Afghanistan combined. Peaceful regime change will not succeed any time soon, given the weakness of the opposition in Iran and North Korea, the problems that U.S. backing would present for those inside the countries, and the limited tools available for the United States to affect their internal politics. Nor is it likely that the U.S. negotiators could soon realize the extensive compromises and breakthroughs necessary to produce a "grand bargain" that would normalize relations and resolve outstanding issues with either nation—should they even desire this. With Iran, in particular, surgical military strikes against known nuclear assets would only set the Iranian nuclear program back a few years and would stiffen Iranian resolve to produce a weapon in the near future. Muddling through with the current approach of stiff sanctions and half-hearted incentives has not worked. We are left, almost by process of elimination, with a strategy of matching the sanctions with genuine compromise including the willingness to accept Iran's right to enrich uranium under stringent international inspections—that could produce first a pause in the enrichment program then its limitation.

If, despite our best efforts, Iran or North Korea or both persist in nuclear pursuits, a combination of security assurances to neighboring states and continued isolation can contain and deter the new nuclear threats either or both would present. Though not the desired outcome, it is far preferable to the consequences of a major regional war in the Middle East or Northeast Asia. These nations are, after all, economically feeble, without military or political alliances or influence. It is the United States that remains the undisputed economic and military superpower with a vast international network of security and financial alliances.

Indeed, curtailing these programs, containing them if nonproliferation efforts fail, and holding them as an example of the high price to be paid for breaking treaty obligations are necessary not just to stop the spread of nuclear weapons but to have any hope of moving toward a world without them. "The vision of a world free of nuclear weapons will hold little attraction if it appears to be impossible to prevent states (or non-state actors) from concealing existing nuclear weapons or building new nuclear weapons in a clandestine manner," warns the Stanford University scholar and nuclear historian David Holloway. "Moreover, the nuclear-weapon states will not eliminate their nuclear forces if new states are acquiring nuclear weapons, i.e., if the nuclear nonproliferation regime appears to be breaking down."[29]

President Obama underscored the vital importance of enforcement in Prague when he declared, along with his vision and his near-term practical steps, that "rules must be binding. Violations must be punished. Words must mean something."

The president is right. Jessica Mathews, Rose Gottemoeller, George Perkovich, Jon B. Wolfsthal, and I wrote of the importance of enforcement in our Carnegie Endowment for International Peace study, *Universal Compliance: A Strategy for Nuclear Security*:

> Perhaps the most ambitious attempt ever made to extend the civilizing reach of the rule of law has been the international effort to constrain the acquisition and use of nuclear weapons, the greatest physical force created by humankind. The United States, the Soviet Union, and other states laid the foundation for this mission in the 1960s with the negotiation of the Nuclear Non-Proliferation Treaty (NPT). In the decades since, states have evolved rules and institutions to govern nuclear exports, safeguard and account for nuclear materials, and control and even reduce the number of nuclear weapons.
>
> The rules are not self-enforcing, as painful experience in Iraq, North Korea, Libya Iran, and elsewhere has shown. Moreover, states and international agencies must struggle to mobilize the power needed to enforce and adapt the rules as conditions change. Doing so involves difficult trade-offs as states seek benefits commensurate with the options they forgo and the costs they bear.[30]

Enforcement of the rules is not a job for one nation. Even if the American public wanted its government to be the world's detective, judge, and executioner—which it does not—it would be impossible even for a nation with all our power. As the authors just quoted wrote in 2005, "The United States cannot defeat the nuclear threat alone, or even with small coalitions of the willing."[31] But the job can be done with the joint efforts of dozens of diverse nations, large and small. It has been done.

There are fewer nations now with nuclear weapons or weapons programs than at any time since the early 1960s. In the 1960s, twenty-three nations were conducting weapons-related research, were discussing the pursuit of weapons, or already had weapons.[32] By the 1980s, the number was down to nineteen.[33] In 2012, the number was down to ten. Indeed, more nations have given up nuclear weapons and weapons programs in the past twenty-five years than have tried to acquire them. Continuing this progress means stopping or containing the programs in Iran and North Korea and continuing to reduce dramatically the existing arsenals. The responsibilities, enforcement, and restrictions must be shared by all. "The nuclear weapon states must show that tougher non-proliferation rules not only benefit the powerful but constrain them as well," we wrote in the Carnegie study. "Non-proliferation is a set of bargains whose fairness must be self-evident if the majority of countries is to support their enforcement."[34]

The methods are well known; the strategies, proven. Global leaders just need the political will to implement policies tested by history. It is very likely that if leading nations jointly continue to engage and contain these last two small but dangerous nuclear-state threats, proceed step-by-step to reduce the number and roles of nuclear weapons worldwide, collectively enforce existing nonproliferation rules, and work steadily to resolve the regional security conflicts that give rise to the proliferation imperative, the world will witness the end of the proliferation of nuclear weapons that began seven decades ago in the deserts of New Mexico.

We can, slowly and steadily, shrink and eventually completely dissipate our nuclear nightmares.

President Barack Obama seems to agree. On a warm December day at the end of 2012, the reelected president addressed his assembled nuclear security team at the National Defense University to commemorate twenty years of achievement of the Nunn-Lugar Cooperative Threat Reduction program. Named after the two senators who sponsored the legislation, Sam Nunn and Dick Lugar, the program has helped Russia and other successor states to the Soviet Union destroy thousands of nuclear-armed missiles and hundreds of silos, submarines, and bombers and deactivate more than 13,000 nuclear warheads that once threatened America and the world.

Just as the president had used his first foreign policy speech after becoming president in 2009 to talk about the elimination of nuclear weapons, he used his first national security speech after winning reelection to reaffirm his personal commitment to this goal and its critical importance to American national security. He talked about the continuing danger of nuclear, biological, and chemical weapons and recalled his trip with Senator Lugar to Ukraine, where they saw teams of workers funded by the U.S. program slowly and carefully taking apart old weapons. "We simply cannot allow the twenty-first century to be darkened by the worst weapons of the twentieth century," he said, then artfully bridged to his policy goals.

> It took decades—and extraordinary sums of money—to build those arsenals. It's going to take decades—and continued investments—to dismantle them. . . .

It's painstaking work. It rarely makes the headlines. But I want each of you to know, and everybody who's participating in this important effort to know that the work you do is absolutely vital to our national security and to our global security.

Missile by missile, warhead by warhead, shell by shell, we're putting a bygone era behind us. Inspired by Sam Nunn and Dick Lugar, we're moving closer to the future we seek. A future where these weapons never threaten our children again. A future where we know the security and peace of a world without nuclear weapons.[35]

Getting to that future is not something that one nation or one government can do. It will have to be a joint enterprise of several leading nations and their publics. The role of the publics in realizing this goal and, more specifically, of the private foundations that support many of the public and expert efforts detailed in this book is the subject of my concluding chapter.

ELEVEN
FOUNDATIONS

Kennette Benedict, who spent many years at the John D. and Catherine T. MacArthur Foundation before becoming publisher of *The Bulletin of the Atomic Scientists*, writes that too often "many of us lucky enough to live in democracies view elections as the only responsibility we have as citizens and leave the policy discussion to the elected and to the experts." We should not treat officials and experts as if they were our guardians, she warns; we should not turn over decisions of immense importance to the nation and to the entire human race to a small group. While appreciative of President Obama's knowledge and leadership, Benedict urges: "To free the world from nuclear danger, citizens in the United States and Russia, in particular, should claim their rightful places in the nuclear discussion, reignite their democracies, and work with each other and with President Obama and President Vladimir Putin to once and for all get rid of nuclear weapons—before they get rid of us."[1] She is right. President Obama during his initial campaign for the presidency and in his efforts for reelection spoke constantly of the need for public involvement to transform entrenched policies. "I can't do it alone" may be one of his most repeated phrases. For all the discussion in this book about Obama's views, the expert policy debates, and the struggles in Congress, in the end, it is the American people who will decide what course the nation takes on nuclear policy. The people create the political space that allows policy makers to take the tough decisions and the political will to actually do so.

It is true, of course, that governments set national security policies. But governments are influenced by many factors in the development of these policies, including public opinion, expert analysis, and domestic political considerations—all of which can have an impact behind the scenes. Money is not always necessary for the people to have their voices heard. But it helps. Ever since Andrew Carnegie gathered a group of distinguished Americans in Washington in December of 1910 to launch with his gift of ten million dollars the Carnegie Endowment for International Peace and charged them to "hasten the abolition of war, the foulest blot upon our civilization," foundations have played important roles in the search for practical, diplomatic solutions to conflicts. This concluding chapter describes in some detail how these efforts are at work on nuclear policy and takes, as a case study, the work of my own foundation, Ploughshares Fund.[2]

Philanthropists want to do good. Whether it is paying forward or giving back, they want to use their money to make a demonstrable improvement in the lives of others. There are two basic approaches that philanthropist may take: direct contributions to aid a relatively small group of people or investments intended to change social policy on a large scale.

The first approach usually funds specific local or national projects that directly help a community or social group. This might be constructing an art museum or hospital wing, supplying foot pumps so Indian farmers can irrigate a hectare of land, or funding an early education program that gives inner-city children the skills they need to succeed in school. There are hundreds of foundations, public and family-run, that pursue these types of programs. One of the largest, the Ford Foundation, awards over $420 million in grants each year to implement its mission to give all people "the opportunity to reach their full potential, contribute to society, and have voice in the decisions that affect them." The grants usually track with the foundation's mission statement:

> We believe the best way to achieve these goals is to encourage initiatives by those living and working closest to where problems are located; to promote collaboration among the nonprofit, government and business sectors; and to ensure participation by men and women from diverse communities and all levels of society. In our experience, such activities help build common understanding, enhance excellence, enable people to improve their lives and reinforce their commitment to society.[3]

In the second approach, individuals and foundations will often try to change public policy by funding research to provide objective, analytical support for policy change, promoting public-education efforts to build support for change or funding organizations that advocate for change. The John D. and Catherine T. MacArthur Foundation, as every listener of NPR knows, "supports creative people and effective institutions committed to building a more just, verdant, and peaceful world." MacArthur gives about $240 million in grants each year on a broad range of issues. It is one of the few foundations to provide substantial grants for international security issues. Under the leadership of its new president, Robert Gallucci, it focuses these latter grants on preventing nuclear terrorism and strengthening stability in the Asia-Pacific region, a key area of nuclear risk and competition.

In 2012, for example, the MacArthur Foundation announced the award of $13.4 million in grants to sixteen organizations to strengthen nuclear security around the globe. Much of the funding was directed to train and support "an elite group of nuclear experts to make policy recommendations for preventing nuclear terrorism and enhancing nuclear non-proliferation."[4] Gallucci explains the foundation's approach:

> The obligation of someone who runs a foundation is to figure out what is the proper place for us. Where should we stand? On which issues? Try to accomplish what and how? How do we use those resources to get the change, the impact on the human condition?
>
> What most foundations, including MacArthur, try to do is to use the money we have . . . and try to have an impact in some areas, but an impact that is outsized, where we have leveraged in some way the amount of money that we have.
>
> Wherever we decide we are going to work, we are looking for a strategic approach . . . looking for leverage, looking for substantial change so at the end

of the day my colleagues and I can go home and say we did right by the confidence that was placed in us by the American people.[5]

Ploughshares Fund takes this leveraging strategy a step further. It is an operating foundation that coordinates grants around a specific strategic objective and then applies the talents of its staff to network the grantees together for near-term policy impact. This model, dubbed "impact philanthropy," provides both a case study in effective grant making and a model for one way that modest grants can achieve an outsized impact and promote significant policy change.

THE BIG CUBE

"The results of work in the big cube are often measurable only by small statistical changes," say Paul Brest and Hal Harvey in their seminal guide to philanthropy, *Money Well Spent*, "and even small changes may take many decades to emerge."[6]

Brest, then president of the William and Flora Hewlett Foundation, and Harvey, then CEO and president of ClimateWorks, developed a three-axes chart of social issues ranging from the "small cube" to the "big cube." Work in the small cube focuses on "local, quality-of-life, reversible problems." Work in the big cube deals with "global, life-threatening, irreversible problems." The latter "tend to require ambitious grantmaking, and require funders with a tolerance for ambiguity and complexity."

> But the advantages of working at the edges of the big cube are profound. When you are successful, your efforts will affect millions of people and can prevent irreversible damage. The patience, the risk, the indirectness of such work can be compensated for by astounding leverage. If you do this right, your money will reach its fullest potential.[7]

Since 1981, Ploughshares Fund has tackled a classic big-cube problem, the global threat of nuclear weapons. This has required the fund's leaders to understand the need to keep their sights set on the horizon while pursuing strategies that make steady progress toward the ultimate goal. Foundations involved in other big-cube problems do the same in their efforts to ameliorate climate change or eradicate a devastating disease. Each victory may seem small, but the key is to identify—and win—those steps that can unlock the more ambitious strategic agenda.

For most of its thirty-two years, Ploughshares Fund has specialized in finding what it has called "the smartest people with the best ideas" for ways to reduce the dangers from nuclear, chemical, and biological weapons. There is a remarkable pool of talented individuals that Ploughshares Fund and other foundations have been pleased to support over the years. Many have been cited in this book. From grassroots organizers to Stanford professors, some of the most talented people in the country have dedicated their lives to these issues. Their success has been the foundation's success.

Brest and Harvey highlighted the fund as a prime example of dedicated work "at the edges of the big cube." Ploughshares Fund, they noted in 2008, has a mission of preventing the use of weapons of mass destruction.

> The fund, using its budget with strategic brilliance, made a principal contribution to the International Campaign to Ban Land Mines. Ploughshares grantees were instrumental in the renegotiations of the Nuclear Non-Proliferation Treaty. The fund supported high-level, off-the-record negotiations between senior U.S. analysts and North Korean officials that may have averted a war during the Clinton administration.
>
> Ploughshares took on a hugely important realm of work that was not heavily supported by philanthropy. It built an expert board of directors, learned its field well, and has had an impact disproportionately large for its size. Given their ambitious choice of goals, it is evident that Ploughshares donors have a tolerance for substantial abstraction and significant risk of failure.[8]

By mid-2009, the fund had more than doubled in size from the $4-million-a-year operation based in San Francisco that Brest and Harvey had critiqued. The visionary founding president, Sally Lillienthal, passed away, and the board hired me as president to carry on her work; open an additional office in Washington, D.C.; and take the organization to a new level. Key to the transition was a skilled and involved board of directors composed of philanthropists, scholars, former senior officials and military leaders, and successful business executives. They provided not only much of the funding but the push for a more active, involved approach.

The board adapted Brest and Harvey's ideas to create a new model of philanthropy to secure a true "victory in the big cube." Largely under the direction of the former executive director Naila Bolus and board chair Roger Hale, the organization designed and implemented an ambitious campaign to build awareness of the importance of the New START treaty in 2010. The agreement between the United States and Russia was not, by itself, a fulfillment of President Barack Obama's pledge "to seek the peace and security of a world without nuclear weapons," but it was a major and essential step in the process, one whose outcome was initially by no means certain.

At the beginning of 2010, the journalist Josh Rogin wrote in *Foreign Policy* that President Obama's nuclear agenda was "faltering out of the starting gate."[9] Negotiations with the Russians over the expired START treaty were dragging on, battle lines were being drawn in Congress, and opponents were successfully framing President Obama as weak, naïve, or worse. But Ploughshares Fund and many of its grantees believed the nation was at a unique historical moment. As Bolus wrote in the *Chronicle of Philanthropy*:

> We and many of our grantees knew that if the Senate defeated New START, progress on the rest of the nuclear security agenda would stop cold. If we played it right, we could help shape a series of victories that together could fundamentally reorient U.S.—and global—nuclear policy. The window, however, would not remain open for long.[10]

The campaign for New START developed an impact-philanthropy model that can be replicated by other foundations. It consists of three essential steps: craft a strategy with clear goals; select grantees and knit them together into a collaborative network; and commit the foundation's assets to provide leadership and amplify the grantees' work. Or, more succinctly: strategy, network, and leadership.

THE NEW START CAMPAIGN

Ploughshares Fund has always been a "hands-on" operation, working closely with its grantees and encouraging various forms of cooperation and integration. Indeed, my first exposure to the fund was in late 1993, when I ended almost ten years of work as a professional staff member of the House Armed Services Committee and the House Government Operations Committee to become executive director of a coalition effort initially funded by Ploughshares Fund and the W. Alton Jones Foundation. Headquartered at the Stimson Center in Washington, D.C., the Coalition for the Non-Proliferation Treaty united twenty arms-control and disarmament organizations in a successful campaign to help win the indefinite extension of the treaty and strengthen the global nonproliferation regime.[11]

The New START campaign took this early model and similar efforts to a new level. The campaign started with the basic understanding that the heavy lifting for the treaty would be done by the administration and the Senate leadership. But in policy debates that are often decided on the margins, the margins matters. Public groups could tip the balance. The key was to focus the efforts of many groups on core, achievable goals.

Strategy, Network, and Leadership

The members of the campaign realized that they had to build political support if the treaty was to pass. They would need respected military and national security leaders making the case for nuclear reductions, editorial boards endorsing the agreement, and passionate constituents in states with swing Senate votes. Ploughshares Fund focused its grants and staff work on mobilizing these critical groups.

The campaign built on respected expert groups long funded by the foundation, including the Arms Control Association and the Council for a Livable World, who were already making the treaty's approval a central part of their work. It then brought in new faces, new communicators, and new energy by adding faith groups, such as the evangelical American Values Network; military leaders in the American Security Project; and communication wizards in the National Security Network and ReThink Media. In all, fifty organizations joined in this national, nonpartisan campaign.

A common problem in coalition efforts is the organizational rivalries that create resentments and jealousies and can rip a coalition apart. As a foundation funding all the groups involved, Ploughshares Fund could stand above and somewhat apart from this dynamic. It was, as one fellow funder called it, "the Switzerland of the arms control movement." It used that position to convene strategy sessions and organize the weekly strategy calls and—when the treaty hit the Senate floor—daily "war room" messaging calls. Because the foundation was intimately involved, its staff was able to quickly deploy additional resources as needed. This was not just funding but having

its registered lobbyist work closely with Hill offices. Its research staff created a twice-weekly "START News" e-mail sent to hundreds of congressional
offices, journalists, and experts; its executive director kept the groups working together; and its grants staff helped establish grassroots call centers and
place full-page ads in newspapers.

Rogin reported on a January 12, 2010, meeting of some fifty think tanks
and advocacy organizations convened in "the K Street conference room of
the Ploughshares Fund" aimed at "marshaling those organizations' combined
resources and preparing a full-on campaign to press their shared goals."[12]
Naila Bolus summarized the effort:

> By the end of the campaign our grantees had recruited a battalion of retired
> military officers, actively engaged both behind-the-scenes and in public fo-
> rums; and placed pro-treaty op-eds and editorials that far outnumbered oppos-
> ing pieces and were consistently on message (a dramatic reversal from the
> outset of the campaign). New allies, particularly from the faith community,
> drastically boosted the impact of organizations and organizers working at the
> grassroots.

This was made possible, she notes, because:

> We flipped our foundation's usual practice. Rather than focusing primarily on
> proposals submitted to us, our grant making evolved into a process of pro-
> actively identifying organizations that could meet particular needs and pro-
> viding resources aimed at encouraging our grantees to focus on tasks at which
> they already excelled.[13]

By urging the organizations involved to concentrate on their comparative advantages, by eliminating redundancies, and by promoting cohesion and efficiency, the campaign maximized the potential of these disparate but now
united groups. One of the campaign members, ReThink Media, said after-
ward that the effort was "among the best-organized and most effective coalitions. In terms of objectives, targets, strategy, tactics and message, advocates
were almost uniformly on the same page."

On December 22, 2010, the last day of the Senate's session, the treaty
squeaked past the two-thirds needed for approval, with seventy-one senators
voting in favor. Undoubtedly, the key factors in their decisions were based on
the facts provided by the administration and the trust they had in the leader-

ship of the Senate Foreign Relations Committee, Senator John Kerry (D-MA) and Senator Richard Lugar (R-IN), who strongly backed the treaty.

But there was an intense, political, and heavily funded campaign against the treaty in the Senate, in Washington think tanks, and in key states. The Heritage Foundation, senior leadership in the Senate organized by Senator Jon Kyl (R-AZ), and major political opponents including Gov. Mitt Romney denounced the treaty in the harshest terms. These kinds of campaigns defeated many other initiatives in 2010 that had also been backed by the administration, Senate leaders, and noted experts. In the case of New START, the nongovernmental effort—buoyed by Ploughshares Fund's impact philanthropy—made a difference.

It is always difficult to measure impact, particularly on big policy issues, but ReThink Media's survey of media coverage provides some interesting tangible evidence of success. A big focus of the campaign was on media, particularly getting objective analysis of the treaty to editorial boards and columnists in key states. This was a job neither an administration nor a Senate committee can do. Before the campaign began, editorials and op-eds opposing the treaty heavily outweighed pro-treaty articles. ReThink's postvote analysis demonstrated the impact of the targeted, strategic effort:

- The analysis found print outreach—placement of letters to the editor, op-eds, and editorials—far outpaced that of the opposition and was more precise in targeting high circulation publications in strategically significant key states.

- Data indicate that in key states where print pieces in favor of ratification most outpaced negative pieces, swing senators were much more likely to support the treaty.

- In states where positive pieces outpaced negative ones by more than fifteen pieces, six out of six senators voted for ratification.

- In the key period from September to December 2010, pro-ratification op-eds outpaced the opposition more than two to one (a dramatic reversal from a year earlier, before the campaign began). Nationwide, 219 op-eds appeared for ratification, while only 89 appeared against (27 of those, or nearly one-third, were in the ultraconservative *Washington Times*.)

- Editorials were a powerful force behind support for the treaty. Around the country, ninety-one appeared in favor of ratification with only twenty against.

- It is no coincidence that states that had a strong group presence on the ground were able to publish a greater number of positive pieces.[14]

"It's worth noting that these outcomes are neither assured nor common," concluded the ReThink Media analysts, "Of particular note was the leadership shown by Ploughshares in bringing people together and providing a common framework for action including a regular process for updating work, identifying areas that needed attention and creating informal working groups."[15]

ORGANIZATIONAL STRUCTURE AND STRATEGY

The New START campaign was just one part of Ploughshares Fund's overall program of grants. It is unlikely that a foundation could succeed only with this campaign approach. Part of the success of the effort was that it was rooted in and part of a deeper, broader philanthropic endeavor.

In 2010, the year of the New START campaign, the fund had an operating budget of $10 million and gave $6.2 million in grants. Over the past five years, the foundation has transitioned from just providing grants to other organizations, to adding value to the projects with its own expert analysis, media outreach, liaison with Congress and the White House, and convening of grantees. All its work is focused on three main areas related to nuclear security: continued reductions in global nuclear arsenals, preventing the spread of nuclear weapons, and reducing conflicts in regions where threats of nuclear weapons, terrorism, and conflict converge.

Efforts to limit and reduce current arsenals are in large part focused on concrete steps to reduce stockpiles in the United States and Russia, which hold 95 percent of all nuclear weapons, but also include efforts to influence U.S. and global nuclear policy. Work to prevent the emergence of new nuclear states and the spread of nuclear arms focuses on two of the most significant threats to the global nonproliferation regime: Iran and North Korea. Finally, to help reduce tensions and resolve regional conflicts in South Asia that could escalate into nuclear crises, the fund supports projects to increase civil-society participation in negotiations, address water conflicts, and increase knowledge and understanding of the conflicts among decision makers in Washington, D.C.

Ploughshares Fund coordinates this work with a staff of fourteen. It maintains a vibrant website and blog highlighting grantee accomplishments and provides all its annual reports online.[16] The organization's social media presence, principally on Facebook and Twitter, is also an important element of its larger online media strategy.

REPLICATING THE MODEL

But can this impact-philanthropy model be replicated? Or were the strategy and tactics unique to a campaign to achieve a specific, time-limited goal such as treaty ratification? Since the New START success, Ploughshares Fund has adapted the model to two efforts, one focused on cutting the budget for nuclear weapons programs and the other on dealing with the challenges of a nuclearizing Iran.

The foundation's leaders paid heed to the advice of Brest and Harvey:

> You can't know in advance whether your philanthropy will have world-chang-
> ing consequences or turn out in retrospect to be money down the drain. But
> you do know in advance that because social change is complex, and causal
> chains are often murky, strategic philanthropy requires real clarity of goals,
> sound analysis, follow-through, and continuous feedback. And this means that
> you can change the odds in your favor through strategies that are based on
> evidence (rather than hope) and through careful planning and execution.[17]

Sound, tested strategy is all the more important because of the scale of the problems this philanthropy is trying to address. Grant dollars are meager compared to the amounts governments and corporations spend on any of the big-cube issues. For example, the federal government spends about $56 billion each year on nuclear weapons and weapons-related programs. Foundations provide about $33 million in grants in this area in any given year, or 0.06 percent of the private and government money invested in contracts, profits, jobs, and large, established institutions. How can foundations hope to make a dent in this issue? By being smart, strategic, and thorough.

For example, before launching its nuclear weapons budget campaign, Ploughshares Fund commissioned three focused analyses from leading budget experts to determine what policy goals might be reasonable for a campaign to address. The recommendations of that process were discussed at a meeting of some twenty groups. Collective campaign goals were agreed upon and collaborative work plans produced. With the campaign underway, the groups have frequent teleconferences and regular in-person meetings with campaign partners intended to assess how the campaigns are going, whether goals are being met, and if the sharing of tasks and expertise is appropriate. This flexible approach allowed the campaign to respond to outside developments.

One example of the campaign's success came in the fall of 2012 when Congress, in the Continuing Resolution for fiscal year 2013, zeroed out a multi-billion-dollar plutonium-bomb plant. The plant, known as the Chemical and Metallurgical Research Replacement facility (or CMRR) was to be built at the Los Alamos National Laboratory in New Mexico. Originally expected to cost under $400 million, its budget had exploded to almost $6 billion. The Congress agreed with the administration's plan to delay the project for five years—effectively killing it. The design team has since been disbanded. Funds from the project are being reprogrammed. And work is beginning on a smaller, cheaper alternative that can provide the necessary plutonium cores at close to the original budget.[18]

To be sure, the delay in the plant's construction was initiated by the administration with the agreement of the lab directors. But this outcome was by no means assured. In two letters that year, nineteen senators wrote the administration demanding that funding for the bomb plant be restored. When this many senators demand something, they usually get it. But not this time. Many of the organizations that are part of the budget campaign—including Nuke Watch New Mexico, the Project on Government Oversight, the Alliance for Nuclear Accountability, the Union of Concerned Scientists, and the Friends Committee on National Legislation—wrote, lobbied, and argued that the plant was unnecessary and urged Congress to cancel it, shining a spotlight on the process. Editorial boards and constituents weighed in, and, to the delight of the organizations, the appropriators held firm and denied the funding. The campaign notched an important initial victory.[19]

Similarly, the Iran campaign networks the talents of more than forty-five organizations to prevent another war in the Middle East and prevent Iran from developing a nuclear weapon. The campaign holds regular meetings and conference calls and maintains a vibrant e-mail listserv that hums with daily debate. It is the only effort of its kind in the country. For almost two years, beginning in early 2011, the effort has developed and amplified reasoned analysis detailing the consequences of military strikes on Iran and promoting the advantages of a negotiated settlement of the crisis.

Each campaign effort is different, with varying tempos and degrees of coordination. For the Iran campaign, it was important to provide for a wide range of views among the participating groups on sanctions, assessments of Iran's progress toward a weapon, and use of force, among others. The campaigns do not direct any group's work but provide platforms for the sharing of information and development of analysis. One of the groups participating, a group of former diplomats and current experts, produced a remarkable paper that was among the most influential reports on Iran published in 2012. *The New Yorker* described its findings:

> A bipartisan group in New York, called the Iran Project, released a report ti-
> tled "Weighing Benefits and Costs of Military Action Against Iran." The group,
> which is composed of thirty-two foreign-policy heavyweights who run the
> gamut from Richard Armitage to Anne-Marie Slaughter, persuasively argues
> that a sustained U.S.-Israeli bombing campaign, supplemented by cyber-
> attacks and covert operations, could delay the Iranian nuclear program by at
> most four years, and that it would do so at considerable cost to American and
> Israeli interests. If Israel were to act alone, it might delay the program by no
> more than two years. In the long run, bombardment would make the Islamic
> Republic all the more likely to go nuclear. Any more lasting objective—such
> as regime change—would require a wholesale invasion and occupation of Iran,
> which, according to the report's authors, would cost more in blood and treasure
> than have the past ten years of war in Iraq and Afghanistan combined.[20]

The report did not make recommendations; rather, it provided a careful assessment of costs and benefits. Simply by objectively presenting this information it helped counter a rush to military strikes as a viable solution to the Iran challenge. Endorsed by Brent Scowcroft, Zbigniew Brzezinski, Sen. Chuck Hagel, Adm. William Fallon, Gen. Anthony Zinni, Anne Marie Slaughter, Jessica Mathews, and many others, it restored the common sense of the center of America's security elite to a debate all too often ruled by exaggerated threats and political pressures from the fringe. That has been the essential point of all Ploughshares Fund's efforts on nuclear policy.

THE NUCLEAR SECURITY FIELD

Ploughshares Fund is just one foundation in a larger field of public and private foundations providing grants and support for nuclear security issues. The number of groups and the amount of funding available are small compared to many other issues, such as climate change, human rights or the environment, but they are not insignificant.

From 2008 through 2011, forty-three foundations provided almost $130 million in grants to individuals and organizations working on nuclear weapons and related issues.[21] The funding has been roughly consistent each year, with almost $33 million granted in 2011. By far, the majority of the grants have been provided by three foundations—the Carnegie Corporation of New York, the John D. and Catherine T. MacArthur Foundation, and Ploughshares Fund—who account for more than 66 percent of all funding in the nuclear security field.

Impact philanthropy is not applicable to many of these foundations, particularly those that eschew advocacy or prefer to concentrate grants on a few large institutional or academic actors. This type of philanthropy is important and part of the overall funding needed in the security field. But for those with the patience and the organizing inclination, impact philanthropy may be the model many have searched for over the years.

John Tirman was one of those pioneers looking to improve on the return of his foundation's investments when he served as executive director of the Winston Foundation for World Peace in Washington, D.C., from 1986 to 1999. He was a champion of advocacy philanthropy, writing approvingly in a 2000 study of how a small group of private donors in the 1970s and 1980s had a "profound impact" on efforts to end the U.S.-Soviet nuclear arms race. He concluded "that philanthropy is most effective when it is able and willing to support a dynamic combination of critical thinkers and social activists."[22]

Tirman believes that foundations willing to fund these efforts in the 1980s helped build "the burgeoning peace movement as an opportunity to contend with the resurgent right and to bypass the inert discourse of the elite institutions of New York and Washington." This was a break from traditional foundation behavior. "The notion that American foundations might support a social and political movement aimed at disrupting longstanding security policy was unorthodox," he writes, "virtually heretical."[23] But by 1984, his foundation and five or six others were funding the analysts and activists trying to stop the arms race, including the Carnegie Corporation of New York, the MacArthur Foundation, Rockefeller Brothers Fund, and the W. Alton Jones Foundation. Ploughshares Fund began operations in this period and in this mold.

Clearly, the desires of Ronald Reagan and Mikhail Gorbachev to move toward the elimination of nuclear weapons (desires many questioned at the time but that are now established fact) were decisive in ending the arms race and making sweeping reductions in nuclear arsenals possible. But "it was the public demand for an end to the nuclear danger that spurred and strengthened these events," argues Tirman. "And American philanthropy, particularly the decisive and risk-taking philanthropy of the early 1980's was a partner in this remarkable story."[24]

Expanding his analysis, Tirman details five critical factors that help explain why political leaders are willing to negotiate peaceful agreements and search for solutions that may fall short of their original aims. These could well serve as guideposts for any successful advocacy campaign:

1. A critical community of intellectuals who informally work in concert to nurture social values that promote, for example, the legitimization of an insurgent group, or preference for nonviolent solutions over military solutions;

2. The rise of activist movements to adopt those values and introduce them, first within their own circles and then with increasing intensity through a variety of techniques into the national or international discussion about the conflict;

3. The growing concordance of measured attitudes in the public that support the new social values and goals . . . ;

4. A noticeable embrace by non-governing elites—leaders of religions, business, news media, universities, etc.—of new social values or something akin to those values; and

5. New initiatives from opposition political parties or similar groups in the political culture that reflect the new social values.[25]

Tirman was writing about mass movements in those decades, but, in many ways, these are the elements of the more limited policy campaigns of the impact-philanthropy model: analytical research, activists, public support, elite validators, and adoption by political leaders.

There continues to be considerable debate about the proper role and past successes of foundation-supported national security enterprises. Mitchel Wallerstein, the former vice president for the Program on Global Security and Sustainability of the MacArthur Foundation, writing in 2008, is less sanguine than Tirman about the impact of the philanthropic efforts "either regarding the modest arms control success achieved during the 1980s and early 1990s . . . or ultimately, in hastening the end of the Cold War."[26]

Wallerstein says that foundations did provide key support for a broad range of policy studies and educational efforts during this period, many of which proved highly influential in policy formation. He also cites the value of their support for specific initiatives, such as the campaign to ban landmines. It is not the impact of these projects that Wallerstein criticizes but the failure of foundations to sustain these efforts, particularly when the sharp partisan politics that emerged in the second Clinton administration made major policy change exceptionally difficult. Many foundations left the field disillusioned or disinterested, short-circuiting a process of policy change that requires sustained effort.

There remained "extremely important 'unfinished business' related to nuclear arms reductions and the security of existing nuclear weapons," argues Wallerstein, including "additional deep reductions in nuclear arms and improved nuclear safety measures, such as warhead de-alerting or de-mating, plutonium disposition, and re-direction of the work of the nuclear weapons designers." Foundations needed to stay the course rather than "abandon or reduce the scope of this work in order to divert resources to other, more contemporary threats, such as biological weapons."[27]

Ten years later, Wallerstein's critique has proved accurate. Fortunately, there remains a core group of dedicated funders, including many cited already in this chapter. They are in it for the long haul, the only perspective one can realistically take when fighting in the big cube. And many would agree with Wallerstein (whose perspective of 1990s partisan politics seems almost quaint compared to how brutal these fights have become in the second decade of the century):

> Funders have learned from experience that if they support only academic policy analysis, however well conceived and innovative, without attending to the far more difficult (and 'messier') questions of how policy is actually made—or changed—in the real world, there was likely to be little tangible progress—especially on a subject as complicated (and potentially frightening) as weapons of mass destruction.[28]

New grant-making foundations, most importantly, the Skoll Global Threat Fund, and new operating foundations, particularly the Nuclear Threat Initiative lead by former senator Sam Nunn and Ted Turner, have joined the field in the past ten years, bringing financial resources, organizing skills, and imaginative new approaches. Many of the projects supported by the Skoll Global Threat Fund are civil society initiatives that mobilize popular opinion and influential individuals around the globe. The fund benefits from some of the other organizations started by its founder, Jeffrey Skoll, particularly the film company Participant Media, which in 2010 released a powerful documentary on nuclear weapon threats, *Countdown to Zero*, to critical acclaim and is working on other projects, including a feature film, *Reykjavik*, starring Michael Douglas as Ronald Reagan and Christoph Waltz as Mikhail Gorbachev. The Nuclear Threat Initiative, in addition to several major projects to secure and eliminate nuclear materials, serves as the secretariat for the work of George Shultz, Henry Kissinger, William Perry, and Sam Nunn and is assembling an international network of partner institutes dedicated to reducing and eliminating nuclear threats. Other major foundations working on these issues include the William and Flora Hewlett Foundation, the Rockefeller Brothers Fund, and Colombe Foundation.

The foundations in the field today are seasoned, savvy, and as tough as the problems they seek to solve. Some favor research and publication; others, public education; others, public advocacy. All have a role to play in continuing this "unfinished business." All believe that the active, sustained involvement of the public is key to sound national security policies and to finally breaking with the Cold War policies that still grip our nuclear enterprises.

Polls clearly show the public wants to reduce nuclear numbers and budgets and favors the eventual elimination of all these weapons. The more the public turns its opinions into action—writing, calling, organizing, and donating—the quicker and more assuredly policy will change. "Now some may argue that it is impossible to expect a majority of citizens to understand the complexity of nuclear strategy," writes Kennette Benedict. On the contrary, she argues, we cannot give a small group of people "sole responsibility for deciding whether or not to kill millions and destroy vast areas of the planet by firing nuclear weapons—without any participation by the people who paid for the weapons with their taxes or by those who voted for the leaders who give the final orders."[29] She is right. Our democratic system requires active citizen involvement. The future of our planet demands it. Then, and only then, will we be able to dispel the nuclear nightmares that have haunted us for far too long.

REMARKS BY PRESIDENT BARACK OBAMA

HRADCANY SQUARE, PRAGUE, CZECH REPUBLIC | APRIL 5, 2009

Thank you so much. Thank you for this wonderful welcome. Thank you to the people of Prague. Thank you to the people of the Czech Republic. Today, I'm proud to stand here with you in the middle of this great city, in the center of Europe. And, to paraphrase one of my predecessors, I am also proud to be the man who brought Michelle Obama to Prague.

To Mr. President, Mr. Prime Minister, to all the dignitaries who are here, thank you for your extraordinary hospitality. And to the people of the Czech Republic, thank you for your friendship to the United States.

I've learned over many years to appreciate the good company and the good humor of the Czech people in my hometown of Chicago. Behind me is a statue of a hero of the Czech people—Tomas Masaryk. In 1918, after America had pledged its support for Czech independence, Masaryk spoke to a crowd in Chicago that was estimated to be over 100,000. I don't think I can match his record—but I am honored to follow his footsteps from Chicago to Prague.

For over a thousand years, Prague has set itself apart from any other city in any other place. You've known war and peace. You've seen empires rise and fall. You've led revolutions in the arts and science, in politics and in poetry. Through it all, the people of Prague have insisted on pursuing their own path, and defining their own destiny. And this city—this Golden City which is both ancient and youthful—stands as a living monument to your unconquerable spirit.

When I was born, the world was divided, and our nations were faced with very different circumstances. Few people would have predicted that someone like me would one day become the President of the United States. Few people would have predicted that an American President would one day be permitted to speak to an audience like this in Prague. Few would have imagined that the Czech Republic would become a free nation, a member of NATO, a leader of a united Europe. Those ideas would have been dismissed as dreams.

We are here today because enough people ignored the voices who told them that the world could not change.

We're here today because of the courage of those who stood up and took risks to say that freedom is a right for all people, no matter what side of a wall they live on, and no matter what they look like. We are here today because of the Prague Spring—because the simple and principled pursuit of liberty and opportunity shamed those who relied on the power of tanks and arms to put down the will of a people.

We are here today because 20 years ago, the people of this city took to the streets to claim the promise of a new day, and the fundamental human rights that had been denied them for far too long. Sametová Revoluce—the Velvet Revolution taught us many things. It showed us that peaceful protest could shake the foundations of an empire, and expose the emptiness of an ideology. It showed us that small countries can play a pivotal role in world events, and that young people can lead the way in overcoming old conflicts. And it proved that moral leadership is more powerful than any weapon.

That's why I'm speaking to you in the center of a Europe that is peaceful, united and free—because ordinary people believed that divisions could be bridged, even when their leaders did not. They believed that walls could come down; that peace could prevail.

We are here today because Americans and Czechs believed against all odds that today could be possible.

Now, we share this common history. But now this generation—our generation—cannot stand still. We, too, have a choice to make. As the world has become less divided, it has become more interconnected. And we've seen events move faster than our ability to control them—a global economy in crisis, a changing climate, the persistent dangers of old conflicts, new threats and the spread of catastrophic weapons.

None of these challenges can be solved quickly or easily. But all of them demand that we listen to one another and work together; that we focus on our common interests, not on occasional differences; and that we reaffirm our shared values, which are stronger than any force that could drive us apart. That is the work that we must carry on. That is the work that I have come to Europe to begin.

To renew our prosperity, we need action coordinated across borders. That means investments to create new jobs. That means resisting the walls of protectionism that stand in the way of growth. That means a change in our financial system, with new rules to prevent abuse and future crisis.

And we have an obligation to our common prosperity and our common humanity to extend a hand to those emerging markets and impoverished people who are suffering the most, even though they may have had very little to do with financial crises, which is why we set aside over a trillion dollars for the International Monetary Fund earlier this week, to make sure that everybody—everybody—receives some assistance.

Now, to protect our planet, now is the time to change the way that we use energy. Together, we must confront climate change by ending the world's dependence on fossil fuels, by tapping the power of new sources of energy like the wind and sun, and calling upon all nations to do their part. And I pledge to you that in this global effort, the United States is now ready to lead.

To provide for our common security, we must strengthen our alliance. NATO was founded 60 years ago, after Communism took over Czechoslovakia. That was when the free world learned too late that it could not afford division. So we came together to forge the strongest alliance that the world has ever known. And we should—stood shoulder to shoulder—year after year, decade after decade—until an Iron Curtain was lifted, and freedom spread like flowing water.

This marks the 10th year of NATO membership for the Czech Republic. And I know that many times in the 20th century, decisions were made without you at the table. Great powers let you down, or determined your destiny without your voice being heard. I am here to say that the United States will never turn its back on the people of this nation. We are bound by shared values, shared history—We are bound by shared values and shared history and the enduring promise of our alliance. NATO's Article V states it clearly: An attack on one is an attack on all. That is a promise for our time, and for all time.

The people of the Czech Republic kept that promise after America was attacked; thousands were killed on our soil, and NATO responded. NATO's mission in Afghanistan is fundamental to the safety of people on both sides of the Atlantic. We are targeting the same al Qaeda terrorists who have struck from New York to London, and helping the Afghan people take responsibility for their future. We are demonstrating that free nations can make common cause on behalf of our common security. And I want you to know that we honor the sacrifices of the Czech people in this endeavor, and mourn the loss of those you've lost.

But no alliance can afford to stand still. We must work together as NATO members so that we have contingency plans in place to deal with new threats, wherever they may come from. We must strengthen our cooperation with one another, and with other nations and institutions around the world, to confront dangers that recognize no borders. And we must pursue constructive relations with Russia on issues of common concern.

Now, one of those issues that I'll focus on today is fundamental to the security of our nations and to the peace of the world—that's the future of nuclear weapons in the 21st century. The existence of thousands of nuclear weapons is the most dangerous legacy of the Cold War. No nuclear war was fought between the United States and the Soviet Union, but generations lived with the knowledge that their world could be erased in a single flash of light. Cities like Prague that existed for centuries, that embodied the beauty and the talent of so much of humanity, would have ceased to exist.

Today, the Cold War has disappeared but thousands of those weapons have not. In a strange turn of history, the threat of global nuclear war has gone down, but the risk of a nuclear attack has gone up. More nations have acquired these weapons. Testing has continued. Black market trade in nuclear secrets and nuclear materials abound. The technology to build a bomb has spread. Terrorists are determined to buy, build or steal one. Our efforts to contain these dangers are centered on a global non-proliferation regime, but as more people and nations break the rules, we could reach the point where the center cannot hold.

Now, understand, this matters to people everywhere. One nuclear weapon exploded in one city—be it New York or Moscow, Islamabad or Mumbai, Tokyo or Tel Aviv, Paris or Prague—could kill hundreds of thousands of people. And no matter where it happens, there is no end to what the consequences might be—for our global safety, our security, our society, our economy, to our ultimate survival.

Some argue that the spread of these weapons cannot be stopped, cannot be checked—that we are destined to live in a world where more nations and more people possess the ultimate tools of destruction. Such fatalism is a deadly adversary, for if we believe that the spread of nuclear weapons is inevitable, then in some way we are admitting to ourselves that the use of nuclear weapons is inevitable.

Just as we stood for freedom in the 20th century, we must stand together for the right of people everywhere to live free from fear in the 21st century. And as nuclear power—as a nuclear power, as the only nuclear power to have used a nuclear weapon, the United States has a moral responsibility to act. We cannot succeed in this endeavor alone, but we can lead it, we can start it.

So today, I state clearly and with conviction America's commitment to seek the peace and security of a world without nuclear weapons. I'm not naïve. This goal will not be reached quickly—perhaps not in my lifetime. It will take patience and persistence. But now we, too, must ignore the voices who tell us that the world cannot change. We have to insist, "Yes, we can."

Now, let me describe to you the trajectory we need to be on. First, the United States will take concrete steps towards a world without nuclear weapons. To put an end to Cold War thinking, we will reduce the role of nuclear weapons in our national security strategy, and urge others to do the same. Make no mistake: As long as these weapons exist, the United States will maintain a safe, secure and effective arsenal to deter any adversary, and guarantee that defense to our allies—including the Czech Republic. But we will begin the work of reducing our arsenal.

To reduce our warheads and stockpiles, we will negotiate a new Strategic Arms Reduction Treaty with the Russians this year. President Medvedev and I began this process in London, and will seek a new agreement by the end of this year that is legally binding and sufficiently bold. And this will set the stage for further cuts, and we will seek to include all nuclear weapons states in this endeavor.

To achieve a global ban on nuclear testing, my administration will immediately and aggressively pursue U.S. ratification of the Comprehensive Test Ban Treaty. After more than five decades of talks, it is time for the testing of nuclear weapons to finally be banned.

And to cut off the building blocks needed for a bomb, the United States will seek a new treaty that verifiably ends the production of fissile materials intended for use in state nuclear weapons. If we are serious about stopping the spread of these weapons, then we should put an end to the dedicated production of weapons-grade materials that create them. That's the first step.

Second, together we will strengthen the Nuclear Non-Proliferation Treaty as a basis for cooperation. The basic bargain is sound: Countries with nuclear weapons will move towards disarmament, countries without nuclear weapons will not acquire them, and all countries can access peaceful nuclear energy. To strengthen the treaty, we should embrace several principles. We need more resources and authority to strengthen international inspections. We need real and immediate consequences for countries caught breaking the rules or trying to leave the treaty without cause.

And we should build a new framework for civil nuclear cooperation, including an international fuel bank, so that countries can access peaceful power without increasing the risks of proliferation. That must be the right of every nation that renounces nuclear weapons, especially developing countries embarking on peaceful programs. And no approach will succeed if it's based on the denial of rights to nations that play by the rules. We must harness the power of nuclear energy on behalf of our efforts to combat climate change, and to advance peace opportunity for all people.

But we go forward with no illusions. Some countries will break the rules. That's why we need a structure in place that ensures when any nation does, they will face consequences. Just this morning, we were reminded again of why we need a new and more rigorous approach to address this threat. North Korea broke the rules once again by testing a rocket that could be used for long range missiles. This provocation underscores the need for action—not just this afternoon at the U.N. Security Council, but in our determination to prevent the spread of these weapons.

Rules must be binding. Violations must be punished. Words must mean something. The world must stand together to prevent the spread of these weapons. Now is the time for a strong international response—now is the time for a strong international response, and North Korea must know that the path to security and respect will never come through threats and illegal weapons. All nations must come together to build a stronger, global regime. And that's why we must stand shoulder to shoulder to pressure the North Koreans to change course.

Iran has yet to build a nuclear weapon. My administration will seek engagement with Iran based on mutual interests and mutual respect. We believe in dialogue. But in that dialogue we will present a clear choice. We want Iran to take its rightful place in the community of nations, politically and economically. We will support Iran's right to peaceful nuclear energy with rigorous inspections. That's a path that the Islamic Republic can take. Or the government can choose increased isolation, international pressure, and a potential nuclear arms race in the region that will increase insecurity for all.

So let me be clear: Iran's nuclear and ballistic missile activity poses a real threat, not just to the United States, but to Iran's neighbors and our allies. The Czech Republic and Poland have been courageous in agreeing to host a defense against these missiles. As long as the threat from Iran persists, we will go forward with a missile defense system that is cost-effective and proven. If the Iranian threat is eliminated, we will have a stronger basis for security, and the driving force for missile defense construction in Europe will be removed.

So, finally, we must ensure that terrorists never acquire a nuclear weapon. This is the most immediate and extreme threat to global security. One terrorist with one nuclear weapon could unleash massive destruction. Al Qaeda has said it seeks a bomb and that it would have no problem with using it. And we know that there is unsecured nuclear material across the globe. To protect our people, we must act with a sense of purpose without delay.

So today I am announcing a new international effort to secure all vulnerable nuclear material around the world within four years. We will set new standards, expand our cooperation with Russia, pursue new partnerships to lock down these sensitive materials.

We must also build on our efforts to break up black markets, detect and intercept materials in transit, and use financial tools to disrupt this dangerous trade. Because this threat will be lasting, we should come together to turn efforts such as the Proliferation Security Initiative and the Global Initiative to Combat Nuclear Terrorism into durable international institutions. And we should start by having a Global Summit on Nuclear Security that the United States will host within the next year.

Now, I know that there are some who will question whether we can act on such a broad agenda. There are those who doubt whether true international cooperation is possible, given inevitable differences among nations. And there are those who hear talk of a world without nuclear weapons and doubt whether it's worth setting a goal that seems impossible to achieve.

But make no mistake: We know where that road leads. When nations and peoples allow themselves to be defined by their differences, the gulf between them widens. When we fail to pursue peace, then it stays forever beyond our grasp. We know the path when we choose fear over hope. To denounce or shrug off a call for cooperation is an easy but also a cowardly thing to do. That's how wars begin. That's where human progress ends.

There is violence and injustice in our world that must be confronted. We must confront it not by splitting apart but by standing together as free nations, as free people. I know that a call to arms can stir the souls of men and women more than a call to lay them down. But that is why the voices for peace and progress must be raised together. Those are the voices that still echo through the streets of Prague. Those are the ghosts of 1968. Those were the joyful sounds of the Velvet Revolution. Those were the Czechs who helped bring down a nuclear-armed empire without firing a shot.

Human destiny will be what we make of it. And here in Prague, let us honor our past by reaching for a better future. Let us bridge our divisions, build upon our hopes, accept our responsibility to leave this world more prosperous and more peaceful than we found it. Together we can do it. Thank you very much. Thank you, Prague.

STATEMENT BY PRESIDENT BARACK OBAMA

ON THE RELEASE OF NUCLEAR POSTURE REVIEW | APRIL 6, 2010

One year ago yesterday in Prague, I outlined a comprehensive agenda to prevent the spread of nuclear weapons and to pursue the peace and security of a world without them. I look forward to advancing this agenda in Prague this week when I sign the new START Treaty with President Medvedev, committing the United States and Russia to substantial reductions in our nuclear arsenals.

Today, my Administration is taking a significant step forward by fulfilling another pledge that I made in Prague—to reduce the role of nuclear weapons in our national security strategy and focus on reducing the nuclear dangers of the 21st century, while sustaining a safe, secure and effective nuclear deterrent for the United States and our allies and partners as long as nuclear weapons exist.

The Nuclear Posture Review, led by the Department of Defense, recognizes that the greatest threat to U.S. and global security is no longer a nuclear exchange between nations, but nuclear terrorism by violent extremists and nuclear proliferation to an increasing number of states. Moreover, it recognizes that our national security and that of our allies and partners can be increasingly defended by America's unsurpassed conventional military capabilities and strong missile defenses.

As a result, we are taking specific and concrete steps to reduce the role of nuclear weapons while preserving our military superiority, deterring aggression and safeguarding the security of the American people.

First, and for the first time, preventing nuclear proliferation and nuclear terrorism is now at the top of America's nuclear agenda, which affirms the central importance of the Nuclear Non-Proliferation Treaty. We have aligned our policies and proposed major funding increases for programs to prevent the spread of nuclear weapons around the world. Our nuclear security summit next week will be an opportunity for 47 nations to commit to specific steps to pursue the goal of securing all vulnerable nuclear materials around the world within four years. And next month in New York, we will work with the wider world to strengthen the global non-proliferation regime to ensure that all nations uphold their responsibilities.

Second, we are further emphasizing the importance of nations meeting their NPT and nuclear non-proliferation obligations through our declaratory policy. The United States is declaring that we will not use or threaten to use nuclear weapons against non-nuclear weapons states that are party to the Nuclear Non-Proliferation Treaty and in compliance with their nuclear non-proliferation obligations. This enables us to sustain our nuclear deterrent for the narrower range of contingencies in which these weapons may still play a role, while providing an additional incentive for nations to meet their NPT obligations. Those nations that fail to meet their obligations will therefore find themselves more isolated, and will recognize that the pursuit of nuclear weapons will not make them more secure.

Finally, we are fulfilling our responsibilities as a nuclear power committed to the NPT. The United States will not conduct nuclear testing and will seek ratification of the Comprehensive Test Ban Treaty. The United States will not develop new nuclear warheads or pursue new military missions or new capabilities for nuclear weapons.

As I stated last year in Prague, so long as nuclear weapons exist, we will maintain a safe, secure and effective arsenal that guarantees the defense of the United States, reassures allies and partners, and deters potential adversaries. To that end, we are seeking substantial investments to improve infrastructure, strengthen science and technology, and retain the human capital we need to sustain our stockpile, while also strengthening the conventional capabilities that are an important part of our deterrent. The nuclear strategy we're announcing today therefore reaffirms America's unwavering commitment to the security of our allies and partners, and advances American national security.

To stop the spread of nuclear weapons, prevent nuclear terrorism, and pursue the day when these weapons do not exist, we will work aggressively to advance every element of our comprehensive agenda—to reduce arsenals, to secure vulnerable nuclear materials, and to strengthen the NPT. These are the steps toward the more secure future that America seeks, and this is the work that we are advancing today.

APPENDIX C
REMARKS BY PRESIDENT BARACK OBAMA

AT THE UNITED NATIONS SECURITY COUNCIL SUMMIT ON NUCLEAR NON-PROLIFERATION AND NUCLEAR DISARMAMENT | SEPTEMBER 24, 2009

I want to thank again everybody who is in attendance. I wish you all good morning. In the six-plus decades that this Security Council has been in existence, only four other meetings of this nature have been convened. I called for this one so that we may address at the highest level a fundamental threat to the security of all peoples and all nations: the spread and use of nuclear weapons.

As I said yesterday, this very institution was founded at the dawn of the atomic age, in part because man's capacity to kill had to be contained. And although we averted a nuclear nightmare during the Cold War, we now face proliferation of a scope and complexity that demands new strategies and new approaches. Just one nuclear weapon exploded in a city—be it New York or Moscow; Tokyo or Beijing; London or Paris—could kill hundreds of thousands of people. And it would badly destabilize our security, our economies, and our very way of life.

Once more, the United Nations has a pivotal role to play in preventing this crisis. The historic resolution we just adopted enshrines our shared commitment to the goal of a world without nuclear weapons. And it brings Security Council agreement on a broad framework for action to reduce nuclear dangers as we work toward that goal. It reflects the agenda I outlined in Prague, and builds on a consensus that all nations have the right to peaceful nuclear energy; that nations with nuclear weapons have the responsibility to move toward disarmament; and those without them have the responsibility to forsake them.

Today, the Security Council endorsed a global effort to lock down all vulnerable nuclear materials within four years. The United States will host a summit next April to advance this goal and help all nations achieve it. This resolution will also help strengthen the institutions and initiatives that combat the smuggling, financing, and theft of proliferation-related materials. It calls on all states to freeze any financial assets that are being used for proliferation. And it calls for stronger safeguards to reduce the likelihood that peaceful nuclear weapons programs can be diverted to a weapons program—that peaceful nuclear programs can be diverted to a weapons program.

The resolution we passed today will also strengthen the Nuclear Non-Proliferation Treaty. We have made it clear that the Security Council has both the authority and the responsibility to respond to violations to this treaty. We've made it clear that the Security Council has both the authority and responsibility to determine and respond as necessary when violations of this treaty threaten international peace and security.

That includes full compliance with Security Council resolutions on Iran and North Korea. Let me be clear: This is not about singling out individual nations—it is about standing up for the rights of all nations who do live up to their responsibilities. The world must stand together. And we must demonstrate that international law is not an empty promise, and that treaties will be enforced.

The next 12 months will be absolutely critical in determining whether this resolution and our overall efforts to stop the spread and use of nuclear weapons are successful. And all nations must do their part to make this work. In America, I have promised that we will pursue a new agreement with Russia to substantially reduce our strategic warheads and launchers. We will move forward with the ratification of the Comprehensive Test Ban Treaty, and open the door to deeper cuts in our own arsenal. In January, we will call upon countries to begin negotiations on a treaty to end the production of fissile material for weapons. And the Non-Proliferation Treaty Review Conference in May will strengthen that agreement.

Now, we harbor no illusions about the difficulty of bringing about a world without nuclear weapons. We know there are plenty of cynics, and that there will be setbacks to prove their point. But there will also be days like today that push us forward—days that tell a different story. It is the story of a world that understands that no difference or division is worth destroying all that we have built and all that we love. It is a recognition that can bring people of different nationalities and ethnicities and ideologies together. In my own country, it has brought Democrats and Republican leaders together—leaders like George Shultz, Bill Perry, Henry Kissinger, and Sam Nunn, who are with us here today. And it was a Republican President, Ronald Reagan, who once articulated the goal we now seek in the starkest of terms. I quote:

"A nuclear war cannot be won and must never be fought. And no matter how great the obstacles may seem, we must never stop our efforts to reduce the weapons of war. We must never stop until all—we must never stop at all until we see the day when nuclear arms have been banished from the face of the Earth."

That is our task. That can be our destiny. And we will leave this meeting with a renewed determination to achieve this shared goal. Thank you.

EXCERPTS FROM PRESIDENT BARACK OBAMA'S

STATE OF THE UNION ADDRESS | JANUARY 27, 2010

Now, even as we prosecute two wars, we're also confronting perhaps the greatest danger to the American people—the threat of nuclear weapons. I've embraced the vision of John F. Kennedy and Ronald Reagan through a strategy that reverses the spread of these weapons and seeks a world without them. To reduce our stockpiles and launchers, while ensuring our deterrent, the United States and Russia are completing negotiations on the farthest-reaching arms control treaty in nearly two decades. And at April's Nuclear Security Summit, we will bring 44 nations together here in Washington, D.C. behind a clear goal: securing all vulnerable nuclear materials around the world in four years, so that they never fall into the hands of terrorists.

Now, these diplomatic efforts have also strengthened our hand in dealing with those nations that insist on violating international agreements in pursuit of nuclear weapons. That's why North Korea now faces increased isolation, and stronger sanctions—sanctions that are being vigorously enforced. That's why the international community is more united, and the Islamic Republic of Iran is more isolated. And as Iran's leaders continue to ignore their obligations, there should be no doubt: They, too, will face growing consequences. That is a promise.

REMARKS BY PRESIDENT BARACK OBAMA

AT NEW START TREATY SIGNING CEREMONY, PRAGUE, CZECH REPUBLIC | APRIL 8, 2010

One year ago this week, I came here to Prague and gave a speech outlining America's comprehensive commitment to stopping the spread of nuclear weapons and seeking the ultimate goal of a world without them. I said then—and I will repeat now—that this is a long-term goal, one that may not even be achieved in my lifetime. But I believed then—as I do now—that the pursuit of that goal will move us further beyond the Cold War, strengthen the global non-proliferation regime, and make the United States, and the world, safer and more secure. One of the steps that I called for last year was the realization of this treaty, so it's very gratifying to be back in Prague today.

I also came to office committed to "resetting" relations between the United States and Russia, and I know that President Medvedev shared that commitment. As he said at our first meeting in London, our relationship had started to drift, making it difficult to cooperate on issues of common interest to our people. And when the United States and Russia are not able to work to-gether on big issues, it's not good for either of our nations, nor is it good for the world.

Together, we've stopped that drift, and proven the benefits of coopera-tion. Today is an important milestone for nuclear security and non-prolifera-tion, and for U.S.-Russia relations. It fulfills our common objective to negoti-ate a new Strategic Arms Reduction Treaty. It includes significant reductions in the nuclear weapons that we will deploy. It cuts our delivery vehicles by roughly half. It includes a comprehensive verification regime, which allows us to further build trust. It enables both sides the flexibility to protect our security, as well as America's unwavering commitment to the security of our European allies. And I look forward to working with the United States Senate to achieve ratification for this important treaty later this year.

Finally, this day demonstrates the determination of the United States and Russia—the two nations that hold over 90 percent of the world's nuclear weapons—to pursue responsible global leadership. Together, we are keeping our commitments under the Nuclear Non-Proliferation Treaty, which must be the foundation for global non-proliferation.

While the New START treaty is an important first step forward, it is just one step on a longer journey. As I said last year in Prague, this treaty will set the stage for further cuts. And going forward, we hope to pursue discussions with Russia on reducing both our strategic and tactical weapons, including non-deployed weapons.

President Medvedev and I have also agreed to expand our discussions on missile defense. This will include regular exchanges of information about our threat assessments, as well as the completion of a joint assessment of emerg-ing ballistic missiles. And as these assessments are completed, I look forward to launching a serious dialogue about Russian-American cooperation on mis-sile defense.

But nuclear weapons are not simply an issue for the United States and Russia—they threaten the common security of all nations. A nuclear weapon in the hands of a terrorist is a danger to people everywhere—from Moscow to New York; from the cities of Europe to South Asia. So next week, 47 nations will come together in Washington to discuss concrete steps that can be taken to secure all vulnerable nuclear materials around the world in four years.

And the spread of nuclear weapons to more states is also an unacceptable risk to global security—raising the specter of arms races from the Middle East to East Asia. Earlier this week, the United States formally changed our policy to make it clear that those [non]-nuclear weapons states that are in compliance with the Nuclear Non-Proliferation Treaty and their non-proliferation obligations will not be threatened by America's nuclear arsenal. This demonstrates, once more, America's commitment to the NPT as a cornerstone of our security strategy. Those nations that follow the rules will find greater security and opportunity. Those nations that refuse to meet their obligations will be isolated, and denied the opportunity that comes with international recognition.

That includes accountability for those that break the rules—otherwise the NPT is just words on a page. That's why the United States and Russia are part of a coalition of nations insisting that the Islamic Republic of Iran face consequences, because they have continually failed to meet their obligations. We are working together at the United Nations Security Council to pass strong sanctions on Iran. And we will not tolerate actions that flout the NPT, risk an arms race in a vital region, and threaten the credibility of the international community and our collective security.

While these issues are a top priority, they are only one part of the U.S.-Russia relationship. Today, I again expressed my deepest condolences for the terrible loss of Russian life in recent terrorist attacks, and we will remain steadfast partners in combating violent extremism. We also discussed the potential to expand our cooperation on behalf of economic growth, trade and investment, as well as technological innovation, and I look forward to discussing these issues further when President Medvedev visits the United States later this year, because there is much we can do on behalf of our security and prosperity if we continue to work together.

When one surveys the many challenges that we face around the world, it's easy to grow complacent, or to abandon the notion that progress can be shared. But I want to repeat what I said last year in Prague: When nations and peoples allow themselves to be defined by their differences, the gulf between them widens. When we fail to pursue peace, then it stays forever beyond our grasp.

This majestic city of Prague is in many ways a monument to human progress. And this ceremony is a testament to the truth that old adversaries can forge new partnerships. I could not help but be struck the other day by the words of Arkady Brish, who helped build the Soviet Union's first atom bomb. At the age of 92, having lived to see the horrors of a World War and the divisions of a Cold War, he said, "We hope humanity will reach the moment when there is no need for nuclear weapons, when there is peace and calm in the world."

It's easy to dismiss those voices. But doing so risks repeating the horrors of the past, while ignoring the history of human progress. The pursuit of peace and calm and cooperation among nations is the work of both leaders and peoples in the 21st century. For we must be as persistent and passionate in our pursuit of progress as any who would stand in our way. Once again, President Medvedev, thank you for your extraordinary leadership.

We recognize, however, that Russia has a significant interest in this issue, and what we've committed to doing is to engaging in a significant discussion not only bilaterally but also having discussions with our European allies and others about a framework in which we can potentially cooperate on issues of missile defense in a way that preserves U.S. national security interests, preserves Russia's national security interests, and allows us to guard against a rogue missile from any source.

So I'm actually optimistic that having completed this treaty, which signals our strong commitment to a reduction in overall nuclear weapons, and that I believe is going to strengthen the Nuclear Non-Proliferation Treaty regime, that sends a signal around the world that the United States and Russia are prepared to once again take leadership in moving in the direction of reducing reliance on nuclear weapons and preventing the spread of nuclear weapons, as well as nuclear materials, that we will have built the kind of trust not only between Presidents but also between governments and between peoples that allows us to move forward in a constructive way.

I've repeatedly said that we will not do anything that endangers or limits my ability as Commander-in-Chief to protect the American people. And we think that missile defense can be an important component of that. But we also want to make clear that the approach that we've taken in no way is intended to change the strategic balance between the United States and Russia. And I'm actually confident that, moving forward, as we have these discussions, it will be part of a broader set of discussions about, for example, how we can take tactical nuclear weapons out of theater, the possibilities of us making more significant cuts not only in deployed but also non-deployed missiles. There are a whole range of issues that I think that we can make significant progress on. I'm confident that this is an important first step in that direction.

APPENDIX F
PLOUGHSHARES FUND

Ploughshares Fund works to build a safe, secure nuclear-weapon-free world by developing and investing in initiatives to reduce and ultimately eliminate the world's nuclear stockpiles and to promote stability in regions of conflict. Ploughshares Fund is supported by individuals, families, and foundations. A public grant-making foundation, Ploughshares Fund is the largest grant maker in the United States dedicated exclusively to peace and security funding. Since is founding in 1981 by San Francisco philanthropist Sally Lilienthal, Ploughshares Fund has invested almost $100 million in the smartest people with the best ideas for keeping our nation safe and all nations at peace. The foundation has given grants to reduce the threats from nuclear weapons and proliferation and to support on-the-ground projects to reduce the incidence of violent conflict and to help rebuild civil society in regions where nuclear weapons are a factor.

The foundation's efforts are rooted in the conviction that civil society has an essential role to play in policy change, sometimes in partnership with government but often by taking leadership when government leaders cannot. We help build a dynamic community of smart, dedicated people with novel, practicable ideas and the resources to put those ideas into action. For thirty-two years, Ploughshares Fund has worked to create and strengthen that community, both by providing support for key individual initiatives on every continent and by enhancing that community's collective impact.

For more information, please visit www.ploughshares.org.

ACKNOWLEDGMENTS

Some books are solitary journeys; this one was a collective enterprise from start to finish. Anne Routon, senior editor at Columbia University Press, made possible the production and publication of my first book, *Bomb Scare: The History and Future of Nuclear Weapons*. Her faith in me and her persistence also yielded this second book, though several years after she initially suggested I write it. Rebecca Remy, my special assistant at Ploughshares Fund, did an amazing job of managing the production of this work, organizing, cajoling, correcting, and encouraging me every step of the way.

I could not have written this book without the dedicated support of several gifted researchers. Benjamin Loehrke, our senior analyst at Ploughshares Fund, helped draft the very first chapter of this book several years ago then looked on in bemusement as I postponed again and again the writing of the other chapters. His patient research underpins the analysis in chapter 6 on budgets and the original article in the *Brown Journal of World Affairs* upon which it is based.

Mary Kaszynski, now with ReThink Media, worked as my research intern for many months and proved absolutely brilliant at budgets and the arcana of nuclear weapons policy. Leah Fae Cochran followed ably in Mary's footsteps and drafted major sections in this book, particularly on Pakistan, Iran, and North Korea. Marianne Fisher helped bring the book into the final lap, and Alyssa Demus, with her keen eye and intellect, was absolutely essential to carrying us over the finish line. I must also thank Rizwan Ladha for his excellent research on Pakistan during his summer internship. I am also grateful to all the publishers who gave me permission to adapt for this book chapters and articles I wrote originally for them.

During this entire, lengthy process, I am very grateful for the support and understanding of my colleagues at Ploughshares Fund. They did not choose me to be their president so that I could write books. But I never doubted that the foundation could spare my weeks of diverted attention as long as we had Philip Yun smoothly steering us as our executive director and chief operating officer, Samara Dun sustaining us as our development director, Paul Carroll judiciously guiding our grants as our program director, Joel Rubin masterfully maneuvering us through the Washington currents as our policy and government affairs director, Margaret Swink ensuring we effectively deliver our message as our communications director, and Cathy Kalin making sure the ship is water tight as our operations director. They, with Lorely Bunoan, Peter Fedewa, and Elizabeth Rogers, form the most effective, innovative, smoothly running operation I have ever had the privilege to join. I thank the board of directors, led by our indefatigable previous chairman, Roger Hale, and our dynamic current chairwoman, Mary Estrin, for its support and encouragement and our generous donors, without whom none of our work would be possible, including this book. Finally, I must thank our program officer, Kelly Bronk, who started helping me with this book four years ago when I hired her to be my assistant and to this day does not believe that I will ever finish it.

While I am honored to serve on the International Security Advisory Board to the secretary of state, the views I express in this book and elsewhere are mine alone and do not necessarily represent those of the U.S. Department of State or of the U.S. government.

Books and jobs come and go, but my family is my rock. I have an amazing wife, Priscilla Labovitz, and two grown and incredibly talented children, Amy and Peter Cirincione, and now a son-in-law, Jon O'Conner. I am not sure if they will read any of this book beyond this page, or have read any of my other books, but their love sustains me, their humor lifts me, and a great deal of what I do, I do for them and their futures.

NOTES

INTRODUCTION

1. McGeorge Bundy, "To Cap the Volcano," *Foreign Affairs* 48, no. 1 (October 1969): 9–10.
2. CNN, "Obama Says Time to Rid World of Nuclear Weapons," July 16, 2008, http://www.cnn.com/2008/POLITICS/07/16/obama.speech/.
3. The poll, conducted by the Program on International Policy Attitudes/Knowledge Networks Poll, March 16–22, 2004, asked, "Based on what you know, do you think the U.S. should or should not participate in the following treaties and agreements? The treaty that would prohibit nuclear weapon test explosions worldwide." See http://www.pollingreport.com/defense.htm.
4. The poll, conducted by GfK Roper Public Affairs & Media, November 3–8, 2010, asked, "Which statement comes closest to your view? No countries should be allowed to have nuclear weapons. (62 percent in favor) Only the United States and its allies should be allowed to have nuclear weapons. (16 percent in favor) Only countries that already have nuclear weapons should be allowed to have them. (15 percent in favor) Any country that is able to develop nuclear weapons (6 percent in favor) should be allowed to have them." See http://www.pollingreport.com/defense.htm.

5. CBS News Poll, November 29–December 2, 2010, http://www.pollingreport.com/defense.htm.

6. The survey, which was statistically reliable to within 5 percent, not only asked Americans if they would cut the defense budget but to identify amounts for which areas they would cut. Given the choice of nuclear arms, ground forces, air power, or missile defense, the largest proportional cut chosen was nuclear weapons, at 27 percent. See R. Jeffrey Smith, "Public Overwhelmingly Supports Large Defense Cuts," Center for Public Integrity, May 10, 2012, http://www.publicintegrity.org/2012/05/10/8856/public-overwhelmingly-supports-large-defense-spending-cuts.

7. President John F. Kennedy, "Address Before the General Assembly of the United Nations," September 25, 1961, http://www.jfklibrary.org/Asset-Viewer/DOPIN64xJUG RKgdHJ9NfgQ.aspx.

8. President Ronald Reagan, "Address to the Nation and Other Countries on United States–Soviet Relations," January 16, 1984, http://www.reagan.utexas.edu/archives/speeches/1984/11684a.htm.

9. See the National Security Advisory Group, William J. Perry, chair, "Worst Weapons in Worst Hands: U.S. Inaction on the Nuclear Terror Threat Since 9/11, and a Path of Action," July, 2005), http://belfercenter.hks.harvard.edu/files/nsag_worst_weapons_in _worst_hands_july2005.pdf, 1.

10. See Stephen I. Schwartz, "Barack Obama and John McCain on Nuclear Security Issues," James Martin Center for Nonproliferation Studies, October 6, 2008, http://cns .miis.edu/stories/080925_obamamacain.htm#_edn6.

11. Carl von Clausewitz, *On War*, trans. J. J. Graham (1873), http://www.clausewitz.com/readings/OnWar1873/BK1ch07.html.

12. President Barack Obama, interview with Charlie Rose, CBS News, July 15, 2012, http://www.cbsnews.com/8301-3445_162-57472476/obama-not-enough-change-in -first-term/.

13. See, for example, Strobe Talbott, "An American President in the Age of Globalization," *Yale Global Online*, November 19, 2012, http://yaleglobal.yale.edu/content/american-president-age-globalization.

14. Conversations with author.

15. Joseph Cirincione, "Obama's Turn on Nuclear Weapons," *Foreign Affairs* 91, no. 1 (January/February 2012), http://www.foreignaffairs.com/articles/137075/joseph-cirincione /obamas-turn-on-nuclear-weapons.

16. Talbott, "An American President in the Age of Globalization."

17. "The Nuclear Agenda," *New York Times*, February 23, 2013, http://www.nytimes .com/2013/02/24/opinion/sunday/the-nuclear-agenda.html.

ONE **PROMISE**

1. The author gratefully acknowledges the research support of Benjamin Loehrke in the preparation of this chapter.

2. Edwin Chen and Hans Nichols, "Obama Condemns North Korea's Launch of a Missile," *Bloomberg*, April 5, 2009, http://www.bloomberg.com/apps/news?pid=20601087&sid=acFUssUbIDvc.

3. William J. Broad, "North Korean Missile Launch Was a Failure, Experts Say," *New York Times*, April 5, 2008, http://www.nytimes.com/2009/04/06/world/asia/06korea.html.

TWO **LEGACY**

1. This chapter is based on my "Strategic Collapse: The Failure of the Bush Nuclear Doctrine," originally published by the Arms Control Association in the November 2008 edition of *Arms Control Today*, http://www.armscontrol.org/act/2008_11/cirincione

2. Glenn Kessler, "Rice: U.S. Has Aided in Nuclear Regulation," *Washington Post*, September 8, 2008, http://www.washingtonpost.com/wp-dyn/content/article/2008/09/07/AR2008090702490.html; also see U.S. Department of State, "Remarks with Moroccan Foreign Minister Fassi Fihri at Press Conference with Secretary of State Condoleezza Rice," September 7, 2008, available from http://www.africom.mil/Newsroom/Transcript/6300/transcript-us-secretary-of-state-condoleezza-rice-.

3. John Bolton, "A Legacy of Betrayal," *Washington Times*, May 12, 1999, http://www.aei.org/article/foreign-and-defense-policy/international-organizations/a-legacy-of-betrayal/.

4. Dafna Linzer, "The NSC's Sesame Street Generation," *Washington Post*, March 12, 2006, http://www.washingtonpost.com/wp-dyn/content/article/2006/03/10/AR2006031002003.html.

5. Gary Schmitt, "Memorandum To: Opinion Leaders," Project for a New American Century, August 2, 2005, http://www.newamericancentury.org/iran-20050802.htm.

6. Elliot Abrams, special assistant to the president and senior director on the National Security Council for Near East and North African affairs (2002–2005) and deputy national security adviser (2005–2008); John Bolton, undersecretary of state for arms control and international security (2001–2005) and U.S. permanent representative to the United Nations (2005); Richard Perle, Defense Policy Board chairman (2001–2003); Paul Wolfowitz, deputy secretary of defense (2001–2005) and State Department International Security Advisory Board chairman (2008).

7. Condoleezza Rice, "Campaign 2000: Promoting the National Interest," *Foreign Affairs* 79, no. 1 (January/February 2000), http://www.foreignaffairs.com/articles/55630/condoleezza-rice/campaign-2000-promoting-the-national-interest; Robert Kagan, "The Benevolent Empire," *Foreign Policy* no. 111 (Summer 1998): 24–34, available from http://people.cas.sc.edu/rosati/a.kaplan.benevolentempire.fp.sum98.pdf.

8. Office of the Press Secretary, the White House, "President Bush Delivers Graduation Speech at West Point," Washington, D.C., June 1, 2002, http://georgewbush-white house.archives.gov/news/releases/2002/06/20020601-3.html.

9. Office of the Press Secretary, the White House, "President Bush Delivers 'State of the Union,'" Washington DC, January 28, 2003, http://georgewbush-whitehouse.archives .gov/news/releases/2003/01/20030128-19.html.

10. Paul Wolfowitz, interview, on "Campaign Against Terror," *Frontline PBS*, April 22, 2002, http://www.pbs.org/wgbh/pages/frontline/shows/campaign/interviews/wolfo witz.html.

11. State Department, "National Strategy to Combat Weapons of Mass Destruction," December 2002, 1, http://www.state.gov/documents/organization/16092.pdf.

12. Department of Defense, "Nuclear Posture Review Report," December 31, 2001.

13. David Sanger, "Bush Outlines Doctrine of Striking Foes First," *New York Times*, September 20, 2002, http://www.nytimes.com/2002/09/20/international/20CND-STRA .html.

14. The Congressional Research Service calculates that the wars in Iraq and Afghanistan had cost $859 billion by mid-2008. The Congressional Budget Office estimates the wars would eventually cost $2.4 trillion. See Amy Belasco, "Cost of Iraq, Afghanistan, and Other Global War on Terror Operations Since 9/11," *CRS Report for Congress*, July 14, 2008; Congressional Budget Office, *Estimated Costs of U.S. Operation in Iraq and Afghanistan and of Other Activities Related to the War on Terrorism Before the House Committee on the Budget*, 110th Cong. (October 24, 2007) (statement of Peter Orszag, vice chairman of Global Banking at Citigroup); See also Travis Sharp and John Andrews, "Analysis of House-Senate Agreement on FY2009 Defense Authorization Bill (S.3001)," Center for Arms Control and Non-Proliferation, September 24, 2008, http://arms controlcenter.org/issues/securityspending/articles/analysis_c110_s3001_conference/ index.html.

15. See David Sanger, "Aftereffects: Nuclear Standoff," *New York Times*, April 21, 2003, http://www.nytimes.com/2003/04/21/world/aftereffects-nuclear-standoff-adminis tration-divided-over-north-korea.html.

16. Office of the Press Secretary, the White House, "President Says Saddam Hussein Must Leave Iraq Within 48 Hours," March 17, 2003, http://georgewbush-whitehouse .archives.gov/news/releases/2003/03/20030317-7.html.

17. Thomas E. Ricks, *Fiasco: The American Military Adventure in Iraq* (New York: Penguin, 2006), 3.

18. Jeffrey M. Jones, "Opposition to Iraq War Reaches New High," Gallup Inc., April 24, 2008, http://www.gallup.com/poll/106783/opposition-iraq-war-reaches-new-high .aspx.

19. Pew Research Center, "U.S. Image Up Slightly, but Still Negative: American Character Gets Mixed Reviews," June 23, 2005.

20. *DCI's Global Intelligence Challenges: Briefing Before the Senate Select Committee on Intelligence*, 109th Congress (February 16, 2005) (testimony of Porter Goss, director of the Central Intelligence Agency); see also, *Current and Projected National Security Threats to the United States Before the Senate Select Committee on Intelligence*, 109th Cong. (February 16, 2005) (testimony of Vice Admiral Lowell E. Jacoby, director of the Defense Intelligence Agency).

21. In 2002 the number of "significant" international terrorist incidents was 136; in 2003 it was 175; and in 2004, it was 651. See U.S. Department of State, "Patterns of Global Terrorism 2002," http://www.state.gov/j/ct/rls/crt/2002/; U.S. Department of State, "Patterns of Global Terrorism 2003," http://www.state.gov/j/ct/rls/crt/2003/. Also see National Counterterrorism Center, "A Chronology of Significant International Terrorism for 2004," April 27, 2008, http://www.fas.org/irp/threat/nctc2004.pdf.

22. Matthew Bunn and Anthony Weir, *Securing the Bomb 2005: The New Global Imperatives* (Cambridge, Mass.: Belfer Center for Science and International Affairs, 2005), 30–32, http://www.nti.org/media/pdfs/securing-the-bomb-2005-fullreport .pdf?_-1322768203; also see National Nuclear Security Administration (NNSA), "Fact Sheet. NNSA Expands Nuclear Security Cooperation With Russia," October 2005.

23. Brian Finlay, "Nuclear Terrorism: U.S. Policies to Reduce the Threat of Nuclear Terror," Partnership for a Secure America, September 2008, http://www.psaonline.org/down loads/NUCLEAR%20report%208-28-08.pdf.

24. Lee Hamilton and Thomas Kean, "WMD Report Card: Evaluating U.S. Policies to Prevent Nuclear, Chemical, and Biological Terrorism Since 2005," Partnership for a Secure America, September 2008), 3, http://www.psaonline.org/downloads/ReportCard%20 8-25-08.pdf.

25. Nicholas Burns, "We Should Talk to Our Enemies," *Newsweek*, October 25, 2008, http:// www.thedailybeast.com/newsweek/2008/10/24/we-should-talk-to-our-enemies. html. Former secretaries of state Madeleine Albright, James Baker, Warren Christopher, Henry Kissinger, and Colin Powell said they favored talking to Iran as part of a strategy to stop Tehran's development of a nuclear weapons program during a forum hosted by The George Washington University on September 15, 2008. Former national security advisers Zbigniew Brzezinski and Brent Scowcroft also praised engagement at a July 2008 event at the Center for Strategic and International Studies.

26. Chuck Hagel and Peter Kaminsky, *America: Our Next Chapter, Tough Questions, Straight Answers* (New York: Harper Collins, 2008), 93.

27. Alex Wagner, "Bush Puts N. Korea Negotiations on Hold, Stresses Verification," *Arms Control Today* (April 2001), http://www.armscontrol.org/print/832.

28. Ibid.

29. Johnathan D. Pollack, "The United States, North Korea, and the End of the Agreed Framework," *Naval War College Review* (Summer 2003): 26, http://www.army.mil/ professionalWriting/volumes/volume1/august_2003/8_03_1.html.

30. Arms Control Association, "Chronology of U.S.-North Korean Nuclear and Missile Diplomacy," (April 2012), http://www.armscontrol.org/factsheets/dprkchron.

31. Office of the Press Secretary, the White House, "President Announces New Measures to Counter the Threat of WMD," February 11, 2004, http://georgewbush-whitehouse.archives.gov/news/releases/2004/02/20040211-4.html.

32. Steve Kingstone, "Brazil Joins World's Nuclear Club," *BBC News*, May 6, 2006, http://news.bbc.co.uk/2/hi/americas/4981202.stm. See Leonor Tomero, "The Future of GNEP: The International Partners," *Bulletin of the Atomic Scientists*, Reports, July 31, 2008, http://www.thebulletin.org/web-edition/reports/the-future-of-gnep/the-future-of-gnep-the-international-partners.

33. Sharon Squassoni, "Risks and Realities: The New Nuclear Energy Revival," *Arms Control Today* (May 2007), http://www.armscontrol.org/act/2007_05/squassoni.

34. Robert Norris, William Arkin, Hans Kristensen, and Joshua Handler, "Russian Nuclear Forces, 2002," *Bulletin of the Atomic Scientists* 58, no. 4 (July/August 2002): 71–73, http://bos.sagepub.com/content/58/4/71.full.

35. Presidents Bush and Vladimir Putin signed SORT in June 2002. Both sides were required to reduce their deployed strategic nuclear weapons to between 1,700 and 2,200 by the end of 2012. Under the proposed START III, negotiated by Presidents Bill Clinton and Boris Yeltsin in 1997, each side would have drawn down to similar numbers of deployed strategic nuclear weapons by 2007, five years earlier than envisioned under SORT. START III would also have provided a framework for discussions on reductions in tactical nuclear weapons and dismantlement of warheads. See Joseph Cirincione, Jon Wolfsthal, and Miriam Rajkumar, *Deadly Arsenals* (Washington, D.C.: Carnegie Endowment for International Peace, 2005), 204–5, 209–11. See Hans Kristensen and Robert Norris, "Nuclear Notebook: U.S. Nuclear Forces, 2008," *Bulletin of the Atomic Scientists* 64, no.1 (March/April 2008): 50–53, http://bos.sagepub.com/content/64/1/50.full.

36. Daryl G. Kimball and Miles A. Pomper, "A World Free of Nuclear Weapons: An Interview with Nuclear Threat Initiative Co-Chairman Sam Nunn," *Arms Control Today* (March 2008), http://www.armscontrol.org/act/2008_03/Nunn.

37. Stephen Hadley, "Policy Consideration in Using Nuclear Weapons," *Duke Journal of Comparative and International Law* 8, no. 23 (Fall 1997): 23, http://scholarship.law.duke.edu/djcil/vol8/iss1/4/.

38. Several of the participants were appointed to senior positions on nuclear policy in the Bush administration, including Linton Brooks, Stephen Cambone, and Robert Joseph. See Keith Payne et al., "Rationale and Requirements for U.S. Nuclear Forces and Arms Control," National Institute for Public Policy, January 2001, http://www.nipp.org/National%20Institute%20Press/Archives/Publication%20Archive%20PDF/volume%201%20complete.pdf.

39. Department of Defense, "Nuclear Posture Review Report," Washington D.C., April 2010, http://www.defense.gov/npr/docs/2010%20Nuclear%20Posture%20Review%20Report.pdf.

40. "Pakistan Demands U.S. Nuclear Deal," *BBC News*, October 2, 2008, http://news.bbc .co.uk/2/hi/south_asia/7648435.stm.

41. Josh Loewenstein, "House Set to Approve Version of U.S.-India Deal With Added Oversight," *CongressNow*, September 25, 2008.

42. Kofi Annan, "A More Secure World: Our Shared Responsibility," Report of the High-Level Panel on Threats, Challenges, and Change, United Nations, December 1, 2004, 3, http://www.un.org/secureworld/report2.pdf.

43. Ian Cobain and Ian Traynor, "Intelligence Report Claims Nuclear Market Thriving," *Guardian*, January 4, 2006, http://www.guardian.co.uk/world/2006/jan/04/iran .armstrade.

44. In April 2008, the former Pentagon director of operational test and evaluation Philip Coyle told the House Oversight and Government Reform Subcommittee on National Security and Foreign Affairs that the antimissile system being deployed in Europe "still has no demonstrated effectiveness to defend the U.S., let alone Europe, against enemy attack under realistic operational conditions." Lisbeth Gronlund, a senior scientist with the Union of Concerned Scientists, commented at the same hearing that "the United States is no closer today to being able to effectively defend against long-range ballistic missiles than it was 25 years ago." See *What Are the Prospects? What Are the Costs? Oversight of Missile Defense Before the House Committee on Oversight and Government Reform*, 110th Cong. (April 2008) (statement of Phillip Coyle, former Pentagon director of operational test and evaluation).

45. Richard Haass "Regime Change and Its Limits," *Foreign Affairs* (July/August 2005), http://www.foreignaffairs.com/articles/60823/richard-n-haass/regime-change -and-its-limits.

46. Nicholas Burns, "We Should Talk to Our Enemies," *The Daily Beast*, August 24, 2008, http://www.thedailybeast.com/newsweek/2008/10/24/we-should-talk-to-our -enemies.html.

47. Wolfgang Panofsky, "Nuclear Insecurity," *Foreign Affairs* (September/October 2007), http://www.foreignaffairs.com/articles/62832/wolfgang-k-h-panofsky/nuclear -insecurity.

48. Barack Obama, "A New Strategy for a New World," speech, Washington, D.C., July 15, 2008, available from http://www.huffingtonpost.com/2008/07/15/read-obamas-iraq -speech-a_n_112871.html.

49. John McCain, remarks by to the Los Angeles World Affairs Council, March 26, 2008, available from http://thinkprogress.org/politics/2008/03/26/20858/ embargoed-mccains-speech-to-the-los-angeles-world-affairs-council/.

50. "2008 Republican Platform," Republican National Convention, Committee on Arrange-
     ments for the 2008 Republican National Convention, August 2008, 2.

51. "Renewing America's Promise" 2008 Democratic Party Platform, Democratic National
     Convention Committee, August 25, 2008, 31–32.

52. Ivo Daalder and Jan Lodal, "The Logic of Zero: Towards a World Without Nuclear
     Weapons," *Foreign Affairs* (November/December 2008): 81.

THREE **PIVOT**

1.   This chapter is based on my "The Nuclear Pivot: Change and Continuity in American
     Nuclear Policy," originally published in *RUSI Journal* 155, no. 3 (June 2010), http://
     www.rusi.org/publications/journal/ref:A4C21D6A2C1BC6/#.UTodN9FtXsI.

2.   Barack Obama, "Remarks by President Barack Obama," Hradcany Square, Prague,
     Czech Republic, April 5, 2009, http://www.whitehouse.gov/the_press_office/
     Remarks-By-President-Barack-Obama-In-Prague-As-Delivered.

3.   Barack Obama, remarks at UN Security Council Meeting, New York, September 24,
     2009, http://www.whitehouse.gov/the-press-office/remarks-president-un-security
     -council-summit-nuclear-non-proliferation-and-nuclear-.

4.   Jim Hoagland, "President Obama's Farsighted Nuclear Strategy," *Washington Post*,
     April 18, 2010, http://www.washingtonpost.com/wp-dyn/content/article/2010/04/16/
     AR2010041603992.html.

5.   United States National Security Council, *National Security Strategy* (Washington, D.C.:
     Government Printing Office, 2010), http://www.whitehouse.gov/sites/default/files/
     rss_viewer/national_security_strategy.pdf.

6.   U.S. Department of Defense, "Nuclear Posture Review Report," Washington, D.C., April
     2010, http://www.defense.gov/npr/docs/2010%20nuclear%20posture%20review%20
     report.pdf.

7.   Ibid., i.

8.   Elaine M. Grossman, "Gates Sees Stark Choice on Nuke Tests, Modernization," *Glob-
     al Security Newswire*, October 29, 2008, http://www.nti.org/gsn/article/gates-sees
     -stark-choice-on-nuke-tests-modernization/.

9.   George Shultz, "Debating Obama's New Nuclear Doctrine," *Wall Street Journal*, April
     13, 2010, http://online.wsj.com/article/SB1000142405270230422250457517420011402
     8206.html.

10. James N. Miller, principal deputy undersecretary for policy at the Department of De-
     fense, remarks to the Defense Writers Group, Washington, D.C., June 4, 2010.

11. Ibid.

12. Ben Armbruster, "Conservatives Falsely Claim New Obama Nuke Policy Prevents Nu-
     clear Retaliation Against Chem/Bio Attack," *Think Progress*, April 7, 2010, http://think
     progress.org/security/2010/04/07/90545/conservatives-nuclear-posture-review/.

13. Charles Krauthammer, "Nuclear Posturing, Obama Style," *National Review Online*, April 9, 2010, http://www.nationalreview.com/articles/229509/nuclear-posturing -obama-style/charles-krauthammer?pg=2.

14. "Nuclear Complex Upgrades Related to START Treaty to Cost $180 billion," Walter Pincus, *Washington Post*, May 14, 2010, http://www.washingtonpost.com/wp-dyn/con tent/article/2010/05/13/AR2010051305031.html.

15. Greg Mello, "The Obama Disarmament Paradox," *Bulletin of the Atomic Scientists*, February 4, 2010, http://www.thebulletin.org/web-edition/op-eds/the-obama -disarmament-paradox.

16. David Alexander, "After Early Successes, Obama Struggles to Implement Disarmament Vision," Reuters, August 31, 2012, http://www.reuters.com/article/2012/08/31/ us-usa-nuclear-arms idUSBRE87U06B20120831.

17. Ambassador Linton Brooks, remarks to the Center for Strategic and International Studies, Washington, D.C., April 16, 2010.

18. Tom Hunter, Michael Anastasio, and George Miller, "Tri-Lab Directors' Statement on the Nuclear Posture Review," Sandia National Laboratory, New Mexico, April 9, 2010, http://www.lanl.gov/newsroom/news-releases/2010/April/04.09-nuclear-posture -review.php.

19. Statement by minister for foreign affairs of Japan on the release of the U.S. Nuclear Posture Review, April 7, 2010; remarks by German federal foreign minister, Berlin, April 8, 2010; statements made by the Ministry of Foreign and European Affairs spokesperson, April 7, 2010; spokesperson's commentary, South Korean Ministry of Foreign Affairs and Trade and the Ministry of National Defense, April 7, 2010.

20. Richard Burt, "Debating Obama's New Nuclear Doctrine," *Wall Street Journal*, April 13, 2010, http://online.wsj.com/article/SB10001424052702304222504575174200114028206.html.

21. James Schlesinger, "The Historical and Modern Context for U.S.-Russian Arms Control," Testimony to the Senate Foreign Relations Committee, April 29, 2010.

22. James Baker, "The History and Lessons on START (Strategic Arms Reduction Treaty)," Testimony to the Senate Foreign Relations Committee, May 19, 2010.

23. William Perry, "The Historical and Modern Context for U.S.-Russian Arms Control," Testimony to the Senate Foreign Relations Committee, April 29, 2010.

24. Statement by David Miliband, foreign secretary of the United Kingdom, March 26, 2010.

25. Marty N. Natalegawa, statement at the NPT Conference, New York, May 3, 2010.

26. Hillary Clinton, statement at the NPT Conference, New York, May 3, 2010.

27. Marty M Natalegawa, statement on behalf of NAM States party to the NPT, May 3, 2010.

28. Daryl G. Kimball, "ACA Welcomes NPT Review Consensus," *Arms Control Association*, May 28, 2010, http://www.armscontrol.org/pressroom/NPTReviewConference2010.

29. John Duncan, "The NPT Review Conference: Capturing Success," *The Foreign and Commonwealth Office Blog*, June 3, 2010.

30. Eben Harell, "A Surprising Consensus on Nuclear Nonproliferation," *Time*, June 2, 2010, http://www.time.com/time/world/article/0,8599,1993339,00.html.

31. Barack Obama, speech at United States Military Academy at West Point Commencement, New York, May 22, 2010, http://www.whitehouse.gov/the-press-office/remarks-president-united-states-military-academy-west-point-commencement.

FOUR **ARSENALS AND ACCIDENTS**

1. This chapter is based on "The Continuing Threat of Nuclear War," by Joseph Cirincione, chap. 18, pp. 381–401, from *Global Catastrophic Risk*, edited by N. Bostrom and M. M. Cirkovic (2008), free permission to use Author's own material by permission of Oxford University Press, www.oup.com.

2. Jonathan Schell, *The Fate of the Earth* (Palo Alto, Calif.: Stanford University Press, 2000), 3.

3. Calculations are based on the following deployed strategic warhead totals: 1992 combined total of 16,840 (U.S. 8,280, USSR 8,560); 2012 combined total of 4,380 (U.S. 1,950, USSR 2,430).

4. Adapted from Federation of American Scientists, "Status of World Nuclear Forces," December 18, 2012, http://www.fas.org/programs/ssp/nukes/nuclearweapons/nuke status.html.

5. Hans M. Kristensen and Robert S. Norris, "NRDC Nuclear Notebook, U.S. Nuclear Forces, 2013," *Bulletin of the Atomic Scientists* 69, no. 3 (March 2013): 84–91; Hans M. Kristensen and Robert S. Norris, "NRDC Nuclear Notebook, Russian Nuclear Forces, 2013," *Bulletin of the Atomic Scientists*, forthcoming; Matthew G. McKinzie, Thomas B. Cochran, Robert S. Norris, and William M. Arkin, *The U.S. Nuclear War Plan: A Time For Change* (New York: Natural Resources Defense Council, 2001), 42, 73, 84.

6. Jeffrey Lewis, "Nightmare on Nuke Street," *Foreign Policy*, October 30, 2012, http://www.foreignpolicy.com/articles/2012/10/30/nightmare_on_nuke_street.

7. Bruce G. Blair, "Primed and Ready," *The Defense Monitor: The Newsletter of the Center for Defense Information* 36, no. 3 (May/June 2007): 2–3.

8. Ibid.

9. Ibid.

10. Ibid.

11. Sam Nunn, speech to the Carnegie International Non-Proliferation Conference, June 21, 2004, http://www.nti.org/media/pdfs/statement_nunnceip_062104.pdf?_=1316466791.

12. Federation of American Scientists, "Status of World Nuclear Forces"; Hans N. Kristensen and Robert S. Norris, "Nonstrategic Nuclear Weapons, 2012," *Bulletin of the Atomic Sciences* 68, no. 5 (September/October 2012): 96–104, http://bos.sagepub.com/content/68/5/96.full.pdf; Kristensen and Norris, "NRDC Nuclear Notebook, Russian Nuclear Forces, 2013."

13. Hans M. Kristensen and Robert S. Norris, "NRDC Nuclear Notebook, French Nuclear Forces, 2008," *Bulletin of the Atomic Scientists* 64, no. 4 (September 2008): 52–54, http://bos.sagepub.com/content/64/4/52.full.

14. Hans M. Kristensen and Robert S. Norris, "NRDC Nuclear Notebook, Chinese Nuclear Forces, 2011," *Bulletin of the Atomic Scientists* 67, no. 6 (November 2011): 81–87, http://bos.sagepub.com/content/67/6/81.full.

15. Hans M. Kristensen and Robert S. Norris, "NRDC Nuclear Notebook, British Forces, 2011," *Bulletin of the Atomic Scientists* 67, no. 5 (September 2011): 89–97, http://bos.sagepub.com/content/57/6/78.full.

16. Shannon N. Kile, Phillip Schell, and Hans Kristensen, "Israeli Nuclear Forces," in *SIPRI Yearbook* (Stockholm: Stockholm International Peace Research Institute, 2012), http://www.sipri.org/research/armaments/nbc/nuclear. For the higher estimate, see Robert S. Norris, William M. Arkin, Hans M. Kristensen, and Joshua Handler, "NRDC Nuclear Notebook, Israeli Nuclear Forces, 2002," *Bulletin of the Atomic Scientists* 58, no. 5 (September 2002): 73–75, http://bos.sagepub.com/content/58/5/73.full.

17. Kile, Schell, and Kristensen, "Israeli Nuclear Forces."

18. Hans M. Kristensen and Robert S. Norris, "NRDC Nuclear Notebook, Indian Forces, 2012," *Bulletin of the Atomic Scientists* 68, no. 4 (July 2012): 96–101, http://bos.sagepub.com/content/68/4/96.full.

19. Hans Kristensen, "North Korea: FAS Says We Have Nukes!" *FAS Strategic Security Blog,* November 27, 2009, http://www.fas.org/blog/ssp/2009/11/dprk.php.

20. Scott Sagan, "A Call for Global Nuclear Disarmament," *Nature,* July 5, 2012, 30, http://cisac.stanford.edu/publications/a_call_for_global_nuclear_disarmament.

21. Ibid., 32.

FIVE CALCULATING ARMAGEDDON

1. This chapter is based on "The Continuing Threat of Nuclear War," by Joseph Cirincione, chap. 18, pp. 381–401, from *Global Catastrophic Risk,* edited by N. Bostrom and M. M. Cirkovic (2008), free permission to use Author's own material by permission of Oxford University Press, www.oup.com.

2. Bruce G. Blaire et al., "Accidental Nuclear War—a Post–Cold War Assessment," *The New England Journal of Medicine* 338, no. 18 (April 1998): 1326–32.

3. Lynn Eden, *Whole World on Fire: Organizations, Knowledge, and Nuclear Weapons Devastation* (Ithaca, N.Y.: Cornell University Press, 2004).

4. Office of Technology Assessment, *The Effects of Nuclear War* (Washington, D.C., 1979), 15, 35; Atomic Archive, "The Effects of Nuclear Weapons," National Science Digital Library, 2001, http://www.atomicarchive.com/Effects/index.shtml.

5. Blaire et al., "Accidental Nuclear War," 1326–32.

6. NRDC used computer software and unclassified databases to model a nuclear conflict and approximate the effects of the use of nuclear weapons based on an estimate of the U.S nuclear war plan. See Matthew G. McKinzie, Thomas B. Cochran, Robert S. Norris, and William M. Arkin, *The U.S Nuclear War Plan: A Time For Change* (New York: Natural Resources Defense Council, 2001), ix–xi, http://www.nrdc.org/nuclear/warplan/warplan_start.pdf.

7. McKinzie et al., *The U.S Nuclear War Plan*, 130.

8. Russian casualties are smaller that U.S. causalities because a higher percentage of Russians still live in rural areas and the lower-yield U.S. weapons produce less fallout. See Office of Technology Assessment, *The Effects of Nuclear War*.

9. Ibid., 4–5.

10. Ibid., 8.

11. Robert T. Batcher, "The Consequences of an Indo-Pakistani Nuclear War," *International Studies Review* 6, no. 4 (December 2004): 137.

12. R. P. Turco, O. B. Toon, T. P. Ackerman, J. B. Pollack, and C. Sagan, "Nuclear Winter: Global Consequences of Multiple Nuclear Explosions," *Science* 222, no. 4630 (December 1983): 1290, http://www.atmos.washington.edu/~ackerman/Articles/Turco_Nuclear_Winter_83.pdf.

13. R. P. Turco, O. B. Toon, T. P. Ackerman, J. B. Pollack, and C. Sagan, "Climate and Smoke: An Appraisal of Nuclear Winter," *Science* 247, no. 4939, (January 1990): 166, http://www.atmos.washington.edu/~ackerman/Articles/Turco_Nuclear_Winter_90.pdf.

14. Ibid.,174.

15. C. Sagan and R. P. Turco, "Nuclear Winter in the Post–Cold War Era," *Journal of Peace Research* 30, no. 4 (November 1993): 369.

16. O. B. Toon, A. Robock, R. P. Turco, C. Bardeen, L. Oman, and G. L. Stenchikov, "Consequences of Regional-Scale Nuclear Conflicts," *Science* 315, no. 5816 (March 2007): 1224–25, http://climate.envsci.rutgers.edu/pdf/SciencePolicyForumNW.pdf; A. Robock, L. Oman, G. L. Stenchikov, O. B Toon, C. Bardeen, and R. P. Turco, "Climatic Consequences of Regional Nuclear Conflicts," *Atmospheric Chemistry and Physics Discussions* (April 2007): 11818.

17. Toon et al., "Consequences of Regional-Scale Nuclear Conflicts," 1224–25.

18. Robock et al., "Climatic Consequences of Regional Nuclear Conflicts," 11823.

19. Ira Helfand, "Nuclear Famine: A Billion People at Risk: Global Impacts of Limited Nuclear War on Agriculture, Food Supplies, and Human Nutrition," Physicians for Social Responsibility, 2012, http://www.psr.org/nuclear-weapons/nuclear-famine-report.pdf.

20. Scott D. Sagan and Kenneth N. Waltz, *The Spread of Nuclear Weapons: A Debate Renewed* (New York: Norton, 2003), 115.

21. Michael Krepon, "From Confrontation to Cooperation," Henry L. Stimson Center, November 17, 2004, http://www.stimson.org/essays/from-confrontation-to-cooperation/.

22. P. R. Chari, "Nuclear Restraint, Nuclear Risk Reduction, and the Security-Insecurity Paradox in South Asia," Henry L. Stimson Center, 2004, http://www.stimson.org/images/uploads/research-pdfs/NRRMChari.pdf.

23. George Perkovich, Jessica Mathew, Joseph Cirincione, Rose Gottemoeller, and Jon Wolfsthal, *Universal Compliance: A Strategy for Nuclear Security* (Washington, D.C.: Carnegie Endowment for International Peace, 2005), 24, 34, and 39, https://www.carnegieendowment.org/files/univ_comp_rpt07_final1.pdf.

SIX EXPLODING BUDGETS

1. This chapter is based on my "The Fiscal Logic of Zero," originally published in the *Brown Journal of World Affairs* in 2011, http://bjwa.org/article.php?id=8ckn4rGp5fRK PQ9cpeFdT6DmLC6sJ4dY3QakmNyI. Benjamin Loehrke, Mary Kaszynski, and Leah Fae Cochran provided valuable research and assistance for the original article and its revision into this greatly expanded chapter.

2. Department of Defense, "Defense Budget Priorities and Choices," January 2012, 2, http://www.defense.gov/news/Defense_Budget_Priorities.pdf.

3. "Consulting the American People on National Defense Spending," Program for Public Consultation, Stimson Center, Center for Public Integrity, May 2012, 17, http://www.stimson.org/images/uploads/research-pdfs/DefenseBudget_May12_rpt1.pdf.

4. Ibid., 29.

5. Ibid.

6. Ibid., 30.

7. Nickolas Roth, "NNSA and Its Terrible, Horrible, No Good, Very Bad Week," *Nukes of Hazard*, October 4, 2012, http://nukesofhazardblog.com/story/2012/10/4/18624/6553.

8. "Editorial: Axing NNSA Should Be Among Options," *The Albuquerque Journal*, November 25, 2012, http://www.abqjournal.com/main/2012/11/25/opinion/axing-nnsa-should-be-among-options.html.

9. Budget estimates from Russell Rumbaugh and Nathan Cohn, *Resolving Ambiguities: Costing Nuclear Weapons* (Washington, D.C.: Stimson Center, 2012), http://www.stimson.org/images/uploads/research-pdfs/RESOLVING_FP_4_no_crop_marks.pdf.

10. Ploughshares Fund, *Working Paper: What Nuclear Weapons Cost Us* (Washington, D.C.: Ploughshares Fund, 2012), 1, http://www.ploughshares.org/sites/default/files/resources/What%20Nuclear%20Weapons%20Cost%20Us%20Final%20(100212).pdf.

11. At the end of fiscal year 2011 (September 2011), China owned $1.27 billion in U.S. Treasury securities, about 8 percent of the U.S. national debt. See U.S. Treasury Department data, available at http://www.treasury.gov/resource-center/data-chart-center/tic/Documents/mfh.txt. For China's defense budget, see Stockholm International Peace Research Institute, "Military Expenditure Database," http://milexdata.sipri.org/result.php4.

12. Roger Altman and Richard Haass, "American Profligacy and American Power," *Foreign Affairs* 89, no. 6 (November/December 2010), http://www.foreignaffairs.com/articles/66778/roger-c-altman-and-richard-n-haass/american-profligacy-and-american-power.

13. Robert Gates, "Statement on Department Budget and Efficiencies," the Pentagon, Washington, D.C., January 6, 2011, http://www.defense.gov/speeches/speech.aspx?speechid=1527.

14. Baker Spring, "Obama's Defense Budget Makes Protecting America Its Lowest Priority," The Heritage Foundation, March 1, 2012, http://www.heritage.org/research/reports/2012/03/obamas-defense-budget-makes-protecting-america-its-lowest-priority.

15. This figure includes $528 billion for the budget of the Department of Defense and $159 billion for the cost of the wars in Iraq and Afghanistan. Figures from White House Office of Management and Budget, Historical Table 5.1, "Budget Authority by Function and Subfunction: 1976–2017," http://www.whitehouse.gov/omb/budget/Historicals.

16. White House Office of Management and Budget, Historical Table 5.1; Stockholm International Peace Research Institute (SIPRI), "The Fifteen Countries with the Highest Military Expenditure in 2011 (Table)," September 2011, http://www.sipri.org/research/armaments/milex/resultoutput/milex_15/the-15-countries-with-the-highest-military-expenditure-in-2011-table/view.

17. Office of the Undersecretary of Defense (Comptroller/CFO), *Overview of Fiscal Year 2013 Budget Request* (Washington, D.C.: Department of Defense, 2012), http://comptroller.defense.gov/defbudget/fy2013/FY2013_Budget_Request_Overview_Book.pdf.

18. Eric Cantor, on *Meet the Press*, NBC, January 23, 2011.

19. Rick Maze, "House GOP Looks to Trim Defense, Vets Spending," *Military Times*, February 7, 2011, http://www.militarytimes.com/news/2011/02/military-republicans-budget-020711w/.

20. Rand Paul, "Defense Cuts Are Essential for Deficit Reduction," December 10, 2010, http://www.randpaul2016.com/2010/12/defense-cuts-are-essential-for-deficit-reduction/.

21. Congressional Budget Office, "Budget Infographic—Discretionary," April 17, 2012, http://www.cbo.gov/publication/43155.

22. National Commission on Fiscal Responsibility and Reform, "The Moment of Truth," December 2010, 20–23, http://www.fiscalcommission.gov/sites/fiscalcommission.gov/files/documents/TheMomentofTruth12_1_2010.pdf.

23. "Solutions," OweNo.com, see http://oweno.com/solutions/.

24. "Securing the National Defense," OweNo.com, http://oweno.com/solutions/securing-the-national-defense/.

25. Todd Harrison, "Defense Funding in the Budget Control Act of 2011," Center for Strategic and Budgetary Assessments, August 2011, http://www.csbaonline.org/publications/2011/08/defense-funding-in-the-budget-control-act-of-2011/.

26. The president's FY13 request for the Pentagon budget exceeded the BCA cap by $4 billion as did the Senate mark of the 2013 National Defense Authorization Act. The House NDAA mark exceeded the cap by $8 billion.

27. "Shields and Brooks on the Job Report, Sequestration, and Tea Party Primary Wins," *PBS Newshour*, August 3, 2012, http://www.pbs.org/newshour/bb/politics/july-dec12/shieldsbrooks_08-03.html.

28. Aaron Mehta, "Dissent Among Republicans Over Defense Spending," Center for Public Integrity, August 15, 2012, http://www.publicintegrity.org/2012/08/15/10695/dissent-among-republicans-over-defense-spending.

29. "Rep. Adam Smith on Defense Issues," *C-SPAN's Newsmakers*, July 22, 2012, http://www.c-span.org/Events/Rep-Adam-Smith-on-Defense-Issues/10737432483-1/.

30. House Armed Services Committee Democrats, "Ranking Member Adam Smith on National Security Aspects of State of the Union," press release, U.S. House of Representatives, February 12, 2013, http://democrats.armedservices.house.gov/index.cfm/press-releases?ContentRecord_id=af720d7e-8f21-48a4-83c8-9a4018d-9f009&ContentType_id=770e20a9-5d2a-40c5-a868-bcf7de9173a9&Group_id=fca18578-e10c-42e8-855a-020244bd590f&MonthDisplay=1&YearDisplay=2013.

31. Thom Shanker, "Senator Urges Bigger Cuts to Nuclear Arsenal," *New York Times*, June 14, 2012, http://www.nytimes.com/2012/06/15/us/politics/senator-levin-urges-bigger-cuts-to-nuclear-arsenal.html.

32. Nuclear Threat Initiative, "Senator Says Nuclear Arsenal Spending Is 'Ripe for Cuts,'" *Global Security Newswire*, June 14, 2012, http://www.nti.org/gsn/article/powerful-senator-says-nuclear-stockpile-spending-ripe-cuts/.

33. Gen. James Cartwright (ret.), remarks by at Global Zero Summit, October 12, 2011.

34. John F. Kennedy, "Address Before the General Assembly of the United Nations," New York City, September 25, 1961, http://www.jfklibrary.org/Asset-Viewer/DOPIN64xJUGRKgdHJ9NfgQ.aspx.

35. The United States produced an estimated 70,000 nuclear weapons since 1945. The stockpile peaked in 1967 with an estimated 31,255 warheads.

36. See notes 10–11.

37. Rumbaugh and Cohn, *Resolving Ambiguities*.

38. Ibid., 6. This includes an estimated $91.8 to $99.1 billion on programs administered by the National Nuclear Security Administration (including funds for weapons activities, administrative costs, and naval reactors) and between $268.9 and $301.7 billion for the Department of Defense to sustain, operate, and modernize the U.S. strategic nuclear arsenal over the next ten years.

39. Ploughshares Fund, *Working Paper: What Nuclear Weapons Cost Us.*

40. Benjamin Loehrke, "Estimated Missile Defense Spending, FY13–FY17," Ploughshares Fund, August 2012, http://www.ploughshares.org/sites/default/files/resources/Ploughshares%20Missile%20Defense%20Estimate%20Budget_0.pdf.

41. To derive these costs and the other costs for nuclear-threat reduction and nuclear-incident management, the study used data for FY08 from analysts Stephen Schwartz and Deepti Choubey then assumed those costs to grow with inflation through FY22. See Schwartz and Choubey, "Nuclear Security Spending: Assessing Costs, Examining Priorities," Carnegie Endowment, 2009, http://www.carnegieendowment.org/2009/01/12/nuclear-security-spending-assessing-costs-examining-priorities/1vl5.

42. Barack Obama, "Remarks by President Barack Obama," Hradcany Square, Prague, Czech Republic, April 5, 2009, http://www.whitehouse.gov/the_press_office/Remarks-By-President-Barack-Obama-In-Prague-As-Delivered/.

43. Jim DeMint, "Will START Treaty Weaken U.S. Missile Defense? Senator Kerry Seems to Hope So," *Jim's Blog*, May 18, 2010, http://blog.heritage.org/2010/05/18/guest-blogger-will-start-treaty-weaken-u-s-missile-defense-senator-kerry-seems-to-hope-so/.

44. Jon Kyl, "The New Start Treaty: Time for a Careful Look," *Wall Street Journal*, July 8, 2010, http://online.wsj.com/article/SB10001424052748704293604575343360850107760.html.

45. Mark Thompson, "A New Nuclear Triad?" *Time*, February 13, 2011, http://nation.time.com/2011/02/13/a-new-nuclear-triad/.

46. Ronald O'Rourke, "Navy Ohio Replacement SSBN(X) Ballistic Missile Submarine Program: Background and Issues for Congress," Congressional Research Service, April 5, 2012, www.fas.org/sgp/crs/weapons/R41129.pdf.

47. Congressional Budget Office, "An Analysis of the Navy's Fiscal Year 2013 Shipbuilding Plan," July 2012, 16–17, http://www.cbo.gov/publication/43468.

48. Ibid.

49. Thirty years ago, U.S. submarines carried 4,782 nuclear warheads. Today the navy deploys about 1,100. See Natural Resources Defense Council, "Table of U.S. Strategic Offensive Force Loadings," http://www.nrdc.org/nuclear/nudb/datab1.asp.

50. Department of Defense, *Nuclear Posture Review Report*, April 2010, iii, http://www.defense.gov/npr/docs/2010%20nuclear%20posture%20review%20report.pdf.

51. Tom Collina, "Fact Sheet: Nuclear Modernization Programs," Arms Control Association, http://www.armscontrol.org/factsheets/USNuclearModernization.

52. Stephen Daggett and Pat Towell, "FY2013 Defense Budget Request: Overview and Context," Congressional Research Service, April 20, 2012, 10, www.fas.org/sgp/crs/natsec/R42489.pdf.

53. Daryl. G. Kimball, "Defuse the Exploding Cost of Nuclear Weapons," Arms Control Association, November 29, 2012, http://www.armscontrol.org/act/2012_12/Focus.

54. Dana J. Johnson, Christopher J. Bowie, Robert P. Hoffa, "Triad, Dyad, Monad: Shaping the U.S. Nuclear Force for the Future," Air Force Association, Mitchell Institute for Airpower Studies, December 2009, http://www.afa.org/mitchell/reports/MP5_Triad_1209.pdf.

55. Jeffrey Lewis, "Minimum Deterrence," *Bulletin of the Atomic Scientists* 64, no. 3 (July/August 2008), http://www.newamerica.net/publications/articles/2008/minimum_deterrence_7552.

56. Dwight Eisenhower, "Atoms for Peace," speech, 207th Plenary Meeting of the United Nations General Assembly, New York, December 8, 1953, http://www.iaea.org/About/history_speech.html.

57. "JFK on Nuclear Weapons and Non-Proliferation," The Carnegie Endowment for International Peace, November 17, 2003, http://carnegieendowment.org/2003/11/17/jfk-on-nuclear-weapons-and-non-proliferation/3zcu.

58. Ivo Daalder and Jan Lodal, "The Logic of Zero," *Foreign Affairs* 87, no. 6 (November/December 2008): 84, http://www.foreignaffairs.com/articles/64608/ivo-daalder-and-jan-lodal/the-logic-of-zero.

59. Valerie Plame Wilson and Queen Noor, interview with Savannah Guthrie, *Today Show*, MSNBC, November 16, 2012, http://video.today.msnbc.msn.com/today/49852931#49852931.

60. Daalder and Lodal, "The Logic of Zero," 90.

61. Steven M. Kosiak, *Spending on the US Strategic Nuclear Forces: Plans and Options for the Twenty-First Century* (Washington, D.C.: Center for Strategic and Budgetary Assessments, 2006), 50, http://www.csbaonline.org/wp-content/uploads/2007/03/2006.09.01-US-Strategic-Nuclear-Forces-Spending.pdf.

62. Benjamin H. Friedman and Christopher Preble, "Budgetary Savings from Military Restraint," CATO Institute, September 23, 2010, http://www.cato.org/sites/cato.org/files/pubs/pdf/PA667.pdf.

63. Benjamin H. Friedman and Justin Logan, "Why the U.S. Military Budget is 'Foolish and Sustainable,'" CATO Institute, May 2012, http://www.cato.org/sites/cato.org/files/articles/logan-friendman-obis-spring-2012.pdf.

64. Daryl Kimball, "Nuclear and Missile Systems We Can't Afford, Don't Need," *Arms Control Association* 3, no. 12 (July 2012), http://www.armscontrol.org/issuebriefs/Nuclear-and-Missile-Systems-We-Cant-Afford-Dont-Need%20.

65. Ibid.

66. Peter Fedewa, "Nuclear Weapons Spending Tops Five Major Cities," Ploughshares Fund, July 2, 2012. http://www.ploughshares.org/blog/2012-07-02/nuclear-weapons-spending-tops-five.

67. Rebeccah Heinrichs and Baker Spring, "Deterrence and Nuclear Targeting in the Twenty-First Century," The Heritage Foundation, November 30, 2012, http://www.heritage.org/research/reports/2012/11/deterrence-and-nuclear-targeting-in-the-21st-century.

68. Ibid.

69. Hans M. Kristensen and Robert S. Norris, "US Nuclear Forces, 2012," *Bulletin of the Atomic Scientists* 68, no. 3 (2012): 84–91, http://bos.sagepub.com/content/68/3/84.full.pdf.

70. Kristensen and Norris, "US Nuclear Forces, 2012."

71. Steven Pifer and Michael O'Hanlon, *The Opportunity: Next Steps in Reducing Nuclear Arms* (Harrisonburg, Va.: R. R. Donnelley, 2012), 178, 188.

72. Ibid.

73. "Modernizing U.S. Strategy, Force Structure, and Posture," Global Zero U.S. Nuclear Policy Commission Report, May 2012, http://www.ndr.de/info/programm/sendungen/streitkraefte_und_strategien/globalzeroreport101.pdf.

74. Ibid., 2.

75. Sidney Drell and James Goodby, "What Are Nuclear Weapons For?" Arms Control Association, April 2005, 14–18, http://www.armscontrol.org/pdf/USNW_2005_Drell-Goodby.pdf.

76. Gareth Evans and Yoriko Kawaguchi, "Eliminating Nuclear Threats: A Practical Agenda for Global Policymakers," Report of the International Commission on Nuclear Non-Proliferation and Disarmament, 2010, http://icnnd.org/Reference/reports/ent/pdf/ICNND_Report-EliminatingNuclearThreats.pdf.

77. Hans Kristensen, Robert Norris, and Ivan Oelrich, "From Counterforce to Minimal Deterrence: A New Nuclear Policy on the Path Toward Eliminating Nuclear Weapons," Federation of American Scientists and the Natural Resources Defense Council, 2009, 42–44, http://www.fas.org/programs/ssp/nukes/doctrine/targeting.pdf.

78. Friedman and Preble, "Budgetary Savings from Military Restraint," 8.

79. James Wood Forsyth Jr., B. Chance Saltzman, and Gary Schaub Jr., "Remembrance of Things Past: The Enduring Value of Nuclear Weapons," *Strategic Studies Quarterly* 1 (2010): 82.

80. Keith Payne, "Zero Nuclear Sense: Is Reckless Disarmament the Plan for Second Obama Term?" *Washington Times*, May 29, 2012, http://www.washingtontimes.com/news/2012/may/29/zero-nuclear-sense/print/#ixzz2CnGDkxtw.

81. Keith Payne, "Maintaining Flexible and Resilient Capabilities for Nuclear Deterrence," *Strategic Studies Quarterly* 5, no. 2 (Summer 2011): 7, http://www.au.af.mil/au/ssq/2011/summer/payne.pdf.

82. Senator Kelly Ayotte, "Ayotte Leads Freshman Senate Republicans in Calling on President to Fulfill Nuclear Modernization Commitment," April 26, 2012, http://www.ayotte.senate.gov/?p=press_release&id=564.

83. John R. Bolton, "What to Do About Syria?" *National Review*, June 11, 2012, http://www.nationalreview.com/articles/302104/what-do-about-syria-john-r-bolton.

84. Senator Jim DeMint, "The New START Treaty Weakens U.S. National Security," *U.S. News & World Report*, August 16, 2010, http://www.usnews.com/opinion/articles/2010/08/16/jim-demint-the-new-start-treaty-weakens-us-national-security.

85. Department of Defense, *Nuclear Posture Review Report*, 11.

86. Jeffrey Lewis, "It's Not You, It's Me," *Foreign Policy*, March 8, 2013, http://www.foreignpolicy.com/articles/2013/03/07/its_not_you_its_me.

87. Barry Blechman and Alexander Bollfrass, eds., *Elements of a Nuclear Disarmament Treaty* (Washington, D.C.: Stimson Center, 2010).

88. Frank Carlucci and William Perry, foreword to *Elements of a Nuclear Disarmament Treaty*, ed. Barry Blechman and Alexander Bollfrass (Washington, D.C.: Stimson Center, 2010), ix, available from http://www.stimson.org/images/uploads/research-pdfs/Preface_Foreword.pdf.

SEVEN **THE 95 PERCENT**

1. This chapter is based on my "Strategic Turn: New U.S. and Russian Views on Nuclear Weapons," was originally published by the American Strategy Program at the New America Foundation in June, 2011, http://www.newamerica.net/publications/policy/strategic_turn.

    The author gratefully acknowledges the research support of Benjamin Loehrke and Sarah Beth Cross in the preparation of this chapter.

2. New START counts each bomber as one weapon although bombers can carry six to sixteen bombs. Thus, the actual number of nuclear weapons allowed under the treaty is greater than 1,550.

3. Lynn Eden, "Underestimating the Consequences of Use of Nuclear Weapons: Condemned to Repeat the Past's Errors?" *Physics and Society* 34, no. 1 (January 2005): 5–7, http://fsi.stanford.edu/publications/underestimating_the_consequences_of_use_of_nuclear_weapons_condemned_to_repeat_the_pasts_errors.

4. R. Jeffrey Smith, "U.S. Nuclear Targeting Unaltered Since 2008," Center for Public Integrity, August 2, 2012, http://www.publicintegrity.org/2012/08/02/10554/us-nuclear-targeting-unaltered-2008.

5. Paul Lettow, *Ronald Reagan and His Quest to Abolish Nuclear Weapons* (New York: Random House, 2005), 243.

6. Mikhail Gorbachev, "Mikhail Gorbachev Calls for Elimination of Nuclear Weapons as Soon as Possible," *Wall Street Journal*, January 31, 2007, http://online.wsj.com/article/SB117021711101593402.html.

7. President George H. W. Bush, "Address to the Nation on Reducing United States and Soviet Nuclear Weapons," Washington, D.C., September 27, 1991, http://www.presidency.ucsb.edu/ws/index.php?pid=20035.

8. Cited in Susan J. Koch, *The Presidential Nuclear Initiatives of 1991–1992* (Washington, D.C: Center for the Study of Weapons of Mass Destruction, National Defense University, 2012), http://www.ndu.edu/press/lib/pdf/CSWMD-CaseStudy/CSWMD_CaseStudy-5.pdf.

9. Johan Bergenas, Miles A. Pomper, William Potter, and Nikolai Sokov, "Reducing and Regulating Tactical (Nonstrategic) Nuclear Weapons in Europe," James C. Martin Center for Nonproliferation Studies, December 2009), 44, http://cns.miis.edu/opapers/pdfs/reducing_tnw_april_2010.pdf.

10. Private discussion with author, March 2010, Washington, D.C.

11. Department of Defense, *Nuclear Posture Review Report*, April 2010, i, http://www.defense.gov/npr/docs/2010%20Nuclear%20Posture%20Review%20Report.pdf.

12. George Shultz, "Debating Obama's New Nuclear Doctrine," *Wall Street Journal*, April 13, 2010, http://online.wsj.com/article/SB10001424052702304222504575174200114028206.html.

13. Philip Taubman, *The Partnership* (New York: HarperCollins, 2012), 325.

14. Hillary Rodham Clinton, "Remarks at the United States Institute of Peace," Renaissance Mayflower Hotel, Washington, D.C., October 21, 2009, http://www.state.gov/secretary/rm/2009a/10/130806.htm.

15. Department of Defense, *Nuclear Posture Review Report*, 12.

16. John Cornyn, "New START in Strategic Context," Floor Statement, United States Senate, December 22, 2010, http://www.cornyn.senate.gov/public/index.cfm?p=NewsReleases&ContentRecord_id=d12fd78a-5244-4336-9760-a26b9377ccc9.

17. Jon Kyl, "Keynote Address at Nixon Policy Conference," Nixon Center, Washington, D.C., May 19, 2010.

18. Baker Spring and Ariel Cohen, "Beware the Next U.S.-Russian Arms Control Treaty," Heritage Foundation, May 27, 2011, http://www.heritage.org/research/reports/2011/05/beware-the-next-us-russian-arms-control-treaty.

19. Daryl G. Kimball, Oliver Meier, and Paul Ingram, "NATO on Nuclear Weapons: Opportunities Missed and Next Steps Forward," *Arms Control Now: Blog of the Arms Control Association*, May 21, 2012, http://armscontrolnow.org/2012/05/21/nato-on-nuclear-weapons-opportunities-missed-and-next-steps-forward/.

20. NATO Press Release 063, "Deterrence and Defence Posture Review," May 20, 2012, http://www.nato.int/cps/en/SID-193D7980-4A881D9C/natolive/official_texts_87597.htm?mode=pressrelease.

21. "U.S. Announces Withdrawal from ABM Treaty, Outlines a 'New Triad,'" *Disarmament Diplomacy* 62 (January–February 2002), http://www.acronym.org.uk/dd/dd62/62nr02.htm.

22. National Security Concept of the Russian Federation, full English translation from *Rossiiskaya Gazeta*, January 18, 2000. Approved by Presidential Decree No. 1300 of December 17, 1999.

23. Yury Fedorov, "New Wine in Old Bottles: The New Salience of Nuclear Weapons," Institut français des relations internationles, Fall 2007, http://www.ifri.org/files/Securite_defense/New_Wine_Fedorov_2007.pdf.

24. Pavel Podvig, "Instrumental Influences: Russia and the 2010 Nuclear Posture Review," *Nonproliferation Review* 18, no. 1 (March 2011): 47, http://www.tandfonline.com/doi/abs/10.1080/10736700.2011.549170.

25. Podvig, "Instrumental Influences," 40.

26. Alexei Arbatov, "Ratification of the Prague Treaty Is Only a State on a Long Path: What Strategy Will Russia Choose?" *Nezavisimoye Voyennoye Obozreniye*, Moscow, February 11, 2011, emphasis added.

27. Ibid.

28. Ibid.

29. Hans M. Kristensen and Robert S. Norris, "Russian Nuclear Forces 2012," *Bulletin of the Atomic Scientists* 68, no. 2 (March/April 2012): 91, http://www.fas.org/blog/ssp/2012/03/russia2012.php.

30. Kevin Rothrock, "Mitt Romney: The American Vladimir Zhirinovsky?" *A Good Treaty,* July 14, 2010, http://www.agoodtreaty.com/2010/07/14/mitt-romney-the-american-zhirinovsky/.

31. Harold Brown and John Deutch, "The Nuclear Disarmament Fantasy," *Wall Street Journal,* November 19, 2007, http://online.wsj.com/article/SB119542524645797257.html.

32. Scott D. Sagan and Jane Vaynman, "Conclusions: Lessons Learned from the 2010 Nuclear Posture Review," *Nonproliferation Review* 18, no. 1 (March 2011): 239–40.

33. Ibid., 239.

34. Ibid., 238.

35. Joseph Biden, remarks at Moscow State University, Moscow, Russia, March 10, 2011, http://www.whitehouse.gov/the-press-office/2011/03/10/vice-president-bidens-remarks-moscow-state-university.

36. Steven Pifer, "The Next Round: The United States and Nuclear Arms Reductions After New START," Arms Control Series, Paper 4, Brookings Institution, November 2010, 8, http://www.brookings.edu/~/media/research/files/articles/2010/11/12-arms-control-pifer/12_arms_control_pifer.pdf.

37. Ibid. Alexei Arbatov provides a lower estimate of 1,000 to 1,100 warheads on 200 ICBMs, 44–60 SLBMs, and 40–50 heavy bombers. See Alexei Arbatov, "Gambit or

Endgame? The New State of Arms Control," Carnegie Endowment for International Peace, March 2011, http://carnegieendowment.org/files/gambit_endgame.pdf. Estimates are counted according to New START counting rules. Russia has not released official estimates of its force composition.

38. U.S. Department of State, "International Security Advisory Board Report on Options for Implementing Additional Nuclear Force Reductions," November 27, 2012, Washington, D.C., http://www.state.gov/t/avc/isab/201191.htm.

39. George P. Shultz, William J. Perry, Henry A. Kissinger, and Sam Nunn, "Next Steps in Reducing Nuclear Risks: The Pace of Nonproliferation Work Today Doesn't Match the Urgency of the Threat," *Wall Street Journal*, March 5, 2013, http://online.wsj.com/article/SB10001424127887324338604578325912939001772.html.

EIGHT **THE MOST DANGEROUS COUNTRY ON EARTH**

1.   Leah Fae Cochran provided substantial research work for this chapter as did Rizwan Ladha earlier. Both worked as research assistants at Ploughshares Fund.

2.   Valerie Plame, interview, *The Daily Beast TV*, June 21, 2012, http://www.thedailybeast.com/videos/2012/06/21/valerie-plame-on-pakistan-s-nuclear-program.html.

3.   Jay Branegan, "You Could Call It the Wonk Wing," *Time*, May 7, 2000, http://www.time.com/time/magazine/article/0,9171,44567,00.html.

4.   Vipin Narang, "Pakistan's Nuclear Posture: Implications for South Asian Stability," Belfer Center, January 2010, http://belfercenter.ksg.harvard.edu/publication/19889/pakistans_nuclear_posture.html. For a more detailed argument, see Vipin Narang, "Posturing for Peace? Pakistan's Nuclear Postures and South Asian Stability," *International Security* 34, no. 3 (Winter 2009/10): 38–78, http://www.mitpressjournals.org/doi/pdf/10.1162/isec.2010.34.3.38.

5.   Jeffrey Goldberg, "Pakistan: Maybe Not the Best Country in Which to Store Nuclear Weapons," *The Atlantic*, August 16, 2012, http://www.theatlantic.com/international/archive/2012/08/pakistan-maybe-not-the-best-country-in-which-to-store-nuclear-weapons/261222/.

6.   Hans M. Kristensen and Robert S. Norris, "Pakistan's Nuclear Forces, 2011," *Bulletin of the Atomic Scientists* 76, no. 4 (July 2011): 91–99, http://bos.sagepub.com/content/67/4/91.full.

7.   Ibid.

8.   International Panel on Fissile Materials, "Global Fissile Material Report 2011: Nuclear Weapon and Fissile Material Stockpiles and Production," 2011, 11, http://fissilematerials.org/library/gfmr11.pdf.

9.   Ibid.; and David Albright and Robert Avagyan, "Construction Progressing Rapidly on the Fourth Heavy Water Reactor at the Khushab Nuclear Site," Institute for Science

and International Security, May 21, 2012, http://isis-online.org/isis-reports/detail/construction-progressing-rapidly-on-the-fourth-heavy-water-reactor-at-the-k/12.

10. Based on calculations of 12–18 kg of HEU or 4–6 kg of plutonium per warhead. See Kristensen and Norris, "Pakistan's Nuclear Forces, 2011," for methodology.

11. Kristensen and Norris, "Pakistan's Nuclear Forces," 96.

12. Ibid., 97.

13. See press release "Naval Chief Inaugurates Naval Strategic Force Headquarters," Inter Services Public Relations, Release no. PR122/2012-ISPR, May 19, 2012, http://www.ispr.gov.pk/front/main.asp?o=t-press_release&id=2067.

14. Bruno Tertrais, "Pakistan's Nuclear and WMD Programmes: Status, Evolution and Risks," International Institute for Strategic Studies, July 2012, 1, http://www.nonproliferation.eu/documents/nonproliferationpapers/brunotertrais5010305e17790.pdf.

15. Shuja Nawaz, "Misfire on Attacks on Pakistani Nukes!" *Foreign Policy*, August 14, 2009, http://afpak.foreignpolicy.com/posts/2009/08/14/misfire_on_attacks_on_pakistani_nukes.

16. Toby Dalton and George Perkovich, "Beware Decline in Pakistani relations," *Politico*, May 16, 2011, http://www.politico.com/news/stories/0511/55014.html.

17. Fareed Zakaria, "The Radicalization of Pakistan's Military," *Washington Post*, June 22, 2011, http://www.washingtonpost.com/opinions/the-radicalization-of-pakistans-military/2011/06/22/AGbCBSgH_story.html; Pervez Hoodbhoy, "A State of Denial," *New York Times*, January 6, 2008, http://www.nytimes.com/2008/01/16/opinion/16iht-edhood.1.9260885.html.

18. Benazir Bhutto, interview, "Pakistan in Crisis," CNN, November 5, 2007, http://transcripts.cnn.com/TRANSCRIPTS/0711/05/sitroom.02.html.

19. Mariana Baabar, "Pak N-Safety Plan," *The News International*, November 10, 2009, http://www.thenews.com.pk/TodaysPrintDetail.aspx?ID=25170&Cat=13&dt=11/10/2009.

20. Shaun Gregory, "Terrorist Tactics in Pakistan Threaten Nuclear Weapons Safety," *CTC Sentinel*, June 1, 2011, http://www.ctc.usma.edu/posts/terrorist-tactics-in-pakistan-threaten-nuclear-weapons-safety.

21. Elaine Grossman, "Mullen: Pakistani Nuclear Controls Should Avert Any Insider Threat," *Global Security Newswire*, July 8, 2011, http://gsn.nti.org/gsn/nw_20110708_3987.php.

22. Toby Dalton, Mark Hibbs, and George Perkovich, "A Criteria-Based Approach to Nuclear Cooperation with Pakistan," Carnegie Endowment for International Peace, June 22, 2011, 12, http://carnegieendowment.org/files/nsg_criteria.pdf.

23. Tertrais, "Pakistan's Nuclear and WMD Programmes," 15.

24. "Pakistani President Defends Nuclear Arsenal Security," *Global Security Newswire*, April 27, 2009, http://www.nti.org/gsn/article/pakistani-president-defends-nuclear-arsenal-security/.

25. Hillary Clinton, interview, "*Spiegel* Interview with Secretary of State Clinton," *Der Spiegel,* November 15, 2009, http://www.spiegel.de/international/world/0,1518,druck -661188,00.html.

26. "State Dept. Says Pakistani Nukes Are Secure," *Global Security Newswire,* June 22, 2011, http://gsn.nti.org/gsn/nw_20110622_2687.php.

27. Grossman, "Mullen: Pakistani Nuclear Controls Should Avert Any Insider Threat."

28. Paul K. Kerr and Mary Beth Nikitin, "Pakistan's Nuclear Weapons: Proliferation and Security Issues," *Congressional Research Service* (RL34248) May 10, 2012, 18, http://fpc .state.gov/documents/organization/169328.pdf.

29. Ibid.

30. Tom Hundley, "Race to the End," *Foreign Policy,* September 10, 2012, http://www .foreignpolicy.com/articles/2012/09/05/race_to_the_end.

31. Dennis Kux, *The United States and Pakistan 1947–2000: Disenchanted Allies* (Washington, D.C.: Woodrow Wilson Center Press, 2001), 18.

32. Paul R. Brass, "The Partition of India and Retributive Genocide in the Punjab, 1946–47: Means, Methods, And Purposes," *Journal of Genocide Research* 5, no. 1 (2003): 71–101, http://faculty.washington.edu/brass/Partition.pdf.

33. For a discussion of how Pakistan's identity affects security calculations, see Stephen P. Cohen, "The Nation and State of Pakistan," *The Washington Quarterly* 25, no. 3 (Summer 2002): 109–22.

34. Benazir Bhutto, *Reconciliation: Islam, Democracy, and the West* (New York: Harper, 2008), 165–166.

35. "The Indo-Pakistani War of 1965," in *A Country Study: Pakistan* (Washington: D.C.: Library of Congress Federal Research Division, 2011), http://lcweb2.loc.gov/frd/cs/ pktoc.html.

36. Office of the Historian, telegram, "Dissent from U.S. Policy Towards East Pakistan," in *Foreign Relations of the United States Series: South Asia Crisis, 1969–1972,* Department of State, April 6, 1971, http://history.state.gov/historicaldocuments/frus1969-76v11/d19.

37. International Institute for Strategic Studies, "Pakistan's Nuclear Programme and Imports," in *Nuclear Black Markets: Pakistan, A. Q. Khan, and the Rise of Proliferation Networks* (London: International Institute for Strategic Studies, 2007), 16, http:// www.iiss.org/publications/strategic-dossiers/nbm/nuclear-black-market -dossier-a-net-assesment/pakistans-nuclear-programme-and-imports-/.

38. Although a U.S. Intelligence Estimate concluded as early as 1986 that Pakistan could assemble a weapon within two weeks if it choose to do so, the Reagan administration had been assuring Congress that there was not a Pakistani bomb program. This was because U.S. aid to the mujahedeen fighting the Russians in Afghanistan could only be dispersed per the Pressler amendment if a president could certify that Pakistan didn't have a nuclear program. In 1987, in the heat of the Brasstacks crisis, A. Q. Khan told a journalist that Pakistan had the ability to build a weapon. Faced with this conundrum,

Reagan choose to use the waiver for national security interest built into the Pressler amendment and continued aid to Pakistan despite the program. See Dennis Kux, *The United States and Pakistan, 1947–2000: Disenchanted Allies* (Washington, D.C.: The Woodrow Wilson Center Press, 2001), 284–86.

39. Owen Bennett Jones, *Pakistan: Eye of the Storm* (New Haven, Conn.: Yale University Press, 2009), 195.

40. Ibid., 207.

41. Ibid.

42. Walter C. Lagwig III, "A Cold Start for Hot Wars," *International Security* 32, no. 3 (Winter 2007/2008): 158, http://belfercenter.ksg.harvard.edu/files/IS3203_pp158-190.pdf.

43. Ibid., 162.

44. Ibid., 165.

45. The visiting group, the Landau Network–Centro Volta, is a group of international experts based in Italy who support global security, disarmament, and cooperation. See http://www.centrovolta.it/landau/.

46. Lagwig, "A Cold Start for Hot Wars," 168. See also Tertrais, "Pakistan's Nuclear and WMD Programmes," 3.

47. Tom Hundley, "Race to the End," *Foreign Policy,* September 5, 2012, http://www .foreignpolicy.com/articles/2012/09/05/race_to_the_end.

48. "WikiLeaks: U.S. on Indian Army's Cold Start Doctrine," December 2, 2010, available at http://www.ndtv.com/article/wikileaks-revelations/wikileaks-us-on-indian-army-s -cold-start-doctrine-69859?cp.

49. International Institute for Strategic Studies, "Pakistan's Nuclear Programme and Imports," 33.

50. Bruce Riedel, *Deadly Embrace: Pakistan, America, and the Future of Global Jihad* (Washington, D.C., Brookings Institution Press, 2011), 91.

51. Ibid., 117.

52. Tertrais, "Pakistan's Nuclear and WMD Programmes: Status, Evolution and Risks," 3, citing N. Salik, *Minimum Deterrence and India Pakistan Nuclear Dialogue: Case Study on Pakistan* (Como: Landau Network-Centro Volta, 2006), 14, http://www.centrovolta.it/ landau/content/binary/01.%20Naeem%20Salik-Minimum%20deterrence%20and%20 India%20Pakistan%20dialogie,%20PAKISTAN.%20Case%20Study%202006.pdf.

53. Johnsthon Marcus, "Will India's Missile Test Trigger Arms Race with China?" *BBC News*, April 20, 2012, http://www.bbc.co.uk/news/world-asia-17770586.

54. Stockholm International Peace Research Institute, "India's Nuclear Forces," in *SIPRI Yearbook 2011* (Stockholm: Stockholm International Peace Research Institute, 2011).

55. Robert S. Norris and Hans M. Kristensen, "India's Nuclear Forces 2012," *Bulletin of the Atomic Scientists* 68, no. 3 (July 2012), http://bos.sagepub.com/content/68/4/96.full.

56. "France Sells Nuclear-Capable Aircraft to India," *Global Security Newswire*, February 7, 2012, http://www.nti.org/gsn/article/france-sells-nuclear-capable-aircraft-india/.

57. "India Test Launches Agni-V Long-Range Missile," *BBC News*, April 19, 2012, http://www.bbc.co.uk/news/world-asia-india-17765653.

58. "India to Achieve N-arm Triad in February," *Times of India*, January 2, 2012, http://articles.timesofindia.indiatimes.com/2012-01-02/india/30580966_1_ins-arihant-first-indigenous-nuclear-submarine-akula-ii.

59. Norris and Kristensen, "India's Nuclear Forces 2010," 76.

60. Jamal Afrifi and Jayshree Bajoria, "China-Pakistan Relations," *Council on Foreign Relations*, July 6, 2010, http://www.cfr.org/china/china-pakistan-relations/p10070.

61. "West Worried by China-Pakistan atomic Ties—Sources," Reuters, June 27, 2012, http://in.reuters.com/article/2012/06/27/nuclear-china-pakistan-idINL6E8HR8SL20120627.

62. James Lamont and Farhan Bokhari, "China and Pakistan: An Alliance Is Built," *Financial Times*, June 30, 2011, http://www.ft.com/cms/s/0/417a48c4-a34d-11e0-8d6d-00144feabdc0.html#axzz2NGlLavzb.

63. Joseph Cirincione, *Bomb Scare: The History and Future of Nuclear Weapons*, pbk. ed. (New York: Columbia University Press, 2008), 160.

64. Ismail Khan, "Prison Term for Helping CIA Find bin Laden," *New York Times*, May 23, 2012, http://www.nytimes.com/2012/05/24/world/asia/doctor-who-helped-find-bin-laden-given-jail-term-official-says.html.

65. Bruce Riedel, "How to Repair the U.S.-Pakistan Relationship," *The Daily Beast*, June 4, 2012, http://www.thedailybeast.com/articles/2012/06/04/how-to-repair-the-u-s-pakistan-relationship.html.

66. Eric Schmidt "Pakistan Opens NATO Supply Line as Clinton Apologizes," *New York Times*, July 3, 2012, http://www.nytimes.com/2012/07/04/world/asia/pakistan-opens-afghan-routes-to-nato-after-us-apology.html; Marcus Weisgerber, "Alternate Afghan Supply Route Tab: $2.1 Billion," *Military Times*, June 30, 2012, http://militarytimes.com/news/2012/06/military-afghanistan-tab-alternate-supply-route-063012d/.

67. Vali Nasr, "No More Bullying Pakistan," *Bloomberg News*, July 5, 2012, http://www.bloomberg.com/news/2012-07-05/u-s-apology-ends-doomed-policy-of-bullying-pakistan-vali-nasr.html.

68. Mike Shuster, "Hard Questions Remain in U.S.-Pakistan Relations." *Morning Edition*, NPR, July 11, 2012, http://www.npr.org/2012/07/11/156578951/hard-questions-remain-in-u-s-pakistan-relations.

69. For a detailed treatment of A. Q. Khans' proliferation of nuclear weapons, see David Albright, *Peddling Peril* (New York: Free Press, 2010).

70. U.S. Department of State, "International Security Advisory Board Report on Pakistan and U.S. Security Strategy," October 9, 2012, Washington, D.C., http://www.state.gov/t/avc/isab/199411.htm.

71. Ibid.

72. Ibid.

73. Richard L. Armitage and Samuel R. Berger, *U.S. Strategy for Pakistan and Afghanistan*, Independent Task Force Report no. 65 (New York: Council on Foreign Relations, 2010).

74. Ibid., 7.

75. "Clever Steps at the Border," *The Economist*, May 12, 2012, http://www.economist.com/node/21554526.

76. Ibid.

77. Haris Anwar and Augustine Anthony, "India, Pakistan Relax Visa Requirements as Part of Peace Process," *Bloomberg*, September 9, 2012, http://www.bloomberg.com/news/2012-09-09/india-pakistan-relax-visa-requirements-as-part-of-peace-process.html.

78. Moeed Yusuf, "The Silver Bullet: India-Pakistan Normalization," U.S. Institute of Peace, May 23, 2011, http://www.usip.org/publications/the-silver-bullet-india-pakistan-normalization.

79. Daniel Markey, "How Cuts Affect U.S.-Pakistan Ties," *Council on Foreign Relations*, July 11, 2011, http://www.cfr.org/pakistan/cuts-affect-us-pakistan-ties/p25453.

80. Owen Bennett Jones, *Pakistan: Eye of the Storm* (New Haven, Conn.: Yale University Press, 2009), 317.

81. Jayshree Bajoria, "Backgrounder: Pakistan's Education System and Links to Extremism," *Council on Foreign Relations*, October 7, 2009, http://www.cfr.org/pakistan/pakistans-education-system-links-extremism/p20364.

82. *Enhanced Partnership with Pakistan Act of 2009*, 111th Cong., S. 1707, *GovTrack*, October 2, 2009, http://www.govtrack.us/congress/billtext.xpd?bill=s111-1707.

83. "Aid to Pakistan by the Numbers: What the United States Spends in Pakistan," Center for Global Development, http://www.cgdev.org/section/initiatives/_active/pakistan/numbers.

84. International Crisis Group, "Reforming Pakistan's Electoral System," Asia Report no. 203, March 30, 2011, 26, http://www.crisisgroup.org/~/media/Files/asia/south-asia/pakistan/203%20Reforming%20Pakistans%20Electoral%20System.ashx.

85. Robert D. Lamb and Sadika Hameed, "Subnational Governance, Service Delivery, and Militancy in Pakistan ," Center for Strategic and International Studies, June 16, 2011, 12, http://csis.org/files/publication/120610_Lamb_SubnatGovernPakistan_web.pdf.

86. Susan B. Epstein and K. Alan Kronstadt, "Pakistan: U.S. Foreign Assistance," Congressional Research Service, R41856, April 10, 2012, http://www.fas.org/sgp/crs/row/R41856.pdf.

87. Armitage and Berger, *U.S. Strategy for Pakistan and Afghanistan*, 50.

88. Riedel, *Deadly Embrace*, 134; Shuja Nawaz, *Pakistan in the Danger Zone: A Tenuous U.S.-Pakistan Relationship* (Washington, D.C.: Atlantic Council, 2010), 18.

89. Yusuf, "The Silver Bullet."

90. Armitage and Berger, *U.S. Strategy for Pakistan and Afghanistan*, 53.

91. Alex Rodriguez, "For Troops on the Siachen Glacier, the Elements Are the Enemy," *Los Angeles Times*, May 20, 2012, http://articles.latimes.com/2012/may/20/world/la-fg-pakistan-glacier-soldiers-20120520.

92. "India, Pakistan Begin Siachen Talks," *AFP*, June 11, 2012, http://tribune.com.pk/story/391988/india-pakistan-begin-siachen-talks/.

93. Micheal Krepon, "Catch and Release," *Arms Control Wonk*, September 10, 2012, http://krepon.armscontrolwonk.com/archive/3531/catch-and-release#more-2770.

94. Riedel, *Deadly Embrace*, 128–29.

95. International Crisis Group, "Reforming Pakistan's Electoral System," 25–26.

96. Armitage and Berger, *U.S. Strategy for Pakistan and Afghanistan*, 53.

97. Daniel Painter, "Why the U.S. Cannot Ignore Pakistan," American Security Project, September 6, 2012, http://americansecurityproject.org/ASP%20Reports/Ref%200081%20-%20Why%20the%20U.S.%20cannot%20ignore%20Pakistan.pdf.

98. Moeed Yusuf, "Stability in the Nuclear Context: Making South Asians Safe," Jinnah Institute, 6, http://www.jinnah-institute.org/images/ji_policybrief_nuclear_security_jan-25-2011.pdf.

99. "Pakistan, India Agree to Set Up Hotline on Terror," *Pak Tribune*, March 30, 2011, http://www.paktribune.com/news/index.shtml?237715; Justin Huggler, "India and Pakistan to Have Nuclear Hotline," *The Independent*, June 21, 2004; Yusuf, "Stability in the Nuclear Context," 6.

100. Mohammed Badrul Alam, "CBMs in South and Northeast Asia: The Sum of Two Parts," Institute of Peace and Conflict Studies, July 16, 2004, http://www.ipcs.org/article/south-asia/cbms-in-south-asia-and-northeast-asia-the-sum-of-1436.html.

101. Dalton, Hibbs, and Perkovich, "A Criteria-Based Approach," 5.

102. A. H. Nayyar, M. V. Ramana and Zia Mian, "Fukushima lessons," *Dawn*, March 27, 2011, http://www.dawn.com/2011/03/27/fukushima-lessons.html.

103. "Ottawa Dialogue Recommends Nuclear Agreements for India and Pakistan," press release, University of Ottawa, July 13, 2011, http://www.uottawa.ca/media/media-release-2370.html.

104. Yusuf, "The Silver Bullet: India-Pakistan Normalization."

105. Nawaz, *Pakistan in the Danger Zone*, 18.

106. Riedel, *Deadly Embrace*, 138.

107. Kerr and Nikitin, "Pakistan's Nuclear Weapons," 8.

108. Dalton, Hibbs, and Perkovich, "A Criteria-Based Approach," 2–3.

109. Armitage and Berger, "U.S. Strategy for Pakistan and Afghanistan," 52.

NINE POSTURE AND PROLIFERATION

1. This chapter is based on my "The Impact of Nuclear Posture on Non-Proliferation," in *In the Eyes of the Experts: Analysis and Comments on America's Strategic Posture*,

Selected Contributions by the Experts of the Congressional Commission on the Strategic Posture of the United States (Washington, D.C.: United States Institute of Peace Press, 2009), 193-200, http://www.usip.org/files/In%20the%20Eyes%20of%20the%20Experts%20full.pdf. I served as an expert advisor to the commission.

2. Cited by Jeffrey Lewis, "Diplomacy 101," Arms Control Wonk, August 2, 2012, http://lewis.armscontrolwonk.com/archive/5547/diplomacy-101.

3. "Interim Report of the Congressional Commission on the Strategic Posture of the United States," facilitated by the U.S. Institute of Peace, December 15, 2008.

4. Director of Central Intelligence, "National Intelligence Estimate: Development of Nuclear Capabilities by Fourth Countries: Likelihood and Consequences," no. 100-2-58, July 1, 1958, 2, 17.

5. Ibid., 17.

6. Director of Central Intelligence, "National Intelligence Estimate: Nuclear Weapons and Delivery Capabilities of Free World Countries Other than the U.S. and UK," No. 4-3-61, September 1961, 5.

7. Ibid.

8. Ibid., 8.

9. Ibid., 9

10. The Committee on Nuclear Proliferation, "A Report to the President," U.S. State Department (Gilpatric Report), January 21, 1965, 7.

11. Ibid, 2.

12. Ibid, 5.

13. Ibid, 7.

14. Ibid, 20.

15. Office of Political Research, "Eight Years Later: New 'Threshold States' Research Study, 'Managing Nuclear Proliferation': The Politics of Limited Choice," Directorate of Intelligence, Central Intelligence Agency, December 1975.

16. National Intelligence Council, "Iran: Nuclear Intentions and Capabilities," November 2007, 7.

17. The ten countries known to have nuclear weapons or believed to be seeking them are, in order of acquisition: United States, Russia, United Kingdom, France, China, Israel, India, Pakistan, North Korea, and Iran.

18. Congressional Commission on the Strategic Posture of the United States, America's Strategic Posture (Washington, D.C.: United States Institute of Peace Press, 2009), 15.

19. Ibid, 17.

20. Department of Defense, Nuclear Posture Review Report, April 2010, 12, http://www.defense.gov/npr/docs/2010%20Nuclear%20Posture%20Review%20Report.pdf.

TEN **THE END OF PROLIFERATION**

1. Colin H. Kahl, Melissa Dalton, and Matthew Irvine, *Atomic Kingdom: If Iran Builds the Bomb, Will Saudi Arabia Be Next?* (Washington, D.C.: Center for a New American Security, 2013), 10.

2. Ibid., 8.

3. Phillip Yun, "Don't Ignore North Korea," *The Hill*, February 6, 2012, http://thehill.com/opinion/op-ed/208999-dont-ignore-north-korea.

4. Mark Hibbs, "Assessing UN Trade Sanctions on North Korea," Carnegie Endowment for International Peace, July 3, 2012, http://carnegieendowment.org/2012/07/03/assessing-nuclear-trade-sanctions-on-north-korea/cj1h.

5. Paul Carroll, "The Mouse That Keeps Roaring: The United States, China, and Solving the North Korea Challenge," *Yale Journal of International Affairs* (September 2012), http://yalejournal.org/2012/09/the-mouse-that-keeps-roaring-the-united-states-china-and-solving-the-north-korean-challenge/.

6. The range of estimates depends on how much plutonium North Korea may have produced and how much plutonium North Korea uses in its warheads. An estimate of 2 kg of plutonium per warhead yields a higher number of warheads; an estimate of 4 kg, fewer warheads. David Albright and Christina Walrond, "North Korea's Estimated Stocks of Plutonium and Weapon-Grade Uranium," Institute for Science and International Security, August 16, 2012, 2, http://isis-online.org/uploads/isis-reports/documents/dprk_fissile_material_production_16Aug2012.pdf.

7. Siegfried S. Hecker, "What to Expect from a North Korean Nuclear Test," *Foreign Policy.com*, February 4, 2013, http://www.foreignpolicy.com/articles/2013/02/04/what_to_expect_from_a_north_korean_nuclear_test.

8. Michael Mazarr and James E. Goodby, "Redefining the Role of Deterrence," in *Deterrence: Its Past and Future*, ed. George P. Shultz, Sidney D. Drell, and James E. Goodby (Palo Alto, Calif.: Hoover Institution Press, 2011), 63.

9. Siegfried S. Hecker, "What I Found in North Korea," *Foreign Affairs*, December 9, 2010, http://www.foreignaffairs.com/articles/67023/siegfried-s-hecker/what-i-found-in-north-korea?page=2.

10. The Chicago Council on Global Affairs, *Foreign Policy in the New Millennium: Results of the 2012 Chicago Council Survey of American Public Opinion and U.S. Foreign Policy*, Dina Smeltz, project director (Chicago, Ill.: Chicago Council on Global Affairs, 2012), http://www.thechicagocouncil.org/UserFiles/File/Task%20Force%20Reports/2012_CCS_Report.pdf.

11. International Institute for Strategic Studies, *Iran's Nuclear, Chemical, and Biological Capabilities: A Net Assessment* (London: The International Institute of Strategic Studies, 2011), 47.

12. Ibid., 58–59.

13. International Atomic Energy Agency, "Implementation of the NPT Safeguards Agreement and Relevant Provisions of Security Council Resolutions in the Islamic Republic of Iran," *Report by the Director General of the IAEA*, September 2, 2011, http://www.iaea.org/Publications/Documents/Board/2011/gov2011-54.pdf.

14. *Addressing the Iranian Nuclear Challenge: Understanding Military Options Before the House Committee on Armed Services*, 112th Cong. (June 20, 2012) (testimony of David Albright, president of the Institute for Science and International Security).

15. Ibid.

16. Benjamin Netanyahu, speech to AIPAC, March 5, 2012. See transcript at http://www.timesofisrael.com/netanyahus-speech-at-aipac-full-text/.

17. Colin H. Kahl, "Not Time to Attack Iran," *Foreign Affairs* (March/April 2012): http://www.foreignaffairs.com/articles/137031/colin-h-kahl/not-time-to-attack-iran.

18. Cited in Friends Committee on National Legislation, "U.S., Israeli Security Officials Warn Against Attacking Iran," 2012, http://fcnl.org/issues/iran/us_israeli_security_officials_warn_against_war_with_iran/index.html.

19. Cited in Matt Duss, "The Neocons' Big Iran Lie," *Salon.com*, February 10, 2012, http://www.salon.com/2012/02/10/the_neocons_big_iran_lie/.

20. Colin Kahl, Melissa Dalton, and Matthew Irvine, *Risk and Rivalry: Iran, Israel, and the Bomb* (Washington, D.C.: Center for a New American Security, 2012), 34, http://www.cnas.org/riskandrivalry.

21. Hillary Clinton, interview, *The Charlie Rose Show*, June 20, 2012, http://thinkprogress.org/security/2012/06/21/504179/clinton-iran-hard-liners-attack-legitimize-regime/.

22. Yossi Melman, "Former Mossad chief: Israel air strike on Iran is the 'stupidest thing I've ever heard'," *Haaretz*, May 7, 2011. http://www.haaretz.com/news/diplomacy-defense/former-mossad-chief-israel-air-strike-on-iran-stupidest-thing-i-have-ever-heard-1.360367.

23. Bill Keller, "Nuclear Mullahs," *New York Times*, September 10, 2012, http://www.nytimes.com/2012/09/10/opinion/keller-nuclear-mullahs.html.

24. Comments of Zbigniew Brzezinski, November 27, 2012, National Iranian American Council, http://www.niacouncil.org/site/News2?page=NewsArticle&id=8713.

25. General John Dempsey, *CNN Global Public Square*, February 17, 2012, http://globalpublicsquare.blogs.cnn.com/2012/02/17/watch-gps-martin-dempsey-on-syria-iran-and-china/.

26. Fareed Zakaria, "Iran is a 'Rational Actor'," *CNN Global Public Square Blog*, March 8, 2012, http://globalpublicsquare.blogs.cnn.com/2012/03/08/zakaria-iran-is-a-rational-actor/.

27. Bill Keller, "Nuclear Mullahs, Continued," *New York Times*, September 12, 2012, http://keller.blogs.nytimes.com/2012/09/11/nuclear-mullahs-continued.

28. I developed this analysis with my colleague Andrew Grotto while serving as vice president for national security and international policy at the Center for American

Progress in the study, *Contain and Engage: A New Strategy for Resolving the Nuclear Crisis with Iran* (Washington, D.C.: Center for American Progress, 2007), http://www.americanprogress.org/issues/security/report/2007/02/28/2682/contain-and-engage-a-new-strategy-for-resolving-the-nuclear-crisis-with-iran/.

29. David Holloway, "Deterrence and Enforcement," in *Deterrence: Its Past and Future*, ed. George P. Shultz, Sidney D. Drell, and James E. Goodby (Palo Alto, Calif.: Hoover Institution Press, 2011).

30. Joseph Cirincione, Jessica Mathews, Rose Gottemoeller, George Perkovich, and Jon B. Wolfsthal, *Universal Compliance: A Strategy for Nuclear Security* (Washington, D.C.: Carnegie Endowment for International Peace, 2005, 2007), 14.

31. Ibid, 24.

32. Argentina, Australia, Brazil, Canada, China, Egypt, France, India, Israel, Italy, Japan, Norway, Romania, South Africa, the Soviet Union, Spain, Sweden, Switzerland, Taiwan, the United Kingdom, the United States, West Germany, and Yugoslavia.

33. Argentina, Brazil, Canada, China, France, India, Iran, Iraq, Israel, Libya, North Korea, Pakistan, South Africa, South Korea, the Soviet Union, Taiwan, the United Kingdom, the United States, and Yugoslavia.

34. Cirincione et al., *Universal Compliance*, 24.

35. Barack Obama, remarks at the Nunn-Lugar Cooperative Threat Reduction Symposium, National War College, Washington, D.C., December 3, 2012, http://www.whitehouse.gov/the-press-office/2012/12/03/remarks-president-nunn-lugar-cooperative-threat-reduction-symposium.

ELEVEN FOUNDATIONS

1. Kennette Benedict, "Democracy and the Bomb," *Bulletin of the Atomic Scientists*, November 15, 2012, http://www.thebulletin.org/web-edition/columnists/kennette-benedict/democracy-and-the-bomb.

2. This chapter is adapted from a paper, "Impact Philanthropy: How Strategic Grants Can Impact National Security Strategy," prepared for the Institute for the Study of Diplomacy at Georgetown University, winter 2013.

3. Ford Foundation, Mission Statement, http://www.fordfoundation.org/about-us/mission.

4. MacArthur Foundation press release, "MacArthur Awards $13.4 Million to Study and Support Enhanced Nuclear Security," March 22, 2012, http://www.macfound.org/press/press-releases/macarthur-awards-13-million-study-and-support-enhanced-nuclear-security/.

5. Robert Gallucci, "The Challenges of Philanthropic Leadership," *Conversations with History*, University of California Television, July 23, 2012, http://uctv.tv/shows/

The-Challenges-of-Philanthropic-Leadership-with-Robert-Gallucci-Conversations
-with-History-24001.

6. Paul Brest and Hal Harvey, *Money Well Spent: A Strategic Plan for Smart Philanthropy*,
    (New York: Bloomberg Press, 2008), 28.

7. Ibid., 26, 28.

8. Ibid., 29.

9. Josh Rogin, "Arms Control Leaders Convene Major Strategy Session," *The Cable*,
    January 12, 2010, http://thecable.foreignpolicy.com/posts/2010/01/12/arms_control
    _leaders_convene_major_strategy_session.

10. Naila Bolus, "A Policy Victory Offers a Blueprint for Grant Makers and Advocacy,"
    The Chronicle of Philanthropy, June 27, 2011, http://philanthropy.com/article/A-
    Policy-Victory-Offers-a/128008/.

11. The MacArthur Foundation, John Merck Foundation, Prospect Hill Foundation,
    Rockefeller Brothers Fund, and Winston Foundation also funded the campaign after
    it began. The campaign operated from December 1, 1993 until it disbanded on July 31,
    1995, having achieved its goal.

12. Rogin, "Arms Control Leaders."

13. Bolus, "A Policy Victory."

14. From unpublished analysis, ReThink Media, "Post START Analysis—Print Outreach
    Revisited," February 2011.

15. ReThink Media, "Post START Analysis."

16. The Ploughshares Fund website is www.ploughshares.org.

17. Brest and Harvey, *Money Well Spent*, 6.

18. See Joseph Cirincione, "A Victory for Good Government," Ploughshares Fund blog,
    September 23, 2012, http://www.ploughshares.org/blog/2012-09-23/victory-good
    -government.

19. For more on the strategic and budgetary analysis motivating the campaign, see Joseph
    Cirincione, "The Fiscal Logic of Zero," *Brown Journal of World Affairs* (Spring/Sum-
    mer 2011), http://bjwa.org/article.php?id=8ckn4rGp5fRKPQ9cpeFdT6DmLC6sJ4dY
    3QakmNyI.

20. Laura Secor, "Road Show," *The New Yorker*, October 8, 2012, http://www.newyorker
    .com/talk/comment/2012/10/08/121008taco_talk_secor.

21. Data are derived from an unpublished report by Carah Ong of the Peace and Security
    Funders Group, "Nuclear Funding, 2008–2011." The group is a collaboration of funders
    initiated by Ploughshares Fund, but the foundation had no influence over the study or
    its conclusions.

22. John Tirman, "Private Wealth and Public Power in the Search for Peace," Dublin Con-
    ference of the International Society for Third Sector Research, July 2000, 2, 3, http://
    www.johntirman.com/ISTR%20paper.pdf.

23. Ibid., 6, 5.

24. Ibid., 11.

25. Ibid., 13.

26. Mitchel B. Wallerstein, "Whither the Role of Private Foundations in Support of Inter-national Security Policy?" *The Nonproliferation Review* (Spring 2002): 86, http://cns.miis.edu/npr/pdfs/91wall.pdf.

27. Ibid., 84, 85.

28. Ibid., 86.

29. Kennette Benedict, "Democracy and the Bomb."

INDEX

UN Special Commission on, 24; U.S. National Intelligence Estimate on, 26; WMD and, 22–23

Irvine, Matthew, 158

Israel, 24, 158, 248n32, 248n33; with Iran, 162–63, 165–67; nondeclaratory policy, 59; nuclear arsenal, 59, *60*; nuclear program, 59, 245n17

Italy, *81*, 154, 241n45, 248n32

Japan, 16, 26, 60, 150, 154, 248n32; famine in, 70; Fukushima, 143; military budget, *81*; plutonium, 158

Jinnah, Mohammed Ali, 127

John D. and Catherine T. MacArthur Foundation, 135, 173, 175–76, 186, 187

John Merck Foundation, 249n11

Johnson, Lyndon B., 151

Jones, James, 14

Jones, Owen Bennett, 129

Jordan, 26, 30, 89

Joseph, Robert, 222n38

Kagan, Robert, 21

Kahl, Colin, 158–59, 165, 166

Kampelman, Max, 106

Kargil crisis, 70–71, 129

Kazakhstan, 148, 154

Kean, Thomas, 27

Keller, Bill, 167, 168

Kennedy, John F., 1, 3, 38, 84, 150, 207

Kerry, John, 4, 138, 139, 181

Khan, Abdul Qadeer (A. Q.), 128, 134, 135, 240n38. *See also* Abdul Qadeer Khan nuclear black market

Khan, Liaquat Ali, 127

Kidwai, Khalid, 130

Kimball, Daryl, 46–47, 91

Kissinger, Henry, 35, 38, 106, 117, 189, 205, 221n25

Klaus, Vaclav, 12

Korea. *See* North Korea; South Korea

Krauthammer, Charles, 42–43, 167–68

Krepon, Michael, 71, 140

Kristensen, Hans, 43, 59, 93, 122–23, 133

Kristol, William, 22

Kyl, Jon, 86, 106–7, 148, 181

Ladwig, Walter, 129–30

Laird, Melvin, 38

Lamb, Robert, 139

Landau Network–Centro Volta, 241n45

land mines, 177, 187–88

launches, accidental, 56–57

LeMay, Curtis, 55

Levin, Carl, 84

Lewis, Jeffrey, 54–55, 88, 96

Libya, 30, 31, 105, 154, 248n33; A. Q. Khan and nuclear black market, 32–33; long-range ballistic missiles, 25; nuclear program, 20, 25

Lillenthal, Sally, 177, 213

Lincoln, Abraham, 6

Lodal, Jan, 35, 89–90

"Logic of Zero, The" (Daalder and Lodal), 35, 89

long-range ballistic missiles: Libya and, 25; in Russia, 52; testing, 16; U.S. and, 52, 53, 223n44

Los Alamos National Laboratory, 78, 160, 184

Lugar, Richard "Dick," 14, 138, 139, 171–72, 181

MacArthur Foundation. *See* John D. and Catherine T. MacArthur Foundation

Manhattan Project, 34

Mao Zedong, 168

Markey, Daniel, 138

Markey, Ed, 32

Norquist, Grover, 83

Norris, Robert S., 59, 93, 122

North Korea, 43, 105, 248n33; as Axis of
Evil, 29; Bush doctrine and, 24; China's
relations with, 160; A. Q. Khan and
nuclear black market, 32–33; as new
nuclear state, 157–58, 159–62; NPT and,
47; nuclear arsenal, 59, 246n6; Nuclear
Non-Proliferation Treaty and withdrawal by, 29, 161; nuclear program,
15, 28–29, 45, 59, 120, 154, 245n17; with
nuclear technology, 160; with nuclear
testing, 16, 20, 28–29, 72, 158, 159, 196;
nuclear warheads, 246n6; plutonium,
29, 160–61, 246n6; sanctions on, 208;
U.S. relations with, 160–61, 196–97

Norway, 154, 248n32

NPR. *See* Nuclear Posture Review

NPT. *See* Non-Proliferation Treaty

nuclear arms race: in South Asia, 19, 67; in
space, 95

nuclear balance, 70–73, 121, 130–33

nuclear bombs, 28–29; blast, 63–65, 100;
fire, 63–65; radiation, 63–65, 66. *See
also* atomic bombs; hydrogen bombs

nuclear forces: Russian, *58*; U.S., *57*

nuclear incident management, budget for,
85, 232n41

Nuclear National Security Administration
(NNSA), 77–78

Nuclear Non-Proliferation Treaty, 15, 36,
46, 72; non-nuclear-weapons states,
60, 153–54; North Korea's withdrawal
from, 29, 161; Review Conference, 25,
32, 39, 46–47, 115–16; Russia and, 110,
170; U.S. and, 170, 196, 200, 204, 211;
U.S.-India deal and, 32, 144

Nuclear Posture Review (NPR): George
W. Bush and, 23, 29, 31, 104–5; Obama
and, 6, 39, 41–42, 43–44, 46–47, 87, 96,

105–6, 116, 199–200, 199–201; strategic
pivot, 105–6; verdict, 155

nuclear programs: China, 245n17; France,
245n17; India, 32, 47, 59, 120, 128–29,
151, 245n17; Iran, 15, 19, 20, 24, 27–28,
38–39, 45, 120, 135, 153, 154, 163–64,
197, 245n17; Iraq, 20; Israel, 59, 245n17;
Libya, 20, 25; North Korea, 15, 28–29,
45, 59, 120, 154, 245n17; Pakistan, 32,
47, 59, 119, 121–22, 128–29, 154, 240n38,
245n17; Russia, 245n17; South Korea,
158; UK, 245n17; U.S., 43, 245n17

nuclear-risk-reduction centers, 142–43

Nuclear Security Summit, 39, 107, 207

Nuclear Threat Initiative, 189

nuclear threat reduction, budget for, 85,
232n41

nuclear warheads: dismantling, 222n35;
North Korea, 246n6; reductions, 116;
Russia, 30, 53, *58*, 115; U.S., 30, 46, 53,
115, 231n35

nuclear weapons: accidents, 54–57; af-
fordability of new, 87–88; arguments
for increase in, 92; balance achieved
with, 70–73, 121, 130–33; with ban
on fissile material production, 16–17;
China and stockpile of, 59, *60*; from
Cold War poised for attack, 30–31, 53,
84; countries known to have, 245n17;
downsizing, 91–96, 136, 170–71; France
and stockpile of, 58–59, *60*; India and
stockpile of, 59, *60*; Israel and stockpile
of, 59, *60*; non-nuclear-weapons states,
60, 153–54; number allowable under
New START, 235n2; number in today's
global arsenal, 1; Pakistan and stockpile
of, 59, *60*; polls on elimination of, 3, 189,
217n4; Russian stockpiles of, 52, 53, *58*,
60; spread of, 51–61; UK and stockpile
of, 59, *60*; U.S.-India deal and spread of,